MORAL COURAGE

MORAL COURAGE

RUSHWORTH M. KIDDER

wm
WILLIAM MORROW
An Imprint of HarperCollins*Publishers*

For Lucha Noerager Vogel
who lit the way

HarperCollins books may be purchased for educational, business, or sales promotional use. For information please write: Special Markets Department, HarperCollins Publishers, Inc., 10 East 53rd Street, New York, NY 10022.

FIRST EDITION

Printed on acid-free paper

Designed by Amy Hill

Library of Congress Cataloging-in-Publication Data

Kidder, Rushworth M.
    Moral courage / Rushworth M. Kidder.
        p.   cm.
    Includes bibliographical references and index.
    ISBN 0-06-059154-4
    1. Courage.   2. Ethics.   I. Title.

BJ1533.C8K45   2005
179'.6—dc22   2004049904

05   06   07   08   09   DIX/QWF   10   9   8   7   6   5   4   3   2   1

Contents

CHAPTER SEVEN

Fakes, Frauds, and Foibles: What Moral Courage Isn't 175

CHAPTER EIGHT

Learning Moral Courage 213

CHAPTER NINE

Practicing Moral Courage in the Public Square 245

Preface

As I talk about moral courage in workshops on ethics, I sometimes notice people staring quizzically back at me. "So what?" they seem to be asking.

My response to their unspoken question is simple: "Don't you wish that Enron's board had had enough moral courage to challenge those phony financial schemes? And aren't you glad that Winston Churchill had enough moral courage to stand up to the Nazis?" Suddenly they get it. Moral courage isn't an esoteric branch of philosophy; it's a practical necessity for modern life. Its presence or absence explains some of the world's greatest successes and failures. Over time, the examples will change, yet the willingness to take tough stands for right in the face of danger will remain, as it has always been, the pinnacle of ethical action.

Moral courage is not restricted to great events and famous individuals. It is relevant not only in the boardroom and the war room but also in the kitchen and the schoolhouse. This book grows out of decades of observation of ethical individuals across the spectrum of human activity. Some are well known, while others lead very private lives. Like two earlier books that flowed from my work with the Institute for Global Ethics, this book is rooted in the experiences of real people, building its argument largely through their stories. The first of those books, *Shared Values for a Troubled World: Conversations with Men and Women of Conscience*, made the case for a common core of global, cross-cultural values. That point is crucial: without the recognition that values don't need to be *imposed* but can instead be *discovered,* ethical discussion can too easily be dismissed as *your values versus my values.* The second book, *How Good People Make Tough Choices: Resolving the Dilemmas of Ethical Living,* built outward from those values. It recognized that ethical issues arise for two reasons. People can be tempted away from core values—by being dishonest, say, in the face of a community commitment to honesty. In that case, ethics is a matter of right versus wrong. Or people can face dilemmas in which two deeply held values are in opposition—fairness, perhaps, versus compassion. In that case, ethics is a matter of right versus right. To address this latter sort of wrenching dilemma, *Tough Choices* proposed a right-versus-right model for values-based decision making.

This book completes the trilogy. It recognizes that while people may have fine values and develop great skill at moral reasoning and ethical decision making, such mental activity counts for little if their decisions sit unimplemented on the shelf. What's so often needed is a third step: the moral courage to put those decisions into action. More broadly, what's needed is the courage to live a moral and ethical life.

The observations underlying this book stretch back well before the founding of the Institute for Global Ethics in 1990. In my former profession as a columnist and correspondent for *The Christian Science Monitor*— a newspaper noted for its depth, balance, global concern, and ethical stance—I found myself interviewing scores of individuals in leadership positions who exhibited, in various ways, a remarkable capacity for resolve in the face of risk. I began to sense that their courage grew out of an ethical commitment, a kind of inner moral compass calibrated by a set of core values. After a while, it became almost axiomatic that to talk to true leaders was to talk to people who demonstrated a kind of daring integrity. What was that courage? Where did it come from? How did they get it? Could they lose it once they had it? Could they teach it to others?

These questions and more came with me into my work at the institute. During the last fifteen years, my colleagues and I have conducted hundreds of seminars and workshops on ethics around the world. These seminars usually require each participant to share a tough, right-versus-right dilemma from his or her own experience. When the discussion is finished and the outcome is finally revealed, I've been struck by how often the result reveals real courage on the part of the teller.

As this recognition of moral courage was growing up within our work at the institute, the importance of it was steadily rising in the world around us. Articles, book chapters, and talks on ethics made reference to this quality. Four years ago, sensing this trend, we drafted a report on moral courage that immediately became the most popular download on our Web site. Since then, we've bent our efforts toward the completion of this book.

I say "we" because a book of this sort has one author but many creators. I am deeply grateful to my colleagues at the institute for their professional insights, their conceptual wrestlings, their suggestions for individuals to interview, and their unflagging encouragement. Without that collective give-and-take over many years, the ideas in this book simply could not have come to fruition. In particular, my thanks go to Graham Phaup, Marilyn Gondek, Patricia Born, Martin Taylor, Paula Mirk, and Sheila Bloom for their pioneering thinking and their practical wisdom; to Martha Bracy, who helped me draft our initial white paper on moral courage; to Jeffrey Spaulding, whose editing of my weekly columns for *Ethics Newsline* (where many of these ideas were worked out) has been immeasurably helpful; to Melissa Parisot for her work on a feminist perspective on moral courage; and to my personal assistant, Marc Fairbrother, who did much of the research for this book and coauthored a part of chapter 8. Great thanks are due to Jonathan Ingbar for educating me on the psychological literature relevant to moral courage, some of which is reflected in sidebars in the following text. I'm indebted to a strongly supportive institute board of directors comprising my good colleagues and friends David Adams, David Anable, Carlos Ramos Garcia, Theodore Gordon, Elizabeth Hart, Anne E. D. Kidder, Janet Norwood, Robert Pratt Jr., Charles Rainwater, George Reid, Philip Smith, Deborah Steckler, Colburn Wilbur, Marcia Worthing, and Mary Margaret Young.

I'm grateful to Lucha Vogel, who more than anyone provided the constant encouragement that finally caused me to commit to this undertaking. I'm most appreciative of conversations with and support from Charlotte Burton, Louise Greeley, Jack Hubbell, Katherine Lazarus, George Moffett, and David Winder. Once again, as in the writing of each of my books, I've drawn strong support from my wife, Elizabeth, whose moral clarity, penetrating analysis, and deep love has so often pointed the way through ambiguities and doubts. And I've been greatly helped by discussions on this topic over the years with our daughters, who both exemplify significant moral courage in their respective professions.

Citations in the text have been assembled into a notes section and are easily traceable by page number and key words. I identify characters in the narratives by full first and last names whenever they have given me permission to do so. If my sources requested anonymity, I used only a first name, invented for the purpose, and sparingly altered details of location, employment, or relationship that might otherwise betray their identities. In each case, however, the narratives used here reflect authentic experiences, captured as I have heard them, and wherever possible verified with the source even when anonymous. Courage, to be moral, must be grounded in ethics—and so must the writing about it.

Camden, Maine
February 2004

CHAPTER ONE

Standing Up for Principle

You gain strength, courage, and confidence by every experience in which you really stop to look fear in the face. You are able to say, "I lived through this horror. I can take the next thing that comes along." . . . *You must do the thing you think you cannot do.*

—Eleanor Roosevelt

Like most private schools, St. Paul's School for Boys posts athletic schedules on its Web site. In the spring of 2001, it listed baseball games, tennis matches, and crew events on its leafy campus in suburban Baltimore. But not lacrosse. Not that spring. Despite being ranked number one in a nationwide lacrosse poll earlier in the year, this prestigious 151-year-old institution canceled its entire varsity season on April 3.

The reason? Earlier in the spring, a sixteen-year-old member of the lacrosse team had a sexual encounter with a fifteen-year-old girl from another private school—and, without her knowledge, videotaped the whole thing. He was apparently mimicking a sequence in *American Pie* (a movie some of the students had recently seen) in which a character broadcasts a live sexual encounter on the Web. When his teammates gathered at another player's home to look at what they thought would be game tapes of an upcoming rival, they saw his video instead.

None of the teammates objected. Nobody tried to stop the showing. Instead, they watched.

What happened next is a tale of moral courage—a lack of it among teammates who failed to stand up against the video, and the expression of it by an administration that took a formidable public stand. Their debate was a wrenching one. At St. Paul's, lacrosse has a sixty-year history. It garners solid alumni support, which translates into funding. And it attracts some of the best young players in the region—so many that St. Paul's runs the risk of being seen, as one administrator put it, as "a 'jocks rule' type of school." But its students are still required to attend chapel. As an institution affiliated with the Episcopal Church, it retains a serious tradition of ethical concern. And it seeks to be a private community dedicated to serious education in a very public world.

What do you do when a popular sport crosses swords with an ethical collapse? In this case, the answer was clear. The headmaster, Robert W. Hallett, stepped in immediately, asking not only (as some who were there recall), "What happened to our school?" but more particularly, "What happened to this young woman?" The boy who made the video was expelled. Thirty varsity players were suspended for three days and sent to counseling with the school's chaplain and psychologist. Eight junior varsity players were made to sit out the rest of the season. And the varsity season was terminated.

"At a minimum," Hallett wrote to parents, "we should expect each boy here will, in the future, have the courage to stand up for, to quote the Lower School prayer, 'The hard right against the easy wrong.' "

He might well have been speaking for his own administration. Choosing the "right" was, in fact, hard. It meant disappointing parents, students, alumni, and national lacrosse fans. It meant facing a spectrum of criticism that ran all the way from "You made a mountain out of a molehill!" to "You let them off too easily!" It put at risk an array of crucial relationships with donors and friends, religious affiliates, advisers and counselors recommending the school to potential enrollees, and the entire Baltimore community. It set in motion a pattern of events that might have either plunged the offending students into deep reflection and self-improvement or pushed them out of the educational arena altogether. And it brought the young woman, who remains anonymous, into the center of a national story over an incident she wanted to put behind her.

Moral courage doesn't always produce an immediate benefit. In this case, however, it did. The student at the center of the controversy later graduated from a local public school. The young woman moved out of state and continued her education. Both appear to have landed on their feet. Hallett, who moved on to an executive position outside education, was swamped with letters praising his stand, which he kept, and requests for interviews on national television, which he turned down. And in the months following the decision, St. Paul's found that requests for admissions materials actually increased, and that a smattering of financial gifts arrived from new donors far beyond the Baltimore community who wanted to express their gratitude.

Standing up for values is the defining feature of moral courage. But *having* values is different from *living by* values—as the twenty-first century is rapidly learning. The U.S. soldiers who abused Iraqi prisoners at Abu Ghraib prison, the CEO of Italian food giant Parmalat who kept quiet as financial malfeasance proliferated, the Olympic athletes who succumbed to steroids, the American president who deceived the world about his sexual escapades—these were not horned and forktailed devils utterly devoid of values. Yet in moments of moral consequence they failed to act with integrity. Why? Because they lacked the moral courage that lifts values from the theoretical to the practical and carries us beyond ethical reasoning into principled action. In the defining moments of our lives—whether as a student watching a videotape or a president facing a nation—values count for little without the willingness to put them into practice. Without moral courage, our brightest virtues rust from lack of use. With it, we build piece by piece a more ethical world.

SHARING THE
QUARTER LOAF

Juan Julio Wicht doesn't look like a hero. He never intended to be a player in a high-stakes global tragedy. A researcher at Peru's University of the Pacific, this soft-spoken priest had been studying national policy issues when he was invited to a gala event at the Japanese embassy in Lima. He thought of himself as a kind of poor academic cousin to the glittering guest list of government ministers, ambassadors, military officers, and business executives assembled there on December 17, 1996.

That was the night that members of the Tupac Amaru Revolutionary Movement shot their way into the embassy grounds. Rounding up the guests crowded around sumptuous buffets, they ended up holding more than four hundred prisoners—the largest hostage taking in history. Dr. Wicht was among them. Speaking to a group of us in Mexico City follow-ing his release, he observed that "there are no words to describe" what went on during that siege. It lasted more than four months. Early on, as the guerrillas sought to reduce their captive population to manageable numbers, they offered him, as a man of the cloth, the opportunity to leave. But as a man of the cloth he refused, choosing instead to remain inside until it was over.

What kept him there? What was it that overcame the natural human impulse for freedom, causing him to put some higher principle ahead of his own needs and opportunities for survival? The ethics of his vocation had something to do with it. But to hear him recount his tale, he was even more committed to staying after seeing a simple demonstration of col-lective moral courage among his fellow captives during their first days together.

Those days, he recalled, were especially intense. The guerrillas were inundated with hostages. There was no food, no place to lie down. Tightly packed into once-lavish embassy rooms, the prisoners squatted together for hours on end. Not wanting to appear to negotiate with the terrorists, the Peruvian government maintained silence. The guerrillas grew increasingly threatening, telling the hostages they would never see their families again. No one knew whether they would eat another meal.

And then someone in Wicht's crowded room found several small loaves of bread. The group calculated how many mouths there were to feed. Slicing carefully, they gave each person a quarter of a loaf. But just after the pieces had been distributed, a newcomer—an ambassador—was shoved in from another room. Without hesitating, one of the hostages divided his already small quarter loaf in half and shared it with his new fellow captive.

In theory, of course, that's not supposed to happen. According to popular interpretations of economics and values, individuals under pressure don't act that way. Humans, we are told, are primarily self-interested. As competition increases for scarce resources, the commitment to such moral values as compassion and sharing goes out the window. In such cases, we're assured, Maslow's hierarchy of needs takes over, insisting that our priorities can be reduced to four words: *food first, ethics later.* So even in a hostage taking, would someone share what might be his or her last loaf of bread? Of course not. To think otherwise is simply naive.

Yet "in that entire experience," Wicht recalled, "I didn't see one sign of selfishness." Was that because all these people were already friends? Hardly. They came from different backgrounds and a variety of countries. "What did we have in common?" he asked rhetorically. His answer was elegantly simple: "We were human beings, and solidarity developed among us." And out of that solidarity—a commonality of values that put something above their own needs—a collective moral courage rose to the surface that put life itself at risk so that others could live.

TESTING THE
CORPORATE METTLE

Eric Duckworth, an ebullient Englishman with an impish wit, notes with self-deprecating modesty that where moral courage is concerned he "usually fails." But "on one occasion when I was young and idealistic," he recalls, "I succeeded—and have been proud of it ever since."

In 1949 Duckworth and his wife were newly married and applying for a mortgage to buy their first home in suburban London. A metallurgist by training, he had joined the Glacier Metal Company, now part of Federal Mogul, a firm that specialized in making bearings for internal combustion engines. Among his tasks were examining damaged bearings returned by customers to determine the causes of the failures, reporting back to the customers, and if necessary recommending changes in production processes to correct the problem.

Most of the time, he recalls, the failures were due to problems such as misuse, improper installation, and lack of lubrication. But "very occasionally," he says, Glacier had supplied a faulty part. As Duckworth got more experience, he came to understand that those occasional faults were not being accurately reported. His boss, the chief metallurgist, regularly tried to cover up such faults by refusing to divulge all the facts. "He salved his conscience," Duckworth recalls, "by saying that he was prepared to commit sins of omission but not of commission."

As a result, bearing failures for which Glacier should have taken responsibility were attributed to mishandling by the end users, and no effort was made to compensate customers.

"After a while," says Duckworth, "I disagreed." He had been with the company for only six months when a particularly egregious case of failure by Glacier came to his attention. Instead of shifting the blame, he "wrote the report with complete honesty." When his boss rejected his findings, Duckworth recalls that "in my altruistic, youthful fervor, I said I would resign."

Moral courage or rash bravado? At the time, says Duckworth, "It was very foolish of me." The sales department, agreeing with the chief metallurgist, protested his report vigorously, certain that such an admission of mistakes would cost them this customer and perhaps many more. Fortunately, Duckworth had already made suggestions that had increased the productivity of the manufacturing line threefold. Those actions, he suspects, had won him the admiration of the CEO, who backed him against his boss. The report was sent to the customer.

Shortly afterward, Duckworth says, "we got back a very congratulatory letter saying that the customer had always suspected concealment in some of our reports." Welcoming the company's newfound candor, they increased their orders as a result.

THE COMMON THREADS OF COURAGE

These three stories—of exploitation in Baltimore, terrorism in Lima, and dishonesty in London—would seem to have little in common. The first happened amid suburban comfort, where the risks were shame, suspension, or expulsion. The second happened at gunpoint, where death was the threat. The third happened in the corporate world, where a career was at stake. One made the local and national papers. Another occurred below the radar during an incident that drew glaring global publicity. The last never reached print until now.

Moral courage comes in a palette of colors. It happens to people who may or may not have any notoriety. Yet it happens in a social context that includes morally courageous actors and—in these three cases, although not always—a supporting cast of others who also exhibit moral courage. Hallett's faculty at St. Paul's, Wicht's fellow captives in Peru, and Duckworth's CEO all resonated to the sound of moral courage, making it easier for the actor to display the courage needed in the moment.

And through each of these tales runs the three-stranded braid that defines morally courageous action: a commitment to moral *principles,* an awareness of the *danger* involved in supporting those principles, and a willing *endurance* of that danger. Think of these three as intersecting domains:

Figure 1. The Three Elements of Moral Courage

Notice how these relationships play out in these three stories:

- At St. Paul's School for Boys the principles involved an expectation of responsible sexual attitudes and behaviors. The danger Hallett and his staff faced had to do with parental wrath and financial hardship. The endurance arose in their collective stand for the "hard right."
- At the Japanese embassy in Peru the principles centered on compassion and responsibility. The danger Wicht faced had to do with pain and discomfort, perhaps even death. The endurance arose in his commitment to be present to help even when he himself might be rendered helpless.
- At the Glacier Metal Company the principles centered on honesty and fairness. The danger facing Duckworth concerned unemployment and self-condemnation. The endurance arose in his willingness—due to a clear understanding of values, youthful chutzpah, or something in between—to risk the full consequences of that danger.

DEFINING COURAGE

Most definitions of courage put it at the intersection of the two bottom circles, danger and endurance. According to the third edition of *Webster's New International Dictionary,* courage is "that quality of mind which enables one to encounter danger and difficulties with firmness, or without fear, or fainting of heart." That definition may be overwrought in using the phrase "without fear": John Wayne's comment that "courage is being scared to death—and saddling up anyway" reflects a recognition, common throughout the literature on courage, that the greatest courage may in fact arise in moments of the greatest fear.

More usefully, the same dictionary cites a simpler definition of courage by General William T. Sherman (after whom the Sherman tank is named) as "a perfect sensibility of the measure of danger and a mental willingness to endure it." Courage, as those two bottom circles suggest, is all about assessing risks and standing up to the hardships they may bring.

In common with other core attributes of humanity, courage is not peculiar to Western culture nor the modern age. Courage, notes the British intellectual Isaiah Berlin, "has, so far as we can tell, been admired in every society known to us." In our modern usage, however, courage typically subdivides into two strands, which we tend to describe as *physical* and *moral.*

Physical courage has to do with the guts to climb up one rock face or rappel down another, the valor to continue running uphill into enemy fire, or the bravery of a mother plucking a drowning child from the surf. For each of these acts, the word *courage* easily springs to mind. We make no requirement that these acts be related to principles, values, or higher-order beliefs in "doing the right thing." On some occasions, to be sure, physical courage may be driven by a sense of honor. It can be shaped by a concern over reputation. It can even be enhanced by a recognition that good things will come by being bold. But while physical courage may be principle-*related*, we don't require that it be principle-*driven*.

Moral courage, however, is just that: driven by principle. When courage is manifested in the service of our values—when it is done not only to demonstrate physical prowess or save lives but also to support virtues and sustain core principles—we tend to use the term *moral courage*. Moral courage is not only about facing physical challenges that could harm your body—it's about facing mental challenges that could wreck your reputation and emotional well-being, your adherence to conscience, your self-esteem, your bank account, your health. If physical courage acts in support of the tangible, moral courage protects the less tangible. It's not property but principles, not valuables but virtues, not physics but metaphysics that moral courage rises to defend. Where the physically courageous individual may be in full agreement with the momentum of the occasion and is often bolstered with cheers of encouragement and team spirit, the morally courageous person often goes against the grain, acting contrary to the accepted norm. Acts of moral courage carry with them risks of humiliation, ridicule, and contempt, not to mention unemployment and loss of social standing.

Simply put, moral courage is *the courage to be moral*. And by moral, as we'll see later, we tend to mean whatever adheres to the five core moral values of *honesty, respect, responsibility, fairness,* and *compassion*. In figure 1, then, the point at which the circle of our deepest values, or principles, intersects with the twin circles of danger and endurance is the point at which we find moral courage most clearly in evidence.

MORAL COURAGE
IN PRACTICE

Some of the evidence for moral courage is found in the lives and practices of admirable world leaders:

- Mahatma Gandhi advocating his philosophy of nonviolence in the struggle for a free India despite repeated internment
- Nelson Mandela enduring eighteen years of degrading imprisonment on Robben Island and still being able to forgive his oppressors in the apartheid regime of South Africa
- Lech Wałesa rising from the shipyards of Gdansk to lead the Solidarity Movement that ultimately played a decisive role in toppling Communism in Poland
- Václav Havel, a dissident playwright, enduring three prison sentences for organizing strong opposition to Communist rule of Czechoslovakia
- Aung San Suu Kyi defiantly resisting her imprisonment in Myanmar and remaining an outspoken voice for democracy

But more frequently it appears in the deeds of ordinary individuals— not necessarily in stories of great moments but in narratives of daily lives that have little to do with broad national and global trends. Consider a few homely examples:

- Early in his career as a consulting engineer, Larry Elder of Palm Desert, California, designed a feed mill for an international company in the nearby Imperial Valley. His design placed all the components of the mill—including a 110-foot-tall bucket elevator—on a concrete slab.

  Needing to calculate the load-bearing capacity of the ground beneath the slab, Elder retained a soils engineer. Only after Elder's design was accepted by the company, however, did the soils engineer realize the slab would be supporting such a tall structure. Given the prevalence of earthquakes in that part of California, he advised Elder to revise his plan by placing the slab on piles—at an additional cost of $25,000.

  Elder concurred. But the company manager rejected the revision and ordered Elder to begin construction. Elder refused, standing his ground despite a series of angry phone calls. "For a new consultant in the area," says Elder, "it seemed like a tough stand to take; but it just seemed right, so I stayed with it."

In the end the manager relented. And despite thirty small earthquakes in the first sixty days after completion, the elevator stayed upright.

• "I have never forgotten an incident that occurred twenty-five years ago, when I was a graduate student in the South in a mental health counseling program," writes a woman who is now a university professor in Florida.

"My job at the time required that I earn a Ph.D., so I was under a great deal of pressure to succeed. The beginning students were randomly paired and expected to work with each other as a client-therapist dyad, each taking the turn of client and then counselor throughout the semester. I was paired with a younger woman, and one evening we met at a local pizza place and settled into getting to know each other over our meal. When the conversation turned to racial issues, my counseling partner began to use the 'N word' in reference to African Americans and to express her negative feelings toward people of color.

"I was shocked that a future therapist would harbor this type of intolerance based on race. At the same time, I was faced with the ethical dilemma of whether to confront her or let it go, as the outcome of my shared clinical work with her would certainly have an impact on my grade in this class. After a few minutes of hearing her use such demeaning language, I could no longer bear my discomfort and asked her not to use the word in my presence. She apologized for offending me, and we went on to other topics of conversation.

"Although this may seem like a minor incident, for me it was a major challenge to my ethics and basic belief in justice, compassion, and respect. I don't think I could live with myself easily if I had not so acted."

Though modest, these examples each evidence the three elements of moral courage: a significant danger (losing future work as an engineer, failing to attain a doctoral degree), a willingness to endure (refusing to compromise, confronting disrespectful language), and a commitment to principle (long-term safety, racial equality).

Sometimes, by contrast, the importance of moral courage appears most vividly by its *absence:*

- A woman in California writes about her uncle, Pete, a quiet man who kept to himself and who served in the U.S. Army in Vietnam. He was stationed there, she says, with "a mishmash of people from all over the country—big cities, small towns, farms. This was downtime—training, rest, routine.

  "My uncle had befriended a big country boy from some tiny Midwestern town. He had grown up on a farm, was a little slow, very shy. One day a bunch of guys were in the process of planning a particularly cruel joke on this country boy. My uncle overheard them, and they invited him to join in. He declined. They went through with their prank, and it was successful.

  "My uncle says he remembers afterward sitting on the bed across from this country boy, who didn't say a word. But his face was full of hurt and humiliation. My uncle said the look on his face said to him, 'You knew, you knew what they were going to do, and you didn't try to stop them.' From that day on he made a vow to himself that never again would he stand by and let someone be hurt if there was something he could do to prevent it."

- When Officer Mike Bocelli was working a bike patrol on August 24, 2003, in Fort Myers, Florida, he cited a man for carrying an open container and having a mutilated driver's license. The man was so upset that he returned several hours later and attempted to slash the tires on the patrol bike of Officer Bocelli's partner. Having no lack of physical courage, Bocelli gave chase and arrested him after a violent scuffle.

Bocelli wanted to include in his written report the fact that the man had slashed the tires—until he realized that the tires had not actually been damaged. So, taking the man's knife, he punctured the tires himself. Three months later Bocelli resigned, having been charged with lying about an arrest and tampering with evidence.

The case surfaced because one of the officers who saw Bocelli slash the tires had the moral courage to stand up against the unspoken but powerful code of fraternal loyalty within police ranks and report the incident to his superiors. Attention then turned to a second officer who saw Bocelli slash the tires but said nothing. His lack of moral courage in failing to notify his superiors cost him a three-week suspension without pay and probation for a year.

• When twenty-seven-year-old Andrew Hamerling, a securities research analyst at Banc of America Securities, analyzed the performance of one of the firms he followed, he concluded that its earnings did not adequately reflect the company's performance. So in September 2001 he drafted a negative report on the company, SBC Communications.

That draft never appeared, largely because SBC, after Hamerling improperly gave them advance notice of his findings, threatened to pull valuable corporate underwriting business from Banc of America. So Hamerling issued a much more positive report. He continued to recommend privately against SBC, however, warning at least one client in an e-mail that its stock would fall because "[SBC] has nothing fundamentally sound going for it."

More than two years later, he was fined and suspended by the National Association of Securities Dealers (his profession's regulatory and disciplinary body) because he "failed to disclose negative facts about the company as well as [his own] actual views in violation of NASD rules." His failure to abide by his conscience cost him this stern rebuke.

Each of these individuals—Pete, the unidentified police officer, and Andrew Hamerling—had an opportunity to express moral courage by taking an action that was ethically right: defending a friend, reporting a perjury, or standing for truth. But Pete was dissuaded by fear of ostracism. Within the police force, the inhibitor was a culture of fidelity to fellow officers. For Hamerling, intimidating threats stifled his conscience. In the end, each paid the price of self-condemnation, sanction, or damage to reputation.

WHY MORAL COURAGE MATTERS

Why should moral courage matter so much to us these days? In part because we see so many examples of its lack—in corporate settings and legal proceedings, in politics and sports and entertainment, in personal and social relationships. But there's another, deeper reason. If courage is indeed one of the core virtues of humanity—as I will argue in the coming pages—we need to find ways to express it, support it, and teach it. The proving of one's own courage, after all, has long been a rite of passage from youth to adulthood. When young men went to war and pioneers took to the wilderness, they were carving out new opportunities for themselves. But they were also testing their mettle beyond the comfortable regulation of civilization.

Times have changed. John Wayne's Wild West has disappeared. The warfare once thought so glorious—and which Aristotle felt was the only place to find true courage—now depends less on the physical courage of the individual warrior and more on technology, information, and weaponry launched from a safe distance. In most developed nations, ordinary citizens rarely have to do what their ancestors routinely did:

train to defend themselves and their loved ones against physical threats. Today, the satisfaction of basic needs typically entails little hazard and demands no physical bravery: fighting traffic on the way to the grocery store is categorically different from battling bears on the way home with the deer you've just speared.

With physical courage less obviously in demand as we move into the twenty-first century, where is courage to be learned and practiced? How will the young, in particular, celebrate this age-old rite of passage? Where, specifically, will the risks come from that test their courage? Will they find those risks in dangerous lifestyles that include unsafe sexual behavior, chemical dependency, and gang activity? Will they find them in newly popular forms of contrived risk taking—extreme sports, survival treks, or even perilous financial ventures? It's as though the young are saying, "If nature, war, and the need for survival are not going to test our courage, we'll invent other ways, for we need to prove to ourselves and others that we really are courageous!"

Is it possible that, among those other ways, the young could begin testing themselves against a courage that is moral rather than physical? If the need for physical courage in everyday life is dwindling, the opposite is happening for moral courage. As the examples in this book indicate—and as daily headlines reconfirm—the opportunities to prove oneself morally courageous are manifold. It may be, in fact, that what most defines maturity in the twenty-first century will be not physical but moral courage.

This book is all about that defining attribute of maturity. What is moral courage, and how does it play out in our lives? Specifically, as we approach situations where moral courage seems to be required, how do we know what to do? What guideposts are available to help us decide whether the issue we face defines the blockbuster moment of our lives or a secondary distraction on the emotional horizon? How can we decide whether to stand and fight or to retreat and retrench? If it seems right to take a stand, how can we tell whether we're being truly bold or merely brazen? How can we nurture and promote moral courage, in ourselves and for others?

There are seven checkpoints along this path:

1. **Assess the situation.** Do I think it calls for courage? Is the problem here a lack of valor or fortitude? Is physical courage all that's needed? Or does this situation need moral courage?

2. **Scan for values.** Moral courage is *the courage to be moral*—to take a stand for values. What are those values? Can I spot them and build on them?

3. **Stand for conscience.** As I think about the uppermost of the three circles in our diagram of moral courage, what principles need to be articulated and defended in this situation? What one or two key values stand out here?

4. **Contemplate the dangers.** Do I have a clear picture of the risks I'm facing? As I examine the second circle, can I properly assess the threats facing me?

5. **Endure the hardship.** Do I have the willingness to endure this situation? If I take this stand—represented by the third circle of our diagram—will the hardship make me give up, or will I be able to persist? What gives me the confidence to persist?

6. **Avoid the pitfalls.** Can I stand firm against the numerous inhibitors of moral courage? Among them are timidity and foolhardiness, which are the opposite and the counterfeit, respectively, of moral courage. Am I alert to these and other traps?

7. **Develop moral courage.** Can moral courage be learned? If moral courage is not simply innate—so that some have it and others don't—how can it be nurtured, taught, practiced, and attained?

Each of the following chapters broadly addresses one of these checkpoints, and each ends with a brief "Moral Courage Checklist" that helps us identify what we're seeing. A final chapter examines the role of moral courage in the public square. Looking at the ways courage applies to some key issues of domestic and international affairs shaping the twenty-first century, this concluding chapter suggests that moral courage is not only a personal but a collective attribute of successful cultures. By the end, several key characteristics of moral courage should become clear. Morally courageous leaders appear to have at least the following five attributes in common:

- Greater confidence in principles than in personalities
- High tolerance for ambiguity, exposure, and personal loss
- Acceptance of deferred gratification and simple rewards
- Independence of thought
- Formidable persistence and determination

There's nothing contrived, academic, or strained about these attributes or checkpoints. They grow up out of hundreds of examples, gathered over years of observation and tested in innumerable conversations with colleagues, friends, and audiences. Not surprisingly, this is a book rooted in real-life stories. Some are drawn from historical accounts or public media sources. But most come from interviews, conversations, letters, and e-mails in the United States and around the world. Where they can be attributed to their sources, I use full first and last names. Where they must remain anonymous, I use only a first—and deliberately invented—name. Even when anonymous, however, these stories are rooted in the accurate details of those who shared them with me: as Pulitzer Prize–winning historian Barbara Tuchman, from whom I have learned so much, once put it, "I do not invent anything, even the weather." Taken together, these stories reflect a natural but invisible decision-making logic that each of us can put into practice as we encounter the demand for moral courage. Continue reading, and this book will continue developing a process for putting that logic into action for ourselves and others.

CHAPTER TWO

Courage, Moral and Physical

Courage without conscience is a wild beast.
—Robert Green Ingersoll

I first heard Viktor Pestov's astonishing tale of moral and physical courage two time zones east of Moscow, where the derelict factory lots and the fields of white-sacked potatoes begin rising toward the mountains that divide Europe from Asia. In the foothills of the Urals, villages are not pretty. They straggle along the margins of highways or cram themselves into steep-hilled river valleys, far from the eyes of all but the most deliberate visitors. Little wonder the Soviets chose such a site for one of their vast networks of gulags, or prison camps. It was there, at Perm-36, that Pestov found himself imprisoned in 1970.

Twenty-eight years later, on a September afternoon in 1998, our charter bus lumbered toward that camp. As we wove through the nearby village, I noticed a slender young woman, baby on hip, standing in a dirt dooryard littered with firewood and cabbages. Buses aren't common here, where old Ladas and farm tractors typically share the road with horse-drawn carts. So she half-turned to watch, her pale Russian features set off by a modern bob of henna-rinsed hair. But her stare was impassive, remote. Beside her, through a blue-framed window, the scarlet geraniums glowed more engagingly than she did.

She would have been a teenager, I judged, when the last government trucks stopped plying this road at night. "Bread," they said on the outside. Inside, they carried political prisoners to Perm-36. She may have known the history of this road, paved in granite cubes by women prisoners from a similar camp in nearby Chusovoy. She may even have seen Perm-36 itself, set behind seven rows of wood, steel, and electrified barbed-wire fences, its two sullen watchtowers jutting up at the corners. She probably heard whispers of its history—that it was built by Stalin in 1946, that it was later converted into the Soviets' principal camp for "particularly dangerous recidivists," that it housed men like Natan Sharansky and Vladimir Bukovsky and Gleb Yakunin, men who published anti-Soviet propaganda and fought for human rights. But she would have known better than to say anything. She would have known not even to seem to take interest in what came along her road. As my bus window passed her, she was already turning back to go inside.

On that afternoon our destination, too, was the gulag. We had flown from Moscow to the gritty industrial city of Perm, then driven another four hours to what had become, only three years earlier, the Gulag Museum. It occupies the restored buildings of the sole remaining labor camp from what Aleksandr Solzhenitsyn famously called the "gulag archipelago." The others were razed as the Soviets closed them, removing evidence of a system so remorseless and pervasive that no Russian family was left untouched. This building, salvaged by the Perm chapter of the Russian human rights group Memorial, is now open to visitors.

Once inside the fences and the squared-log, whitewashed barrack, I lingered behind the group to sit for a moment on a thin, rutted mattress in one of the cells. Behind me, the afternoon sun stared indifferently through iron window bars, just as it did when this cell was occupied. On the opposite wall was the metal-sheathed wooden door with its ominous peephole. Across the room were a toilet, a sink, two red-topped stools, and a small bureau. On the bunk above lay a flimsy cotton shirt and trousers, their gray and maroon horizontal stripes no match for the brutal cold. On the brown floor stood two crude lumps of black leather that had once been shoes. A naked bulb adorned the ceiling. Mounted on the wall was a diminutive green radiator.

Who had lived here? I wondered. Was it Balus Gajauskas, who spent thirty-eight years in Soviet camps for collecting documents about the Lithuanian resistance and translating Solzhenitsyn, afterward to become a member of the Lithuanian Assembly? Was it Levko Lukyanenko, who for founding an illegal political party in his native Ukraine spent twenty years in exile and ten years in this camp, later to serve as Ukraine's ambassador to Canada? Across the entire archipelago, estimates are that a quarter of the prisoners were political dissidents. Another quarter were probably common criminals. The rest? Hapless Soviet citizens who fell afoul of the law—caught being absent from work, stealing a pocketful of grain to feed starving children, talking with foreigners. Some of them survived the knife-edged Russian winters at Perm-36, the bread-and-water rations with soup only on alternate days, the numbing drudgery of assembling electrical parts for clothes irons, the daily forty-five minutes of "exercise" in a nine-foot-square metal-lined cube open to the skies, its top laced with barbed wire. But many never made it. In the 172 camps in the Perm region alone, archives indicate that three hundred thousand people died. An estimate of the number of Soviet citizens killed by their own government in the gulag years: thirty million.

What kind of wholesale moral collapse could have produced a calamity of that proportion? How could it have been kept hidden for so long? Why was it only in 1987 that it became possible for Russians to talk openly about the gulags? Why was the last prisoner in the gulags released only seven years before we arrived by bus that day?

Staring at the heavy black shoes in that cell, I recalled a comment made a few days earlier by one of our friends from Moscow. "In Russia," she said, "nothing is predictable, even the past." As Russians reassess that past—in part because of the efforts of those keeping this fledgling

museum alive—they are recalibrating the future and redefining themselves. And what they are discovering, amid the gray and grisly perver-
sions of organizational depravity, are extraordinary stories of moral
courage that gleam with primary-colored brilliance.

One such story comes from Pestov. A former prisoner in this camp
and now a member of the Gulag Museum's board, he accompanied us on
our visit, pointing out the buildings where he once lived and worked.
Later that day, as our bus retraced its way to Perm, I plunked down onto
the seat beside him. What had brought him there? I asked. What was his
story?

A thin-faced man with black hair and earnest eyes, he told me through
a translator that he was twenty years old in 1967 when the Soviets
launched their massive jubilee to celebrate fifty years of Communist
prosperity. His family was quite well off, living not far from Perm in Ekaterinburg (known in those days as Sverdlovsk), where his mother worked
for the KGB and his father headed a medical facility.

One day a friend took Pestov to visit some relatives living in a building
in the middle of the city. They went inside, he said, and started "going
downstairs—down and down and down," until they came to a lightless,
airless room with a dirt floor. "This fact struck me," he said. "The authorities are celebrating the fiftieth anniversary, yet these people live in such
terrible conditions."

So he began taking an interest in political issues, especially the events in
Czechoslovakia. There, Party Secretary Alexander Dubcek was beginning
to talk about freedom in what would become a massive human-rights
protest known as the Prague Spring. Without his parents knowing—that
would have been "impossible," he said—Pestov began listening to Voice of
America and discussing the news of the day with his friend. Then came
August 20, 1968. He was working as a mechanic at a candy factory, he said,
when he heard a noontime radio news bulletin about Soviet tanks rolling
into Prague to crush the uprising.

"We must do something about this," he told his friend. Within
months, joined by his brother, they had set up a clandestine group called

Free Russia. Pestov warned the members that they had a year at best before they got arrested. They all agreed it was worth the risk. So they bought a typewriter and carbon paper and began writing and publishing pamphlets—laboriously retyping until they had perhaps one hundred copies of each edition to distribute.

That, of course, was the challenge: distribution. At night they sneaked out to stick pamphlets onto walls. By day they fluttered them out of upper-story windows during public parades. They barely escaped when, after one such launch, the police chased them up through the attics. But ingenuity was their strong suit. Another pamphleteer, working in a different city at the time, told them about sneaking into the trolley yards at night and, after the cleaners had washed the cars, plastering pamphlets onto the damp rooftops. The next day, as the trolleys began moving, the sun and wind would dry the papers, which would blow off here and there along the trolley routes to be picked up by passersby. Or at night they would climb out onto the steep roofs of city buildings and stick pamphlets to the slates with pellets of wet bread. In the morning the pigeons would eat the bread, releasing the pamphlets to the wind.

Whatever the method, one thing was sure: the KGB was never far behind. As it happened, Pestov's group had a bit more time than he had estimated. They were not arrested until May 20, 1970, betrayed by an acquaintance they had invited to help with a particularly large distribution. Pestov's mother lost her job immediately and never worked again. His father was demoted to an X-ray technician. Pestov served five years in prison, much of it at Perm-36.

Why did he do it? Of all the agonizing ethical dilemmas facing humanity, few are more wrenching than the choice between what's right for the world and what's right for your family. Pestov felt the force of that dilemma as he thought of his parents' fate. "Since it all happened because of me," he told me, "I felt very guilty."

But he also felt the immensity of his social and moral purpose. What he was fighting against, he said, was the idea that "someone will think for you, someone will make decisions for you." And what he was fighting for was a principle, which he articulated very simply: "A person should be master of his own fate," he said, and there should be "one law for everyone."

His real concern was that Communist repression was making a lasting imprint on the conscience of the entire Russian culture. "Those years of lawlessness brought us to the level of slaves," he said. "Take any director of a [private] stockholding company: he is just like a small czar. If you make a protest, he'll fire you."

I asked what made him most proud of what he did.

He thought for a moment. Then he said, "I believe I did the right thing. I wasn't silent. I was saying and doing what I had to do. There was a very small contribution of mine to the fact that the Communists were pushed out of power."

By now the landscape whizzing past Pestov's window had drifted into darkness, and the lights of Perm were glowing in the distance. I thought of the young woman in the village dooryard. What does she know of Pestov? Probably nothing. His is not a famous name, nor, through his work as director of a small independent library in Ekaterinburg, is it apt to become so. Yet he is one of the heroes of a story so vast and consequential that it reverberates daily and hourly through her life—the story of a Communist experiment that failed, of an ideology proved hollow, of a moral courage that challenged the established order and survived the worst that human meanness and the Siberian climate could deliver. It is because of the Pestovs of this world that she is freer now than her family has ever been. She may not know that. It may take a generation for the legacy of lawlessness to wear off. Maybe in her own life she will remain immobilized by fear, inert and disengaged. But if her children walk up that cobblestone road, they will encounter not a gulag but a museum commemorating people who had the courage to do the right thing.

"The courage to do the right thing" is about as concise a definition of moral courage as you can find. But was Pestov expressing moral or physical courage? From the first time he laid a finger to a typewriter key, he knew he was in danger. But what sort of danger? Was it, as is so often the case with moral courage, a danger to his reputation, his standing in the community? Had that been his concern, he would have sworn allegiance to parents and party. Was it, instead, a danger to his sense of self-worth, his inner commitment to principles, an outrage that impelled him to fight for a higher sense of justice? That's nearer the mark. But wasn't he also showing courage in the face of danger to his physical well-being and even his life? Running through those attics from the police, it must have occurred to him that they were armed and he was not—and that his pursuers weren't apt to spend time in a moral debate over whether or not to shoot a criminal during hot pursuit for clearly treasonous acts. He must have known, too, the tales that were circulating of the gulags, of the numbers of Russian citizens who had simply disappeared, and of the unexplained deaths in captivity.

As Pestov's story indicates, moral and physical courage often coexist. But what distinguishes them? How do we describe these two branches?

PHYSICAL COURAGE

In common usage, courage usually means *physical courage*. Our English word *courage*, derived from the Latin *cor*, or heart, appears in *The Canterbury Tales* (around 1387) in Chaucer's description of the "smale foweles" (little birds) that "maken melodye" because nature "priketh" (urges) them to do so in their "corages." At that time, says the *Oxford English Dictionary*, *courage* meant spirit, mind, disposition, or nature. In the slow transmutations of time, it came to mean, according to the *OED*, "what is in one's mind or thoughts; purpose; inclination"—a definition squaring with Shakespeare's line "I'd such a courage to do him good." Alongside these, however, its medieval meaning persists as "that quality of mind which shows itself in facing danger without fear; bravery, valour." It is, in words John Milton puts into Satan's mouth in *Paradise Lost*, "courage never to submit or yield."

But if in life, as Charles Caleb Colton wrote, "imitation is the sincerest of flattery," so in linguistics a plethora of synonyms can suggest the significance of a concept. The richness of the idea of courage comes through in the lush verbiage of my 1926 edition of *Webster's New International Dictionary*. It lists *daring, fearlessness, resolution, hardihood, audacity, firmness, mettle,* and *pluck* as synonyms for courage, before articulating the following "modifications" of the core idea:

> COURAGE (the generic term) is that firmness of spirit which meets danger without fear. BRAVERY . . . is daring, often defiant, DAUNTLESSNESS, lofty and unintimidated, GALLANTRY, dashing and adventurous, courage. BOLDNESS is the opposite of (sometimes the outgrowth of conscious resistance against) timidity; INTREPIDITY is cool fearlessness; VALOR, personal bravery, esp[ecially] in battle; PROWESS, valor united with skill. FORTITUDE is passive courage, esp. as shown in enduring pain or adversity with a steadfast and unbroken spirit. HEROISM, which may call into exercise all these modifications of courage, is contempt of danger from a noble and self-forgetful devotion to some great cause or purpose.

In support, the dictionary cites references to the poets John Milton, Percy Bysshe Shelley, Thomas Gray, William Wordsworth, and Samuel Taylor Coleridge, novelists George Meredith and William Thackeray, historian Edward Gibbon, and even a botanist, Joseph Reynolds Green.

By whatever name, the concept, translated into English as *courage,* has been treated in detail by Herodotus, Plato, Aristotle, and a host of other classical philosophers and poets—not to mention its extensive consideration by theologians in Christianity, Judaism, and other faith traditions. It is, opined Samuel Johnson, "the greatest of all virtues; because, unless a man has that virtue, he has no security for preserving any other." Or as C. S. Lewis puts it in the explicitly Christian context of *The Screwtape Letters,* "courage is not simply *one* of the virtues, but the form of every virtue at the testing point, which means at the point of highest reality." Explaining, he notes that "a chastity or honesty or mercy which yields to danger will be chaste or honest or merciful only on conditions. Pilate was merciful till it became risky."

Yet courage is different from other virtues. In *The Mystery of Courage,* William Ian Miller observes that courage is more interesting than its opposite. Reflecting on courage as expressed largely in military experience, Miller observes that "courage makes for better stories than its corresponding vice," which is "quite a contrast with other virtues," since most vices "are better material for gripping attention than their corresponding virtues." Miller also notes that "courage and its corresponding vice, cowardice, are more at the mercy of social and cultural context than some of the simpler virtues and vices."

Miller's point reminds us why our definitions of physical courage need updating over time, and how behaviors that in some eras seem immensely brave (jousting, dueling, smoking in public, going over Niagara Falls in a barrel) can in other periods look foolish or trivial. It also reminds us why courage remains such a publicly admired virtue. It lends itself to storytelling:

- Looking back on the events of September 11, 2001, we can understand why the stories of firefighters, police officers, and emergency medical teams produced such gripping tales, and why they will readily be memorialized.
- When American balladeer Burl Ives sang about a lone World War II infantryman, Roger Young, who "volunteered to meet his doom" so that "a company of men might live to fight" in the Solomon Islands, he conferred a kind of immortality on an otherwise unknown soldier.
- The nonprofit Giraffe Project, which has handed out more than 946 "commendations" since 1982, celebrates "people with vision and courage" who are "willing to stick their necks out" and sees itself as "training tomorrow's heroes."
- In Postman's Park in central London, visitors can still read early-twentieth-century tile plaques commemorating "heroic self-

sacrifice" in the stories of William Goodrum (a signalman who on February 28, 1880, "lost his life at Kingsland Road Bridge in saving a workman from death under an approaching train from Kew"), Alice Ayers ("Daughter of a bricklayer's labourer who by intrepid conduct saved 3 children from a burning house in Union Street Borough at the cost of her own young life, April 24, 1885"), Mary Rogers ("Stewardess of the Stella [who] self-sacrificed by giving up her life belt and voluntarily going down in the sinking ship" on March 30, 1899), and fifty other British men and women.

Heroism, the common theme of these stories, often suggests an out-size, extreme, or radical sort of valor. Taking our word *hero* from the Greek (where it has also come to mean a sandwich of such gargantuan proportions as to be manageable only by heroic appetites), we've expanded it beyond its original meaning as a person worthy of public honor for mythic or legendary courage, strength, and accomplishments. It now includes not only illustrious warriors but those who deserve special admiration for exceptional deeds of any sort. And since exceptional deeds are the stuff of good storytelling, it's not surprising that the word also means the principle character in a play, novel, film, or other narrative. While Miller notes that "the distinction between heroism and courage is not consistently maintained, and no great weight should be put upon it," the word usefully reminds us that courage is contextual, that exceptional valor is often in the eye of the beholder, and that, as the aphorism reminds us, "no man is a hero to his valet."

MORAL COURAGE

Moral courage, by contrast, has a far less robust etymology. In his garrulous and personable book *On Moral Courage,* the twentieth-century Scottish novelist Compton Mackenzie (one of whose tales became the immortal comic film *Tight Little Island*) notes that *moral courage* is "a late arrival in English." It shows up first in a series of aphorisms in Charles Caleb Colton's *Lacon* (1822)—the most famous of which, concerning imitation and flattery, is cited above. Not surprisingly that first reference comes about as a way to distinguish moral from physical courage, as Colton notes that "Oliver Cromwell's hypocrisy neutralized his moral courage, never his physical." Forty years later, in 1862, Sir James Fitzjames Stephen, who would afterward become a notable British judge, undertook what Mackenzie calls "the first attempt to define precisely moral courage" when he wrote, "Moral courage is readiness to expose oneself to suffering or inconvenience which does not affect the body. It arises from firmness of moral principle and is independent of the physical constitution."

Writing a century later, after the term had gradually settled into currency, Mackenzie takes Stephen to task over the word *inconvenience,* which he sees as "hardly a felicitous alternative to suffering." Moral courage, Mackenzie writes, "would be too assertive a claim for an expression of opinion or a course of action which merely led to interference with one's personal comfort or ease. Mental suffering, opprobrium or unpopularity are surely more appropriate to moral courage than inconvenience." Adding his own terms to this list, the noted English philosopher Henry Sidgwick, writing early in the twentieth century, defined moral courage as characterizing people "facing the pains and dangers of social disapproval in the performance of what they believe to be duty."

In the remainder of his book, Mackenzie teases out various other challenges facing those who would exhibit moral courage, describing them as "the courage of shocking conventional opinion" or "letting down the side." He notes that "one of the hardest tests of a man's moral courage is his ability to face the disapproval even of his friends for an action which strikes at all the traditions of his class but which nevertheless he feels compelled to take in order to be at ease with his own conscience." That test, in his view, is one not many of his nation's leaders would be

"Danger Invites Rescue"

When the legendary American jurist Benjamin N. Cardozo penned his well-known dictum "danger invites rescue," he was defending the natural reactions of those who run to aid others in distress. He was also, by extension, explaining why moral courage is so appealing to the public mind.

The case he was adjudicating, *Wagner v. International Railway* (1921), focused on a man injured while trying to rescue a cousin who had been accidentally thrown from a railway car. Should that man, Arthur Wagner, be considered as much a victim of the railway's negligence as his cousin? Of course he should, opined Cardozo. "The cry of distress is the summons to relief," he wrote, adding "the wrong that imperils life is a wrong to the imperilled victim; it is a wrong also to his rescuer." Noting that "the emergency begets the man," he went on to say that "the law does not discriminate between the rescuer oblivious of peril and the one who counts the cost. It is enough that the act, whether impulsive or deliberate, is the child of the occasion."

Cardozo's precedent makes it clear that physical courage in the service of others—in this case, Wagner's willingness to walk 445 feet along the elevated tracks in the darkness in search of his cousin— should not be unrewarded. When Wagner came to grief by falling, as he did, from the trestle, he ought not to be further punished for doing something that might seem to others imprudent or foolish. Intuitively, Cardozo's demand seems right: Wagner should be rewarded. Our sense of ethics takes comfort in seeing a recompense for his impulse to help.

In a similar way, we long to see moral courage rewarded. It seems right to us that acts of mental bravery—where we endure hardship to defend principles from significant risk—ought to be supported by public approbation. Our literature, in fact, is filled with such stories, where heroes who have the courage of their convictions win the day. Never mind that moral courage sometimes arises in a fog of ambiguity, where (in Cardozo's words) our heroes have to "choose at once, in agitation and with imperfect knowledge." And never mind that acts of moral courage often subject themselves to alternative explanations as being stupid, or hopelessly impulsive, or perversely willful—particularly while the issues are still in the air and the conclusion has yet to appear. We long to live in a world where our heroes are not penalized for their actions—a world in which, when "danger invites rescue," rescue will be applauded.

Cardozo's comment helps explain, too, why moral cowardice is so repellent. We scorn as spineless the would-be rescuers who pause, weigh their options, and refuse to act because they might risk public repudiation or personal shame. By contrast, the willingness to forge ahead where others quail is what so often distinguishes leaders from followers—provided that the action is impelled by an unselfish motive, such as a desire to relieve another's distress.

Not everyone, thankfully, has opportunities to strike out along a darkened track to find a cousin's body. But life still provides plenty of opportunities in which moral danger invites courageous and principle-based rescue. Responding to that invitation remains one of the hallmarks of true leadership.

able to pass. "In nine cases out of ten," Mackenzie observes, "the man educated at a public [i.e., independent] school will surrender his private convictions for what he believes to be the value of unity."

One of his central examples of moral courage, to which he devotes a chapter, centers on the abdication of England's King Edward VIII, who gave up his throne in 1936 to marry an American divorcée in an age when such a marriage would have scandalized the nation. In a radio broadcast on December 11 from Windsor Castle heard around the world, King Edward implored his people to "believe me when I tell you that I have found it impossible to carry the heavy burden of responsibility, and to discharge my duties as King as I would wish to do, without the help and support of the woman I love." Contrasting the two kinds of courage, Mackenzie notes that "physical courage was a characteristic of the Hanoverians . . . but the first outstanding act of moral courage by a sovereign had to wait until King Edward VIII." Yet Mackenzie is aware of the fine line of separation, the crossing of which could have turned the king's "act of tremendous moral courage" into "a piece of royal willfulness." It is "not always easy," he concludes, "to distinguish between a gesture of moral courage and a display of self-opinionated conceit."

Wrapping some of these ideas together, William Ian Miller defines moral courage as "the capacity to overcome the fear of shame and humiliation in order to admit one's mistakes, to confess a wrong, to reject evil conformity, to denounce injustice, and also to defy immoral or imprudent orders." His list of the obstacles to moral courage includes "derision, ostracism, loss of status, demotion, loss of job," which he describes as "not trivial." Distinguishing moral from physical courage, he notes that moral courage, while not requiring physical courage, can be undone by physical cowardice, and that while physical courage "decays under the intense and relentless demands of combat," moral courage "grows by the doing of deeds that require" us to put it into practice. "Standing up for what we think is right is not easy, but it may well get easier if we cultivate the habit of doing so."

Turning to the focal point of his argument—military courage in its various manifestations—Miller notes that "moral courage is the courage of the military leader who is willing to risk his reputation for courage, to suffer shame, in the interests of reason and effective action toward the goal of ultimate victory." And he quotes General Ulysses S. Grant: "No doubt the majority of the duels fought have been for want of moral courage on the part of those engaged to decline." Elsewhere, Grant appeared dismissive of moral courage, knowing that, as Miller says, "it is capable of being falsely claimed by suspected cowards."

But perhaps the role of moral courage in military action is manifested most powerfully in cases where it is absent—as it was in General Sir Redvers Henry Buller, the British commander in chief during the Boer War of 1880–81. Contemporary accounts that described him as the perfect model to lead the British Army into an expedition in South Africa focused on his physical stature: "big-boned, square-jawed, strong-minded, strong-headed." He was also, as Norman Dixon notes in *On the Psychology of Military Incompetence*, "undoubtedly brave when it came to physical danger." What was lacking was moral courage. That he was out of touch with or heedless of his soldiers was perhaps part of the organizational culture of the Victorian age, when officers were, as Dixon observes, "so busy being gentlemen, in or out of gorgeous uniforms, that they had little time for their men and a total absence of concern for the latter's welfare." More important, Buller had a habit of choosing incompetent subordinates, giving them no responsibility and refusing to take any blame when they failed. On taking his command, Buller "lost no time trying to rid himself of any direct responsibility for the conduct of the war, by handing over the reins to subordinate commanders to whom he gave no further directives." Within five days he lost three battles. Overall, in thirty-one months of fighting, the British lost twenty-two thousand men.

If it's true that top leadership can commit catastrophic blunders through a lack of moral courage, it's also true that subordinates can promote those disasters. They can fail to speak out for alternative views with sufficient force—a problem found beyond military circles as well, as the recent report of the *Columbia* Accident Investigation Board indicated. They placed much of the blame for the February 1, 2003, breakup of the U.S. space shuttle on a "broken safety culture" of the National Aeronautics and Space Administration that did not encourage a free interchange of viewpoints. Subordinates can also provide incompetent judgments. Dixon describes Douglas Haig, commander in chief of British Armies on the Western Front between 1915 and 1918, as a man of physical bravery but moral cowardice who, on finding that one of his generals had withheld crucial intelligence on enemy movements and strength, refused to discipline him. "It requires greater moral courage to fire a congenial subordinate whom one knows personally," concludes Dixon, "than to accept the death of an army whom one does not. Haig evidently lacked this particular brand of moral courage."

The point, for Dixon, is that moral courage is indispensable to military leadership; its absence is sometimes obscured by physical courage; and the qualities that take its place—"moral cowardice, indecisiveness, secretiveness and sensitivity to criticism"—combine to produce supreme incompetence.

Scanning the above examples, it is clear that the term *moral courage,* while relatively fresh from the linguistic mint, describes a venerable idea. Still, with the exception of a short sermon published in the nineteenth century, the catalog of the Library of Congress lists no book simply titled *Moral Courage.* And only in the last decade have more than a few books been published with that phrase anywhere in their titles. Even Miller's notable compendium, *The Mystery of Courage,* devotes only a scant seventeen pages to the topic of moral courage—and then adds a palliative to the chapter heading, calling it "Moral Courage and Civility."

Yet the term is suddenly becoming popular. It is increasingly showing up in conference titles, in school curricula, and in prizes and awards. As this book goes to print, a Google search reveals more than 821,000 entries for moral courage—citing everything from a Moral Courage Award in Hillsborough County, Florida (to be given to "individuals and/or groups who demonstrate high ethical standards and moral courage, and whose actions have made a difference in the community"), to a Web-based compendium of news stories about athletes compiled by the Sports Ethics Institute under the heading of "Integrity and Moral Courage in Sports." More recently, Senator John McCain, in his 2004 book *Why Courage Matters*—a post–9/11 examination of his own and others' courage— writes briefly about moral courage, calling it "the enforcing virtue, the one that makes all the others possible," and describing it as "the courage to keep your virtue when facing unwanted consequences."

Why this efflorescence of interest? Compton Mackenzie, who admits to addressing the topic from a secular rather than a spiritual perspective, speculates that only with the decline of belief in an afterlife does the focus of human attention shift to present-day existence. Since "the assurance of another life beyond the grave has come to seem to more and more people less certain," he observes, "a feeling for the value of human life has become deeper and more widespread." There may be, he adds, "some significance in the fact that the first definition of moral courage was not made until the security of faith was being assailed by the development of human knowledge." If moral courage reaches its highest purpose in defending human life and values, it must start with the assumption that human values are of paramount importance and that no life is expendable—two rather modern assumptions.

William Ian Miller, taking a different tack, notes that "there is little need to carve out a notion of moral courage in an age in which it was so clearly understood that courage of whatever sort meant that your body was ultimately at risk." When *every* sort of courage risked physical destruction, in other words, why bother to parse the finer distinctions between the moral and the physical? But by the nineteenth century, Miller argues, European upper- and middle-class culture had attained enough security that "people could undertake to support unpopular causes, to stand up against injustice, and not die or be imprisoned." The price they paid was "loss of social standing, being despised by 'decent' people . . . [and] often serious economic costs," but not a risk to life and limb. So it proves in our age, when the outrage of Brown & Williamson Tobacco Corporation whistleblower Jeffrey Wigand could lead to his firing rather than to his murder, or when those objecting to the excessive compensation of New York Stock Exchange chairman Richard Grasso could see him removed from office rather than have their own heads removed, as might well have happened had any of their ancestors publicly criticized the wealth of Henry VIII.

It would appear, then, that a taxonomy of moral courage is beginning to coalesce under three headings:

- **Motives.** There appear to be some deep-rooted impulses for moral courage: firmness of moral principle (Stephen); duty (Sidgwick); being at ease with one's own conscience, private convictions (Mackenzie); a desire to reject evil conformity, denounce injustice, or defy immoral orders (Miller).

- **Inhibitions.** Those motives, however, face two sorts of restraints: *counterfeits,* such as willfulness and self-opinionated conceit (Mackenzie), and *obstacles,* such as a refusal to take blame, moral cowardice, indecisiveness, secretiveness, sensitivity to criticism (Dixon), and a desire for acceptance (Mackenzie).
- **Risks.** Most important, moral courage encounters an entire constellation of hazards, variously described as suffering, inconvenience (Stephen); mental suffering, opprobrium, unpopularity, shocking conventional opinion, letting down the side, disapproval of friends (Mackenzie); the pains and dangers of social disapproval (Sidgwick); shame, humiliation, derision, ostracism, loss of status, demotion, and loss of job (Miller).

While none of the formal definitions in this chapter quite accounts for Viktor Pestov's experience, this taxonomy begins to define it. Spreading his hand-typed pamphlets across Sverdlovsk in 1968, Pestov risked no social standing. He was unconcerned about the opprobrium of government authorities. He seems not to have contemplated the risk of mental suffering. Any fear of "letting down the side" paled in comparison to his willingness to see his parents' careers ruined. And while he no doubt encountered plenty of shame, derision, and humiliation at the hands of the guards at Perm-36, the brutal physicalities of his situation must have taxed his endurance far more deeply.

Yet were we to dismiss Pestov's case as merely one of physical courage, the very concrete at Perm-36 would cry out in objection. So would our own intuitions. To be sure, he knew the risks to his physical well-being. Grim tales of the gulags were in circulation during his youth. Yet his circumstance reminds us of an entirely different side of moral courage, which consists less in overcoming the negative than in sustaining the positive. It does not back you fearfully into dangerous corners so much as draw you inexorably toward first principles. It is less about risks, hazards, obstacles, and counterfeits than about values, virtues, standards, and rightness.

Whatever definition we shape will need to accommodate both these dimensions, the positive as well as the negative. It will need to help us understand not only what Pestov feared and overcame but also what he held in highest regard and dared not abandon. It will need, in other words, to recognize that at bottom moral courage is *the courage to be moral.* Whether that definition has any practical value will depend on whether we can successfully define *moral,* which is the topic of the next chapter.

Moral Courage Checklist
Step 1: Assess the Situation

Does my situation require courage? I may be experiencing a timorous, shrinking sense. It may manifest itself in physiological symptoms such as clammy hands and trembling knees, or as a mental wish to avoid, procrastinate, deny, flee, or melt into the woodwork. And it may be a mix of both.

The first need is to analyze the situation. What is the *central* concern? Is it a fear of bodily harm? If so, the situation requires valor and bravery of a physical sort. But if the central concern has to do with a risk to reputation or friendship, or with a conviction that a fundamental principle needs to be honored, the need is for moral courage.

To further assess the situation, ask yourself five questions:

1. What motives make me want to act? Duty? Conscience? Outrage at injustice?

2. What inhibitions would keep me from acting? These may be the opposites of my motives (refusal to take responsibility, shamelessness, indifference) or they may be counterfeits: stubborn willfulness, priggish moralizing, a desire for self-aggrandizement.

➤

3. What risks do I perceive? Could I suffer ostracism, disrepute, shame, derision? Might the hurt I occasion to family, friends, or colleagues outweigh any help the world may get from my act?

4. Am I the one most suited to this action, or is this a stand someone else should take?

5. If there's no one else suited to take this stand, am I prepared to endure the consequences?

CHAPTER THREE

The Courage to Be Moral

If humanity is to survive and avoid new catastrophes, then the global political order has to be accompanied by a sincere and mutual respect among the various spheres of civilization, culture, nations, or continents, and by honest efforts on their part to seek and find the values or basic moral imperatives they have in common.

—Václav Havel

Though she's now the chief executive of a financial services firm, Valerie would be the first to tell you she comes from a modest family background. She has no personal wealth behind her. No trust funds cushioned her upbringing. No family business spun off profits in her direction. She didn't grow up at country clubs or on yachts, nor did she rub shoulders with friends whose parents sat on boards or dispensed charitable largesse throughout the community. Quite the opposite.

"When I was twelve, my father lost our home and family business in a bankruptcy," she recalls. "He walked out, discouraged and angry, never helping in any way through the years." She and her mother "moved from two new cars, fancy schools and clothes, and household help to a small farming town where we were clearly poor." Smart and hardworking, she learned money management as a vocation, picking it up not from well-heeled family members but through careful study in academic and professional circles.

Given her current line of work, those are important points. Her business has only one client: a large, multigenerational family of substantial wealth. As head of the Family Office, Valerie's task is to manage more than fifty employees in a variety of professions—law, accounting, auditing, financial planning—who provide whatever services the hundreds of family members need as they grow and sustain their many-faceted fortunes.

In the eight years Valerie has been in this position, she's done exceedingly well by her clients. Her contract, which pays her nicely but not extravagantly, reflects their satisfaction with her work. She's happy with her job. She respects the family. She has found plenty to keep her professionally satisfied. Which is why she was surprised by the moral courage she suddenly had to display not long ago in the face of a powerful temptation.

She was approached by the founder of another financial services firm, whom she thought of as a reputable man. His search for a new chief executive had led him to her doorstep. Being content where she was, Valerie had no difficulty initially deflecting the offer. Soon a sweeter deal was on the table. It multiplied her salary considerably and provided the potential for significant additional benefits. No longer quite so sure of her position, she struggled with the offer, hesitating to take it. The longer she stalled, the more the offer continued to rise, until she could no longer resist discussing it with the founder of the firm.

The more he talked, the more she found him persuasive. It was, indeed, a most attractive job. It would properly reward her for a record of excellent work. It would crown an already exemplary career with a satisfying sense of accomplishment. And although she never set out to be a "textbook case" of anything, this job could catapult her into a category she'd always admired: the self-made American success story.

So the negotiations moved forward to a final offer. In it, the founder stipulated that she should begin work immediately. Under Valerie's Family Office contract, however, she had a clear obligation to give the family six months' notice that she was leaving. The only way to avoid that requirement would be for her to indicate that she was dissatisfied with her current employer, or that she needed to move on for the sake of her professional growth and had initiated the conversation with the other company herself, neither of which was true. The founder of the offering firm, anticipating this problem, included the text of a letter from Valerie to the Family Office asserting these very things. All that was needed was Valerie's signature.

Taken aback by that request, she told the founder she could not do such a thing. She saw it as fundamentally dishonest under the law, irresponsible to her prior commitments, and disrespectful to a family she liked very much. The founder, however, had anticipated that response as well. His counteroffer was immediate: an additional $1 million to secure her signature.

Valerie never wavered. Something deep in her nature—call it conscience, conviction, principles, values, integrity—gave her the courage to refuse. Her explanation was simple. She told the founder she could not work for someone who requested her to lie or break a promise made in good faith to her employer. While the request itself concerned her mightily, she was even more troubled by what it told her about her prospective employer—and, by extension, the organizational culture he was probably creating at his firm. Rejecting an offer that was extraordinary by every measure, Valerie remained at the Family Office. Nor did she use that incident as a source of leverage with the family to increase her compensation. She remains well paid, though she has never become rich.

Does that matter? Given her background, she admits that "a really good income was probably more of a temptation to me than most people. I remember on my thirteenth birthday deciding that this was a valuable experience, being really poor, but *once* was enough."

She learned, she said, that "girls had to get educations and make good livings to support themselves and their families. And if they want to get married they shouldn't marry flashy and high maintenance, like Dad, they should marry steady and true and committed."

The qualities identified by that thirteen-year-old—steady and true and committed—were still there decades later when this temptation arose. So was something else. "I have learned to think financial *serenity*," she says, "not financial *security.*" Taken together, those values under-girded her courage to resist that temptation. Today, she's sure enough of her decision that she can still look herself in the mirror and know she did the right thing.

But what if, like the witch's mirror in the fable of Snow White, hers could talk back? What would it tell her?

Maybe it would say, "Foolish girl! You had a promise of immense future wealth right in your hands, and you walked away. You know you've never had much, and this was your chance to make it *really* big. Call that moral courage? I call it stupidity."

Or maybe it would say, "Good for you. You resisted one of the most subtle temptations that life can toss up. Even if he hadn't turned out to be a wholesale prevaricator, even if he didn't start deceiving you as well as others, even if that were the last lie he'd ever been party to—you couldn't have accepted those terms and still lived by your values. You'd have com-promised the most important thing about yourself—your character. You stood up to that lie. That took real moral courage."

At its simplest, then, moral courage is *the courage to be moral.* But what, the mirror might ask, does *moral* mean? Valerie's experience reveals her reliance on three values: *honesty, responsibility,* and *respect.* That's not surprising. Those are three of the core values that define our sense of the word *moral.* With two others—*fairness* and *compassion*—they make up the five-fingered hand that appears to constitute humanity's common moral framework.

Humanity's common moral framework. Can there be such a thing? Given the global diversity of culture, ethnicity, race, religion, gender, political persuasion, economic disparity, and educational attainment, is it possible to discover a core of shared values operating across all these variations? Is it possible that the moral relativism so vigorously espoused in the twentieth century is simply a hypothesized intellectual conve-nience rather than an empirical fact? Is there really a deep ethic, a sub-strate of moral values that provides constant aspirational direction to human endeavor throughout the world?

Or is morality simply a set of personal and fungible guidelines for behavior, shifting with each situation, varying widely from culture to culture, and easily negotiable on occasions where, as in Valerie's case, an extra $1 million suddenly appears on the table?

Based on our research at the Institute for Global Ethics, the former appears to be true. It's becoming clear that, wherever we go in the world and ask, "What do you think are the core moral and ethical values held in highest regard in your community?" we hear the same five answers: *honesty, responsibility, respect, fairness,* and *compassion.* As the following sections indicate, the evidence for this five-fingered hand of values—drawn from global interviewing, facilitated discourse, survey research, and textual analysis—goes very deep.

GLOBAL INTERVIEWING

In the early 1990s, I conducted face-to-face interviews with twenty-four people from sixteen countries. Each interviewee, in the eyes of his or her peers, was something of an ethical standard-bearer—"a keeper of the conscience of their community," as I described them at the time, "a center of moral gravity." To each I put a common question: If you could help create a global code of ethics, what would be in it? What moral values would you bring to the table from your own culture and background?

The resulting interviews came together in 1994 in my book *Shared Values for a Troubled World: Conversations with Men and Women of Conscience.* If the interviewees could have addressed these questions together in the same room rather than in the pages of a book, they would have emerged, I felt, with the following list of common values:

- Love
- Truthfulness
- Fairness
- Freedom

- Unity
- Tolerance
- Responsibility
- Respect for life

This list is not in priority order. And the words are less important than the ideas: "Love," for example, might have been reported as *compassion, caring, kindness,* or *empathy,* while "truthfulness" could have appeared as *integrity* or *honesty.* Yet however diverse their backgrounds, these interviewees appeared to hold in common these eight major moral ideas.

These interviews were, of course, examples of journalism. As such, they depended on a relationship of trust between writer and reader regarding some key questions. Why were these interviewees selected? What were they asked? How were their responses interpreted? Which of their comments were reported, and which were not? Only when the reader believes the reporter has worked hard to achieve objectivity will that trust be created.

At its best, then, journalism is flawed. It typically gets the story first and tells it in compelling ways. But it doesn't always get it right. For that, three other methodologies are helpful: facilitated discourse, survey research, and textual analysis. Each of these methods seeks to extend the pool of participants, ensure greater levels of objectivity, and impose higher standards of validity. If, as has been noted, "the plural of *anecdotes* is *data,*" these methods seek to move from storytelling to social science, building from narratives to numbers in an effort to create other kinds of arguments.

FACILITATED DISCOURSE

Our work with facilitated discourse began in the early 1990s with the institute's Ethical Fitness Seminar. To date, the institute estimates that some eighteen thousand people have gone through some version of this seminar in the United States and a range of other countries that includes Australia, Bangladesh, Belgium, Brazil, Canada, Chile, China, El Salvador, Germany, Guatemala, Hong Kong, India, Indonesia, Ireland, Jamaica, Japan, Mexico, New Zealand, Poland, Singapore, South Africa, Taiwan, Thailand, Turkey, the United Arab Emirates, and the United Kingdom.

Central to the seminar is an exercise that asks, "What are our values?" Like the question at the core of *Shared Values,* this one seeks to identify a core of shared values through what we call "The Schoolhouse Exercise." Imagine, we say, that this group of participants in our seminar room is a school board. If they are Americans, they understand what that means: a body of locally elected officials having budgetary authority over the community's tax-supported schools. If they are from other countries, the formula is varied to recognize some entity—perhaps a board of governors or a parent-teacher organization—that has significant input into the community's schools.

Imagine, we continue, that our school board has just constructed a new school building for the ten-to-fourteen-year-old population—in American parlance, a "middle school." On the lintel above the entrance we plan to carve the basic moral values that we want to hand on to the next generation. But we need to be sure they reflect the views of the entire community. The list should be broad enough to apply to everyone who walks through that door—students, teachers, coaches, counselors, government inspectors, administrators, custodians, cafeteria workers, parents, siblings, other relatives, social workers, journalists, and ordinary citizens. While they are primarily aimed at the students, these are not "*their* values" but "*our* values."

What shall be put above that door? We start by assembling a list, on a blackboard or a flip chart, of as many values as the group can bring forward in fifteen minutes. A typical list, in no particular order, looks something like table 1.

Kindness	Respect	Loyalty
Honesty	Compassion	Tolerance
Love	Freedom	Caring
Fairness	Initiative	Patience
Industriousness	Unity	Sincerity
Equity	Conscience	Hope
Perseverance	Logic	Teamwork
Common good	Character	Faith
Integrity	Peace	Support
Trust	Diligence	Knowledge
Responsibility	Honor	Dedication
Dignity	Cooperation	Creativity
Courage	Justice	Brotherhood
Charity	Individualism	Parity
Understanding	Discipline	Selflessness
Awareness	Community	Balance
Leadership	Truth	Safety

Table 1. Proposed Shared Values

Each participant then takes a moment to write down, individually, the five values he or she wants to see above the door. Then, gathering in small teams, the participants arrive at a consensus on the five values their group wants to bring forward. Finally, each group reports its finding to the whole seminar. With some further discussion—often aimed at putting broadly synonymous terms together, combining *fairness* and *justice,* for instance, or *respect* and *tolerance*—the team lists are brought together into a single seminar-wide list of five shared values. That in itself is often an eye-opener for the participants, proof that a diverse group really can arrive at a shared statement of values. But it's more than that. It's at this point that the seminar leader shares with the group the list of values he or she expected them to find:

- Honesty
- Respect
- Responsibility
- Fairness
- Compassion

How does the leader know what to expect? Because, after doing this process hundreds of times with scores of different facilitators, we find an almost uncanny commonality in those five answers. The list produced by a particular group, of course, may not be identical to the one above. Theirs may speak of candor, tolerance, commitment, equality, kindness, or other roughly synonymous words. But the overarching moral ideas behind the words are so often the same that our seminar leaders feel comfortable using this list of five as a benchmark.

One facilitator, Jenny Smucker, conducted twenty-four such exercises over a fourteen-month period in 1994–95 for some 250 citizens of Orrville, Ohio, in connection with a local character education program. Each exercise was open to the public, convening in various places around town on weekday evenings or Saturday mornings. Here, too, the same five values emerged, as illustrated by the cumulative chart she kept of the number of groups choosing each of these terms as one of its top five.

Value	Number of Groups Choosing
Honesty/Integrity/Truthful	24
Respect/Self-respect	22
Work Ethic/Responsibility	22
Compassion/Empathy/Love	19
Self-control/Self-discipline/Discipline	14
Courage	12
Fairness/Justice	12
Cooperation	7

➤

Value	Number of Groups Choosing
Commitment	6
Accountability	5
Trustworthiness/Trust	4
Kindness	3
Open-minded/Unprejudiced/Equality	3
Belief in God	2
Caring	2
Courtesy	2
Golden Rule	2
Hope	2
Loyalty	2
Patience	2
Tolerance	2
Unselfish	2
Chastity	1
Dedication	1
Dependability	1
Pride	1
Respect for Community	1
Vision	1
Wisdom	1

Table 2. Values, Orrville, Ohio

Here again, the key terms that surfaced in nineteen or more of these twenty-four sessions were (to use the labels we've used elsewhere) responsibility, compassion, honesty, and respect—with fairness (12), typically our fifth value, tied with courage and barely eased out by self-control (14).

Is this commonality a purely American phenomenon? No. A 1996 session I conducted in simultaneous translation with the editors of National Television of Chile at their Santiago headquarters generated a similar list:

- Solidaridad
- Responsabilidad
- Libertad
- Tolerancia
- Verdad/Honestidad
- Justicia

Likewise, a session in Tokyo conducted with a group of Becton Dickinson's Japanese executives on July 16, 1998, led by an ethics trainer for BD, produced the results shown in table 3.

正直	Honesty
自由	Freedom
責任	Responsibility
公平	Fairness
愛	Love

Table 3. BD Values, Tokyo, Japan

On January 26, 2000, a similar session was conducted in Suzhou, China, with thirty-one Chinese BD executives. Table 4 lists the now-familiar top values.

Value	Percent
Responsibility	93
Fairness	55
Respect	55
Truth	44

Table 4. BD Values, Suzhou, China

But are these results only available from elites, or when working with certain professions or educational levels? We don't think so. We've done this work with more than seven thousand prisoners in North Carolina.

We've done it at the John Marshall High School in Los Angeles, where at last count fifty-eight languages were spoken by its low-income, inner-city students. We've worked with environmental organizations and military personnel, federal agencies and church groups, police departments and hospitals, professional associations and urban schools. We've had participants as young as eight years old and others who are in their nineties. What we're finding confirms our hypothesis, which is that a broad consensus around five values—honesty, responsibility, fairness, respect, and compassion—surfaces wherever you do this work, without reference to nationality, race, gender, religion, economic status, or political persuasion.

To be sure, facilitated discourse, like journalism, has its own limitations. Facilitators can load the question, planting ideas in the heads of their participants or approving of some answers more than others. So we typically ask, as the Schoolhouse session is concluding, whether the audience agrees that the facilitator ran the meeting rather than manipulated it. Almost invariably the group says "you facilitated" rather than "you coerced."

Even so, two other limitations may arise here. First, seminars typically comprise a self-selected set of participants who already believe that ethics matters. Are such people more attuned to conversations about values than others, and therefore more aware of a common core of values than those new to the topic? Second, any seminar promotes a group mentality. The Schoolhouse Exercise, in particular, makes anonymity impossible. Does that fact intensify or even create the convergence we observe around common responses? To address these issues, survey research is needed.

SURVEY RESEARCH

In 1996 the institute teamed with the Gallup Organization to conduct the first of a number of values surveys. This one, a self-administered questionnaire, was distributed at the State of the World Forum, a meeting in

San Francisco cochaired by Mikhail Gorbachev, Oscar Arias, former U.N. High Commissioner for Refugees Rudd Lubbers, and others. Of some 650 attendees, 272 responded to our survey. They came from forty different countries and fifty different faith groups. Presented with a list of fifteen possible values—a set based on our earlier research—respondents were asked to select the five values most important to them in their daily lives. The results appear in figure 2.

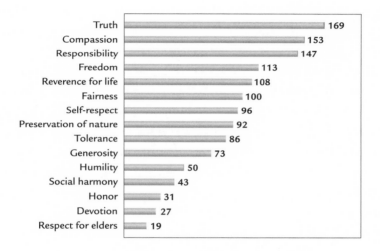

Figure 2. State of the World Forum Values

The results fall into three sets.

- A top level that includes *truth, compassion,* and *responsibility*
- A middle tier including *freedom, reverence for life, fairness, self-respect, preservation of nature, tolerance,* and *generosity*
- A bottom set comprising *humility, social harmony, honor, devotion,* and *respect for elders*

The top three are among the five we regularly find in our seminars. In fact, if *self-respect* can be read as standing for *respect* in general, that five-fingered hand of values is embraced within the top seven values in this survey. Further disaggregating the data, we found no statistically significant distinction between the values held by males and females, nor between native English speakers and those raised speaking another language. Perhaps more important, there was no distinction between the values chosen by those who were "strongly religious" and those who said they were "not at all religious." This data suggests that some attributes popularly thought to relate most directly to values—including religion and gender—are not particularly good predictors of the values actually chosen. Evident, instead, is the commonality of our core values across a spectrum of key differences.

In March of 1998 the institute sent surveys to the one thousand top executives of a leading U.S. financial services company. Of the 710 replies, 562 came from the United States and 128 from other countries. The executives were asked to select, from a list of thirteen values, the five personal values most important to them. A second question, referring to the same list of thirteen, asked them to identify the five values that "should guide the formation of an ethics program" at their company. The results appear in figure 3.

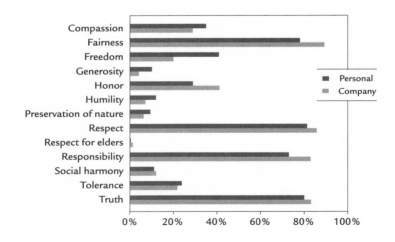

Figure 3. Executive Values

Again, the four top values are not surprising—*fairness, respect, responsibility,* and *truth*—although *compassion,* strong among State of the
World Forum respondents but typically less prominent in corporate
settings, drops off steeply to sixth place behind *freedom* (as a personal
value) and *honor* (as a company value). These executives, however, don't
see themselves as Jekylls and Hydes. As the lack of distinction between
personal and company values suggests, they don't feel they must apply
one set of values at home and another at work. That commonality should
make this firm a very attractive employer—an honor that, in fact,
the firm regularly achieves on annual lists of America's best places to
work.

In December of 1998 the institute administered the identical survey to
405 employees of another financial services company, which had merged
with the corporation over the summer. While industry gossip identified
these as very different firms, figure 4 suggests that, at bottom, employees
of the two firms almost precisely share their personal values.

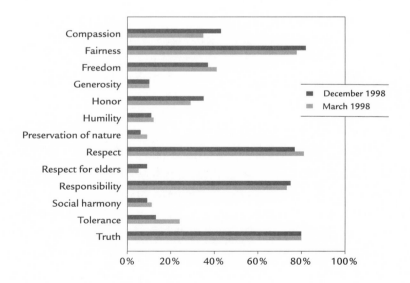

Figure 4. Executive Values in a Merger

In 1998 this data was taken as one predictor of the potential success of the merger—a prediction that has since proved true.

The following year, we organized two values surveys for the Illinois Community College Board, which oversees the state's forty-nine-campus, one-million-student system of two-year colleges. The first survey, conducted by the Gallup Organization, polled a random sample of 735 adults, eighteen years and older, drawn from the general population of Illinois. Meanwhile a second survey, conducted by the institute, was mailed to randomly identified staff members, faculty, and students, producing 1,659 responses with participation from all the campuses. Each survey presented respondents with identical lists of fifteen values and asked them to select the five that were most important to them in their daily lives. The results appear in table 5.

Value	Community College (%)	Statewide (%)
Responsibility	76	63
Truth	71	71
Fairness	55	48
Compassion	50	44
Self-respect	50	49

Table 5. Community and Statewide Values, Illinois

Again, the expected five core values top the list among campus respondents—and, with *freedom* added, are part of the top six in the eyes of the Illinois public. As our report noted, this commonality "helps explode two myths about values," which are, first, that "since everyone has different values, there is no core of values that can be taught" and, second, that "the general public has a very different set of values from those found on community college campuses." Later in the Gallup survey, in fact, these myths were dismissed even more formidably: when the issue turned to money, 85 percent of Illinois citizens disagreed with the assertion that "no tax money should be spent teaching values in community colleges."

In March of 2000 the institute and the Gallup Organization conducted a telephone survey for the Nathan Cummings Foundation of 763 undergraduates from forty-eight states (only South Dakota and Delaware were not represented) who were *not* actively involved in environmental issues. They were read a list of fifteen values and asked to rate each on a scale ranging from 1 ("not at all important") to 5 ("extremely important"). Unlike earlier institute lists, this one included a number of values that were explicitly environmental and others that were more materialistic in nature. The results appear in table 6.

Value*	Percent[†]
Honesty	78.8
Respect	70.6
Responsibility	64.1
Equality	59.2
Fairness	56.4
Compassion	52.4
Spirituality	44.0
World Peace	42.5
Social Justice	40.2
Preventing Pollution	26.9
Environmental Protection	24.0
Unity with Nature	14.5
Authority	13.2
Wealth	8.0
Social Status	5.1

* *Values rated 1 ("not at all important") to 5 ("extremely important") as guiding principles in students' lives.*

[†] *Percent responding "5."*

Table 6. Undergraduate Values

Again, despite the popularity on campuses of terms like "spirituality," "world peace," "environmental protection," and "unity with nature," the students chose the familiar set of values. In fact, if "equality" and "fairness" can be blended together—as participants in our seminars often do—the top five on this list are identical with the top five we typically find.

As part of its ethics training program, BD (Becton Dickinson and Company) surveyed participants about their core values. Each employee was asked to identify his or her "top five" values. By August 2001, with 420 responses in hand, the results looked like figure 5.

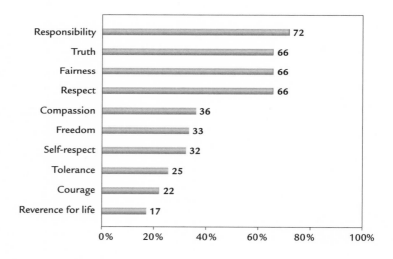

Figure 5. Values at BD

Again, as at the financial services firm surveyed earlier, the top four are predictable—with a sharp drop between them and the fifth, compassion.

In the fall of 2000 the institute teamed with O'Neil Associates of Tempe, Arizona, in a values survey for Maricopa Community College District in the Greater Phoenix area. The survey captured data from 1,458 randomly selected county residents, faculty and staff of the college, and students. Among the questions was one asking them to rate the importance of fourteen values in their personal lives. Table 7 reports the average ratings for all college respondents (450 residential and adjunct faculty) and 566 staff, compared to a 505-participant sample from the general public in Maricopa County.

Value*	College	Public
Truth	3.75	3.44
Responsibility	3.72	3.37
Respect	3.66	3.31
Fairness	3.60	3.28
Freedom	3.58	3.42
Reverence for Life	3.53	3.35
Honor	3.51	3.34
Compassion	3.39	3.12
Tolerance	3.29	2.98
Devotion	3.14	3.07
Social Harmony	3.12	2.82
Preservation of Nature	3.09	2.88
Generosity	3.06	2.90
Humility	3.02	2.84

* Average ratings for moral values by Maricopa Colleges sample and for general public (scale: 1 = "not very important"; 2 = "moderately important"; 3 = "very important"; 4 = "extremely important").

Table 7. Maricopa Colleges Values

Again, the same core values rise to the top. And although the public rates every value lower on the scale than do the college participants, the general distribution of the rankings is very much the same. That phenomenon parallels a distinction in the responses of men and women: women faculty, staff, and students rated all fourteen values higher than men, and by statistically significant margins for ten of the values. Yet the overall rankings of values from highest to lowest for men and women dif-

fered very little, with the top eight being in the same order for both gen-
ders. When religion and politics were factored in, there was no significant
difference in response for the top values: whether or not the respondents
were deeply religious and where they fell on the liberal-to-conservative
scale had no bearing on their choice of the top values—although significant variations appeared for values lower down the scale.

In May of 2001 the institute distributed a values survey to key English-
speaking managers and employees of CARE Bangladesh. Responses were
received from 135 employees. As part of the survey, respondents were
asked to choose from a list of thirteen values the five most important to
them. Respondents also had the opportunity to add one "other" value not
on the list. The results are shown in table 8.

Value*	Chosen (%) [†]
Responsibility	88
Respect	79
Fairness	78
Truth	70
Freedom	47
Tolerance	32
Compassion	22
Social Harmony	17
Honor	13
Other	12
Preservation of Nature	12
Humility	11
Generosity	5
Respect for Elders	4

* *Moral values chosen by respondents as important to them.*
[†] *Percentage of respondents choosing the value.*

Table 8. CARE Bangladesh Values

Again, the same values appear in common. The only differences among respondents' values choices were that women were more likely than men to choose humility; younger respondents chose generosity more often than older respondents; and employees with shorter job tenures were more likely than others to choose honor, while those with longer tenures were more likely to choose respect. Otherwise, the values reflect no differences based on the demographics.

Like facilitated discourse, survey research methodology points toward a core of five shared values. But it, too, has limitations. Unlike the seminar methodology, it provides no realistic way to allow each individual to propose his or her own set of fifty to seventy-five potential values from which to select five. Nor, given the limits of time and funding, is it often feasible to ask open-ended questions. Finally, the human mind can't easily hold in thought a long list (especially when read over the phone) and then select the five most important. So the most successful surveys involve a telephone solicitation followed by the mailing of a questionnaire. That not only requires a far shorter list of values from which to choose—typically between thirteen and seventeen—but also tends to limit the responses to the universe of those who can read and write.

Is there, then, a way to capture a sense of the values *already seen to be held in high regard* within a particular culture? That's where textual analysis proves useful.

TEXTUAL ANALYSIS

Much has been written about corporate codes of ethics. Some are aimed largely at compliance, detailing a series of *don'ts* for their employees to avoid. Others concentrate on values, setting forth the virtues and standards to which employees ought to aspire. The former are often lengthy, sometimes cumbersome, and rarely memorable. The latter, by contrast, can generally be reduced to a set of core values. Not surprisingly, those values bear a strong resemblance to the ones we find through facilitated discourse and survey research.

In a single page, for example, Levi Strauss adumbrated six "Ethical Principles" described as "the values that set the ground rules for all that we do as employees." Each was followed by one or several sentences expanding on its meaning and application. The values are:

- Honesty
- Promise-keeping
- Fairness
- Respect for others
- Compassion
- Integrity

If *promise-keeping* is a form of *responsibility,* this code squares exactly with our five core values, adding a sixth, *integrity,* as a kind of summary or capstone.

In a slightly longer format, McDonnell Douglas (prior to its merger with Boeing) developed a code that centered on core values but expanded on each one. Its code noted that its employees should strive to be:

- *Honest* and trustworthy in all our relationships
- Reliable in carrying out assignments and *responsibilities*
- Truthful and accurate in what we say and write
- Cooperative and constructive in all work undertaken
- *Fair* and considerate in our treatment of fellow employees, customers, and all other persons
- Law-abiding in all our activities
- Committed to accomplishing all tasks in a superior way
- Economical in utilizing company resources
- Dedicated in service to our company and to improvement of the quality of life in the world in which we live

In the italicized words, their code picked up three of our five core values—adding a fourth, *respect*, if that is what is implied by the adjectives "cooperative and constructive."

The list of corporate examples could go on and on. Turning from corporate to academic life, it is instructive to select a single value from the five—honesty, for example—and note its central role in a number of codes:

- In its publication titled *The Fundamental Values of Academic Integrity*, the Center for Academic Integrity notes that "an academic community of integrity advances the quest for truth and knowledge by requiring intellectual and personal honesty in learning, teaching, research, and service."
- The "Carolinian Creed" at the University of South Carolina asks students to agree to "practice personal and academic integrity" defined in such a way as to "eliminate the practice of plagiarism or borrowing another student's homework, lying, deceit, excusemaking, and infidelity or disloyalty in personal relationships. . . ."
- The Honor Code of the United States Air Force Academy states succinctly that "we will not lie, steal, or cheat, nor tolerate among us anyone who does."
- The Air Force Academy's two-part injunction—against doing these acts oneself and against tolerating them in others—is picked up by the Haas School of Business at the University of California, Berkeley, in its undergraduate code of ethics: "Neither this school, its students, nor its professional associations will condone cheating, lying, or any other misrepresentations. Moreover, anyone who willingly conceals these activities will be considered accomplices and equally culpable."

In similar ways, the other core values echo through the literature of ethics codes.

Among the most interesting trends, however, is the movement toward ethics in government. A report issued in 2000 by the Organization for Economic Cooperation and Development, titled *Trust in Government: Ethics Measures in OECD Countries,* bluntly asserts that "integrity has become the fundamental condition for governments to provide a trustworthy and effective framework for the economic and social life of their citizens." From an extensive survey of its twenty-nine member nations, the report lists "the 8 most frequently stated core public service values" and notes the number of countries articulating them in their own public documents, shown in table 9.

Value	Number of Countries
Impartiality	24
Legality	22
Integrity	18
Transparency	14
Efficiency	14
Equality	11
Responsibility	11
Justice	10

Table 9. OECD Values

If for *integrity* we can read *honesty* and for *justice* we substitute *fairness*—and if *impartiality* (further defined in the report as "neutrality" and "objectivity") covers some of the ideas underlying *respect*—then this list (which already includes *responsibility*) covers four of the five core values we find in our surveys and seminars.

GLOBAL COMMONALITIES—
AND DIFFERENCES

The proposition that universals exist is neither new nor surprising. In 1945 the American anthropologist George P. Murdock, countering a trend among his colleagues to focus on cultural diversity rather than similarity, noted seventy-three elements of what he called "the common denominator of culture" that included everything from property rights and puberty customs to ethics and etiquette. Several decades later, looking more specifically at what he calls "spiritual values," psychologist Abraham H. Maslow argued that such values are not "the exclusive possession of organized churches" but are "well within the jurisdiction of a suitably enlarged science" and therefore are "the general responsibility of *all* mankind." He then went on to specify a list of fourteen "Being-values"—including truth (or honesty), justice (or fairness), goodness (or benevolence), wholeness, and uniqueness—that he called "the irreducible, intrinsic values of . . . reality."

More recently, reviewing a broad range of scholarly work on universal values, Yale sociologist Wendell Bell has noted that

> . . . the path toward a harmonious global society and moral community is well marked by widely shared human values. Markers include values such as individual responsibility, treating others as we wish them to treat us, respect for life, treating all other people with dignity (without regard to distinctions of age, sex, race, skin color, physical or mental ability, language, religion, political view, or national or social origin), patience, understanding and acceptance of one another, forgiveness, solidarity and relatedness with other people of the world, kindliness and generosity, caring for others, compassion, love for one another, equality between men and women, nonviolence, economic and social justice, peace and global order, nature-friendly ways of life, respect for human rights

and fundamental values, constancy and trustworthiness, truthfulness and honesty, moderation and modesty, loyalty, safety and security, freedom as long as no harm is done to others, tolerance, and sexuality that expresses and reinforces a loving relationship lived by equal partners.

Building on that platform, the research reported here does not focus on behaviors, nor on points of politeness, nor on values that exist primarily in a cultural, an economic, a political, or even an aesthetic dimension. It looks specifically at the moral values, those that address the difference between right and wrong or good and evil. What is true of the larger picture remains true in this narrower, more sharply focused range: there is indeed a core of shared values, widely held across numerous cultures, that appears to express itself through the five moral ideas of honesty, fairness, respect, responsibility, and compassion.

To say that much, however, is not to end the argument. If it is true, as anthropologist Paul Bohannan argues, that "human moralities throughout the world have a fascinating similarity beneath superficial differences," two issues remain. First, are those similarities real or merely linguistic—an appearance of sameness induced by similar words that, when translated back into their original language, have distinctly different meanings? Second, if these similarities are real, why is there so much variation among individuals and cultures?

The first question deserves ongoing examination. Early research by the institute suggests that respondents in India, Japan, and the United States, when asked to choose among five definitions for such core values as responsibility, honesty, and fairness, did indeed coalesce around the same definition for each term. And it is a matter less of research than of simple observation that mothers everywhere, if asked what values they most want their children to be grounded in and to express, will come up with very similar definitions of love, respect, and responsibility. But more research needs to be done.

The second question—why is there so much variation among individuals and cultures holding the same values?—speaks to issues of priority and of moral boundaries. It is apparent that people holding the same core values may place radically different priorities on them. Our research suggests, for instance, that in both Suzhou, China, and Orrville, Ohio, "truth" is one of the top four values. It led the list as the value most frequently chosen in Jenny Smucker's sessions in Ohio (see table 2, page 47); however, in China (see table 4, page 49) it was viewed as important by less than half the participants. That priority probably hints at the way those values will be put into practice: citizens in Orrville put honesty above everything else, but executives in China feel that way about another value, responsibility, which tops their list.

MORAL BOUNDARIES AND MORAL RELATIVISM

Another explanation for the obvious variations among individuals and cultures lies in the perimeter within which we exercise our values—the invisible but formidable boundaries that constrain our moral sensibilities. It is perfectly possible for individuals to express these five core values vibrantly and profoundly within a small circle of family, friends, and community, while failing to extend them outward to a broader world. On the thin end of the scale, one thinks of the Mafia, famous for close devotion to family and for a deep sense of respect and responsibility with one another, but notoriously indifferent to the moral dignity of those outside its narrow circle. At the broader end, one thinks of those towering figures of moral authority—Jesus, Gandhi, and others—for whom no individual lay beyond the bounds of their moral concern. For most of us who fall between these poles, the progress toward a greater morality equates with an expansion of that circle of concern. We understand and subscribe to these core values. We move beyond theory into practice, applying them in our daily lives. And we aspire to do it better each day. But have we reached—and have our communities reached—beyond our zones of

Courage and Moral Values

Where does courage come from, and what is it made of? Among the more interesting answers (for those who love to count) are those developed by psychologists Christopher Peterson, Martin Seligman, and colleagues at the University of Pennsylvania. They see courage as one of six "core virtues" made up of four of their twenty-four "character strengths."

"There is astonishing convergence across the millennia and across cultures about virtue and strength," writes Seligman in his 2002 book *Authentic Happiness*. "Confucius, Aristotle, Aquinas, the Bushido Samurai Code, the *Bhagavad-Gita,* and other venerable traditions disagree on the details, but all of these codes include six core virtues," which he elsewhere enumerates as "wisdom, courage, humanity, justice, temperance, and transcendence."

Unpacking the virtue of courage, Peterson and Seligman define it largely in its moral rather than physical dimension. Noting that courage entails "the exercise of will to accomplish goals in the face of opposition, external or internal," they see it as comprising bravery, industry, honesty, and vitality.

Bravery, they write, is "not the equivalent of fearlessness" but rather the "ability to do what needs to be done despite fear." It entails "*not* shrinking from threat, challenge, difficulty, or pain; speaking up for what is right even if there is opposition; acting on convictions even if unpopular." Because this definition "includes physical bravery but is not limited to it," it extends courage "beyond the domain of battle to saying or doing the unpopular but correct thing, to facing a terminal illness with equanimity, and to resisting peer pressure regarding a morally questionable shortcut"—extending it, in other words, into the realm of moral courage.

Putting it into practice brings fulfillment. "We feel good when we do the right thing, whether standing up for justice in the face of an angry group or giving a toast at a wedding despite knocking knees," they write. "When we can act regardless of our fear, segregating our physiology from the rest of us, we are fulfilled."

The three other constituents of courage include:

- "Industry: Finishing what one starts; persisting in a course of action in spite of obstacles; 'getting it out the door'; taking pleasure in completing tasks.

- "Honesty: Speaking the truth but more broadly presenting oneself in a genuine way; being without pretense; taking responsibility for one's feelings and actions.

- "Vitality: Approaching life with excitement and energy; *not* doing things halfway or halfheartedly; living life as an adventure; feeling alive and activated."

Why does this matter? Because, say Peterson and Seligman, "we believe that good character can be cultivated, but to do so, we need conceptual and empirical tools to craft and evaluate appropriate interventions." Such tools will, they hope, help "reclaim the study of character"—and presumably its virtues, including courage—"as a legitimate topic of psychological inquiry and informed societal discourse."

comfort to the point where our moral obligation extends to everyone? Few can say yes.

But moral values, in many ways, are aspirational as well as normative. They tell us not only what we are but what we ought to become. We can fault ourselves for failing to practice them. But we can only perceive that we've failed if there exists a standard against which to fail. The aspiration contained in a set of shared moral values—large and ill-defined as they may be—provides that standard.

And that, finally, suggests one other benefit of this modest research. It helps lay to rest the ghostly assertion of moral relativism that still haunts our conversations. The notion that there can be no shared values because everyone is an individual possessed of his or her own unique values is, quite simply, unsustained by either scholarship or observation. Try making that case in Orrville, Ohio, after twenty-four citizen seminars identified the city's shared values, and you'll be laughed out of town. Try asserting that the college communities in Illinois have "different values" from the citizenry of that state, and the research simply won't permit that conclusion. Try convincing the member states of the OECD that each has wholly different ideas of the values underlying public service, and the argument falls to bits. It is increasingly obvious that this five-fingered hand of shared moral values exists—and that its existence can be verified universally, independently, and through a variety of methodologies.

Why is that important? The presence of these five values helps us structure a definition of the term *moral* that raises it from the realm of linguistic opacity, demystifies it, and puts it back into public circulation. That which is moral, in other words, is widely seen to be that which is honest, responsible, respectful, fair, and compassionate. Conversely, the opposites of these five ideas define unethical behavior: that which is immoral is that which is dishonest, irresponsible, disrespectful, unfair, or lacking in compassion. Here the focus should be on the word *or*. In order for a behavior to qualify as unethical, it need not fail in all five categories. Even if someone is responsible, respectful, fair, and compassionate, being dishonest is surely enough to cause most observers to say, "You're unethical!" Just as a complete hand needs all five fingers, so the wholeness of moral action needs all five ideas operating together. Take any one away, and it's immediately clear that something is incomplete. It's no accident that a word we use almost synonymously with ethics—*integrity*—comes from the Latin word *integer,* meaning entire, whole, unbroken, a single integer.

COURAGE:
A VALUE UNLIKE THE OTHERS

In recent years we've discerned a quiet trend in our seminars at the Institute for Global Ethics. As some of the lists above indicate, there's a growing desire to add a sixth value to the mix: courage. Participants who select it often observe that without courage the other values are inoperative. Even the most sophisticated awareness of values, the most sustained capacity for moral reasoning, needs to be made active—a point Confucius made in noting that "to see what is right and not to do it is want of courage."

But courage alone may or may not constitute a moral force. In the philosophers' distinction between terminal and instrumental values—between the fundamental, intrinsic virtues of humanity and the strategic, operational values that lubricate human behavior—concepts like diligence, patience, and perseverance fall into the latter category. So does courage. The question "Why is courage important?" should stimulate a response like "In order to attain fairness, responsibility, truth, or the other intrinsic values." But ask "Why is truth important?" and you may simply get a slack-jawed stare of incomprehension. Truth isn't useful to *get* anywhere. It's the *where* toward which humanity ought to be headed, the ultimate terminus of our journey. Courage is different. It's important not for its own sake but because it leads to higher things. It has, as Susan Sontag writes, "no moral value in itself, for courage is not, in itself, a moral virtue. Vicious scoundrels, murderers, terrorists, may be brave. To describe courage as a virtue, we need an adjective: We speak of 'moral courage'—because there is such a thing as amoral courage, too."

The term *moral* is commonly used in two distinct ways. It defines those areas of concern that consider questions of right and wrong—as opposed to, say, *political* (which considers questions of power) or *economic* (which considers questions of wealth). But we also use the term to mean *good, right,* or *just.* In the phrase "moral dilemma," for example, it refers to the first sense: we understand it to mean "a dilemma about right and wrong," not "a good dilemma." But when we say, "that was a highly moral act," we use it as a term of praise for something right and proper, rather than simply as a description of an act operating in the realm of good or bad choices.

That ambiguity carries over into the meaning of *moral courage.* To be sure, the phrase refers, in a somewhat neutral way, to a courage that oper-

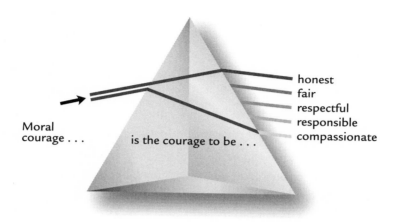

Figure 6. Understanding Values Prism

ates within the realm of concern for good and bad, right and wrong. But if by *moral* we mean that which is good, then *moral courage* also means the positive courage to be ethical. That, it would seem, is the way the public intuitively wants to use it. And if by *ethical* we mean taking action that accords with the core values of honesty, fairness, respect, responsibility, and compassion, then *moral courage* means the courage to invoke and practice those values. Pass the white light of moral courage through the prism of our understanding of values, in other words, and it breaks out into a five-banded spectrum: the courage to be honest, to be fair, to be respectful, to be responsible, and to be compassionate. And if the word *values* is in some way synonymous with *convictions*, then moral courage is, as it's often characterized, "the courage of your convictions" in these five key areas.

That line of reasoning suggests why the trend we've noted—the desire to add *courage* as a sixth element to the definition of moral—doesn't quite work. Courage isn't like the other values, but what is it?

- Rather than being the next pearl on a string with the other five, perhaps moral courage is the string itself, holding the others together.

- Maybe moral courage is a catalyst, which, like a substance added to a chemical reaction, mightily speeds up the interaction among the reagents and emerges unchanged when it's all over.
- Or perhaps moral courage is the hardware upon which the software of the other values operates, or even the operating system running in the background and allowing our values programs to function.

Whatever the metaphor, courage seems a necessary element in the ethics equation. What good is a conviction about honesty or fairness without a willingness to put those values into action in the face of adversity? Of what use is a code of ethics that hangs on the wall, unimplemented? Without the courage to act, virtuous conviction is pointless and paralytic.

Yet courage without virtuous conviction is empty—or perverse. Nazi officers, Mafia hit men, and others of Susan Sontag's "vicious scoundrels" need physical courage, of course, to wreak mayhem among the innocent. But they also need a kind of "immoral" courage to implement a cluster of distinctly bad values—self-seeking, lust, revenge, wrath, and others of the Seven Deadlies. Think of Timothy McVeigh, the Oklahoma City bomber. One of his lawyers, Richard Burr, tried to paint him with the colors of moral courage. For years, he said, his client had been "deeply concerned about the overreaching of federal law enforcement authorities. When that overreach became apparent to him in his own case, it overrode other considerations." The implication is that he acted out of moral courage. Yet McVeigh seemed indifferent to the five core values. He showed little respect for others and no compassion for his victims. The only responsibility he felt, apparently, was to take the law into his own hands, subverting justice and fairness. And his dishonesty showed up in the various deceptions he pursued to meet his ends. It's hard to see anything moral or ethical here, although he had an odd sort of daring and bravado.

But must every evidence of courage be thought of as true moral courage? Here Aristotle's conceptions help. He defined moral virtue as an "intermediate" between a defect and an excess. Courage, he said, lay balanced between the defect of cowardice and the excess of rashness. Put another way, one can think of courage as flanked by two alternatives: its opposite, the cowering timidity that dares not act, and its counterfeit, the bravura and foolhardiness that looks a bit like courage but isn't. The courage that is truly moral, then, has built into it a moderating restraint. If it falls backward, it becomes its own negative. If it lapses into excess, it turns into a caricature of itself.

MORAL COURAGE DEFINED

What, then, is moral courage? It can be defined as the quality of mind and spirit that enables one to face up to ethical challenges firmly and confidently, without flinching or retreating.

- It is a "quality of mind" as well as "spirit" because, like all ethical endeavors, it partakes of both the rational and the intuitional capacities, both left-brain and right-brain activity, both the processes of intellectual discourse and the feelings of rightness and wrongness inherent in each individual.
- It enables us to "face up" to problems—not necessarily to resolve them, and certainly not to promise that we will master them, but to address them squarely, frontally, and with determination.
- It requires action that is both "firmly" persistent and "confidently" assured that its tools—the moral, mental, and emotional elements of argumentation and persuasion—are sound enough to weather serious resistance.
- Finally, it requires us to act "without flinching or retreating" in the face of persuasions, from the subtle to the violent, that make us want to turn tail and run.

But moral courage does not, it seems, require fearlessness—at least in its beginnings. There is little indication that those who triumph in moral courage have never felt an ounce of fear—that they have never, in John Wayne's words, been scared to death as they saddled up for battle. Rather, moral courage may be a means whereby one overcomes fear through practical action.

Think of moral courage, then, as laying at the intersection of three conceptual fields: principles, danger, and endurance.

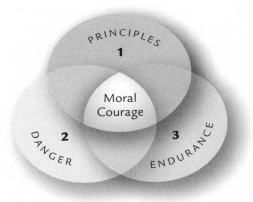

Figure 7. The Three Elements of Moral Courage

At the center stands moral courage. As with courage of any sort, there must be a full awareness of the danger involved—circle 2 in our diagram. The sleepwalker on a ridgepole can't be said to be courageous until, awakening to the risk, he or she overcomes fear and presses on. The same is true for the ingenue wandering innocently through a den of thieves, the skater unwittingly crossing a patch of thin ice to help a fallen friend, or the police officer arresting a drug kingpin without calling in backup and without knowing whom he's got. Without an awareness of danger, there's no courage—just a foolhardiness that a person of greater prudence would probably have avoided.

Nor is there courage without the willingness to endure indicated by circle 3. To have seen the danger and fled—or to have waffled, fiddled, delayed, or otherwise compromised—is also to have lacked courage. The business executive who uncovers accounting chicanery and dares not speak up is clearly lacking in courage—as is the parent who finds evidence of a child's drug use and says nothing, the church members who remain mum as some of the clergy molest children or abscond with funds, or the candidate who finds she's funded by laundered mob money and fails to sever the financial cords. Without the willingness to endure hardship, there's no courage.

Finally, of course, the absence of any conviction about values (circle 1) disqualifies an act from being *morally* courageous—though it may still show signs of *physical* courage. The high-school basketball coach who intervenes bodily to break up a fight between players twice his size manifests physical courage. But the same coach, benching the offending player despite the certainty that his team will lose the championship without him, is standing on principles that go beyond the merely physical. That's moral courage.

A recognition of that dimension of principles and values, then, is crucial to moral courage. Think of the story that opens this chapter. It was Valerie's recognition of principles that caused her to turn down millions, keep her integrity intact, and (we suspect) save herself from serious further compromises. How can we better recognize this dimension of values, work it into the fabric of our decision making, and embed it into the culture of our organizations? That's the subject of the next chapter, which focuses on circle 1 and the concept of the key value as a tool for developing and practicing moral courage.

Moral Courage Checklist
Step 2: Scan for Values

If I've already concluded from step 1 that moral rather than physical courage is called for, this next step requires me to drill deeper into the moral dimension. What values characterize my situation?

Are they primarily economic, social, political, artistic, educational, scientific, or drawn from various other realms? Or are they genuinely moral, having to do with the fundamental distinctions between right and wrong? If they truly are the latter, they'll show up as honesty, responsibility, respect, fairness, and compassion.

But they may not always be easy to discern. You may have to analyze the situation carefully and interpret it in the light of these values—understanding that, for example, a keen sense of loyalty may be a form of responsibility, while a disciplined devotion to accuracy could be a version of honesty.

More commonly, however, a situation that calls for moral courage will require you to be alert to the opposites of these values—since it is usually the lack of values, not their presence, that requires courageous action. Is the core problem I'm facing created because of dishonesty? Irresponsibility? Disrespect? Unfairness? Lack of compassion? Here, five questions are in order:

1. How pervasive is this lack of values? While it's tempting to think that a collapse of several values is more alarming than a failure of just one, remember that we identify as unethical a lapse in *any one* of these five values.

2. If more than one value has been breached, how does that shape my response? It may be that a public expression of moral courage requires us to focus on one value rather than to take on several all at once.

3. Does this failure to express a moral value rise to a level of significance, or does it remain trivial? Dishonesty, for example, is almost always significant. But is this a case where someone made a minor misstatement in a meeting, realized later that it was wrong, and let it stand because the effort to correct it would be too disruptive of a conversation that had already moved on?

4. Can I distinguish the significant from the trivial? Here four tests apply. Issues that are significant are

   a. Immediate, producing clear and present effects
   b. Severe, causing serious harm
   c. Irreversible, unable to be overturned by subsequent action
   d. Widespread, affecting broad numbers

   Issues that operate in only some of these categories are less threatening than those that operate in all four. While that limitation doesn't automatically make them trivial, it helps us to focus our energies where they are most needed.

5. Am I clear enough on my own values to take on the failings of another? The most powerful corrective to disrespect, for instance, comes from someone who regularly practices respect. But don't fall for the fallacy of perfectionism, under which you shrink from speaking up because you yourself are not 100 percent flawless. Leaders lead when they are out in front of others along the trail, not only when they have already reached the final goal.

CHAPTER FOUR

The First Circle:
Applying the Values

When you see what is right, have the courage to do it.
—Chinese proverb

"Can I run an idea by you?"

That's the way so many calls begin on a company's internal ethics hotline—a hesitant voice, feeling its way forward, listening for faint signals of trust and reassurance from the other end of the line.

The callers, usually employees, have seen things they think could be wrong. But they're not sure whether the problem lies in the objective facts or simply in their own perception of them. They don't feel they can raise their concerns within their department. They don't want to reveal their identity. But they're bothered enough to pick up the phone and reach out for guidance—taking the first tentative steps along the path to moral courage.

The question on the phone that morning, Nancy Thomas-Moore remembers, had all those threads woven through it. She was staffing the hotline at the Weyerhaeuser Corporation's head office in Federal Way, Washington, in the early 1990s when an unknown woman called from an undisclosed location somewhere in the firm's sprawling network of facilities.

"What's the policy on a manager belonging to a country club?" Thomas-Moore remembers the employee asking her. "Is the company supposed to be paying the dues?"

Thomas-Moore, who is now the firm's director of ethics and business conduct, said she wasn't sure, but that she'd check. Not wanting to push the caller for more information—not even wanting to ask her name— Thomas-Moore simply invited her to call back in a few days.

And so, like a stately dance, a relationship began to develop through a number of calls. A few days later, when the voice reappeared on the line, Thomas-Moore was able to tell her that the company used to pay club dues on some occasions, but that it no longer did. Gradually, as she listened to the ensuing calls, more details emerged.

The employee—let's call her Dolores—was the human resources manager at a cardboard manufacturing plant in a rural American town. Typical to such facilities, she was part of a small management team— in this case, only ten people—overseeing an operation of some three-hundred hourly employees. While working on budgets for the coming year with the plant's comptroller, she had noticed an odd entry in the books. When she questioned it, the comptroller said it was to cover dues at the local country club for their boss, the plant manager. He also told her that the boss had recently charged the company a significant sum to buy champagne for his daughter's wedding at the club. The boss said he would pay it back, said the comptroller, but he never did.

Dolores was perplexed. The comptroller, she knew, had an obligation to report fraud to headquarters. But he told her he hadn't spoken up and didn't plan to, fearful of losing his job. After all, the plant manager had the authority to hire and fire his team, including the comptroller and Dolores. But if the comptroller wouldn't speak up, she asked herself, who would? Her own reporting channel was strictly to the plant manager: she had no regular relationship with anyone higher in the company. Yet she

felt sure that her own employment would be jeopardized if she con-
fronted the boss with her concerns. After all, he was a well-known figure
in the small community where she and her family also lived, and where
everyone knew everyone else. Even if she revealed the problem to someone higher in the company, she worried that, in a situation where so few
people had access to the plant's financial information, her boss could
quickly trace that revelation back to her.

In their phone calls, Thomas-Moore assured Dolores she was doing
the right thing by bringing the situation to light. She explained that, given
the nature of the company's isolated, small-town plants, it wasn't surprising she felt some trepidation. She'd seen it happen before. "When you
have your own little empire," she told Dolores, referring to the boss,
"there's nobody watching over you." She suggested having an internal
audit team from headquarters go in and investigate.

Dolores agreed, but not without some misgivings. What if the team
found nothing serious—a charge for champagne mistakenly put on the
boss's club account rather than his personal credit card, a full restitution
already in the works, an innocent misunderstanding on the boss's part
about a change in company policy concerning club dues? There was real
risk involved for Dolores and her family, particularly in a community
with few other employment opportunities. But Thomas-Moore remembers the tone of voice that came through Dolores's conversations.

"She was fairly—I wouldn't say 'black-and-white' or 'righteous,' but
'This is not right!' " Thomas-Moore recalls. "She felt it was so wrong. She
was outraged."

While Dolores was troubled about the consequences she herself might
face, she was more concerned about values she knew were important. In
the end, those values prevailed. She agreed to supply information to the
security team, which came in to investigate. The comptroller came forth
with more details. The boss's manager came to town, took the boss to
lunch, and was about to tell him he was fired when the boss handed him
his resignation.

And Dolores? She's still with the company and has advanced in her career. In the end, she was vindicated in her decision. Her values trumped her fears, in a modest but classic expression of moral courage.

THE COURAGE TO
BLOW THE WHISTLE

In situations involving whistle-blowing, values trump fears—otherwise, the whistles would remain silent. That doesn't mean such stories all have happy endings: whistle-blowing remains a risky activity. Dolores's situation occurred at about the time that the revised U.S. federal Whistle-blower Protection Act went into effect in 1989, and before the current concerns about the dangers of exposing corporate or governmental wrongdoing had matured into public fascination in such movies as *The Insider* and *Erin Brockovich.*

Technically, Dolores was not a whistle-blower. "There is an agreed-upon definition [of whistle-blowing]," writes Roberta Ann Johnson in *Whistleblowing: When It Works—and Why* (1993), "that has four component parts: (1) An individual acts with the intention of making information public; (2) the information is conveyed to parties outside the organization who make it public and a part of the public record; (3) the information has to do with possible or actual nontrivial wrongdoing in an organization; and (4) the person exposing the agency is not a journalist or ordinary citizen but a member or former member of the organization." While Dolores was an insider exposing nontrivial information, she was working through internal channels with no interest in making a public case. Had those channels stalemated her actions, would she have gone public? Was she a whistle-blower in the making? Did Thomas-Moore's patient responsiveness head off what could have been an unpleasant public-relations issue for Weyerhaeuser?

We'll never know, but the fact that Dolores wasn't a full-fledged public whistle-blower didn't diminish her expression of moral courage. To think otherwise would be to relegate moral courage to a few high-profile cases—like that of Roger Boisjoly, the Morton Thiokol engineer who tried to stop the fatal launch of the space shuttle *Challenger* in 1986 by warning about a possible cold-weather O-ring failure; or Paul van Buitenen, the Dutch auditor for the European Commission whose 1998 memos revealed deep and endemic fraud in the Brussels hierarchy; or General Maxwell Taylor, who turned down an appointment as Supreme Allied Commander of NATO in 1959 and retired rather than supporting the administration's "massive retaliation" policy of containing Soviet expansionism by relying heavily on a nuclear response. These three clearly expressed moral courage. They faced tough choices in deciding to go public. And they achieved significant results:

- Boisjoly's testimony shook NASA to the core, calling attention to a space program he described as "oversold and underfunded" and foreshadowing the failures in NASA's organizational culture and structure that came to light following the disintegration of the space shuttle *Columbia* in 2003.
- Van Buitenen's exposés of a massive gravy train of nepotism and absenteeism surrounding European Commissioner Edith Cresson led to the resignation of the entire commission in 1999.
- The book General Taylor wrote immediately on retiring, *The Uncertain Trumpet,* made such an impact on President-elect John F. Kennedy that he ultimately persuaded Taylor to return to active duty as chairman of the Joint Chiefs of Staff. "Seldom," writes Colonel Harry J. Maihafer in reviewing Taylor's decision to go public with his concerns, "has one person's act of moral courage had such far-reaching effect."

But the moral courage these three needed to weigh consequences and take action was no different in kind from the courage expressed in less high-profile circumstances. "So often, whistle-blowers don't think that far ahead about the consequences and risks of whistle-blowing," says

Why Be Courageous?

Are heroes nuts? Is moral courage just plain weird?

One of the leading twentieth-century American psychoanalysts, Heinz Kohut, puts the issue more delicately in his essay "On Courage." "When we scrutinize the personalities and the behaviors of unusually courageous people," he wrote in the early 1970s, "there is the possibility that we are dealing with mentally deranged individuals." In fact, Kohut dismisses that idea. Instead he sets himself the task of "defining the psychological constellation which allows an exceptional few to oppose the pressures exerted on them and to remain faithful to their ideals and to themselves, while all the others, the multitudes, change their ideals and swim with the current." He sets out, in other words, to account for moral courage.

His chief finding—not surprising from the founder of self-psychology—is that courage entails a commitment to what he calls "the nuclear self . . . which contains not only the individual's most enduring values and ideals but also his most deeply anchored goals, purposes and ambitions." What prompts the heroic individual to "move forward, despite intimidation from within and without" along his "lonely road, even if it means his individual destruction"? The answer, for Kohut, is that he is "compelled" to "shape the pattern of his life—his thoughts, deeds and attitudes—in accordance with the design of his nuclear self." Moral courage, then, is an alignment of outward acts with inner principles.

Kohut had fled Vienna as the Nazis advanced in 1938, a few months after Sigmund Freud. The illustrations he used in this essay, from Nazi resisters and classical tragedy, make it plain that this alignment is not necessarily easy. "Almost all heroic individuals," he states, "face grave crises while they are still on the road to reaching the ultimate decision that they will remain faithful to their selves, whatever the cost." Yet he also notes that such individuals are "generally not beset by fear of the consequences they will suffer as a result of their actions. They seem unafraid of isolation, social ostracism, or punishment." Their "crises" are more interior, a battle (to use the terminology of ethics) about rule-based principles rather than ends-based outcomes.

Are they psychotic? No, says Kohut, citing three features that indicate their normalcy: "the presence of a fine sense of humor; the ability to respond to others with subtle empathy; and, generally at the time when the ultimate heroic decision has been reached and the agonizing consequences have to be faced, the suffusion of the personality with a profound sense of inner peace and serenity—a mental state akin to wisdom." That peace, as Kohut notes, "never fails to impress the observer, including even persecutors, torturers and executioners." It is the result of an "ultimate state of . . . balance [that] blends the personality with the central values of the self," producing "the experience of conscious pleasure that his ideals and his total personality have now become one."

To the range of theories explaining why some people express moral courage, then, Kohut has added two others: they can't help themselves, and it's pleasurable. The need for alignment is simply too great, and the resulting delight too serene, to do anything else. That may seem an odd conclusion, given many of the stories about whistle-blowers and others in this book. But it's a useful reminder nonetheless of the powerful effect moral courage has on its agents.

Dana Gold, a former staff attorney and director of operations at the Government Accountability Project, a major whistle-blower organization based in Seattle. After observing and working with scores of whistle-blowers over the years, she feels the moral courage required to decide to blow the whistle is rooted in values. "It comes down to an internal core [belief] that overrides even a sense of logic or fear of the consequences," she says, adding that for many whistle-blowers "it's about deeply held values that are defining for people—about being their best selves."

Aligning Values with Actions

That best self, for many of us, comes to the surface when we feel our values are most closely aligned with our actions—when we have the courage to become the moral agent we long to be. While the process of alignment can be complex, it frequently involves a few clear steps. After we recognize the point explored in the previous chapter—that values are indeed at stake—it appears that we move forward from awareness to action through some version of the following three stages:

1. We **focus** on one or two key values.
2. We **dismantle** the right-versus-wrong arguments that might lure us into inaction.
3. We **recognize** that no higher right value ought to draw us into a different course.

As a first step, Dolores knew that values were at stake—that something, as she told Nancy Thomas-Moore, was "not right." Of the five values commonly identified with moral principles—honesty, fairness, responsibility, respect, and compassion—she seems to have zeroed in on the first two, which provided her with the clearest framework for her decision. To her, her boss's action was blatantly dishonest. It was also unfair, in that he appropriated company resources through modalities unavailable to executives who chose to live honestly. And while the situation certainly involved issues of responsibility, she seems to have seen those largely in relation to herself: did *she* have the courage to do the responsible thing? Responsibility, in fact, is a fixed feature of every morally courageous decision, in relation to the individual actor who must decide whether or not to act. To be sure, Dolores's boss was being irresponsible as well. But his action went well past irresponsibility into downright dishonesty and unfairness. Remove those two antivalues from this tale—leaving her boss simply with a garden-variety irresponsibility shared by many a bad manager rather than a pernicious deceptiveness and elitism that so many employees find intolerable—and the occasion for Dolores's moral courage disappears.

Second, Dolores was not—as far as we know—tempted to do wrong. She didn't feel drawn to collude with the comptroller in hiding the fraudulence from headquarters. Nor was she tempted to hurl a bomb into the boss's office or poison his coffee. Her choices all lay well within the bounds of legality and ethics. Yet she still faced a struggle within herself about whether or not to speak up—as many whistle-blowers must. The arguments for keeping quiet sometimes arise from commonplace excuses—loyalty to the group, too much else going on, so little time, a mortgage to pay, kids in college, "there are others who can help," or even "maybe I'm insane." At times, however, they can reflect full-fledged "bystander apathy," a term that gained currency in describing the 1964 murder of Kitty Genovese, whose cries for help were heard by thirty-eight neighbors in Queens, New York, not one of whom stepped forward to help. In Dolores's case, she could not live with an apathetic, bystanding self, and the issue seemed too clear-cut and important to succumb to the more ordinary excuses for inaction. A sense of outrage took over—albeit slowly—and gradually closed off all the avenues of argumentation that urged passivity.

Third, Dolores was not drawn away from her concerns for honesty and fairness by some other, higher idea in her pantheon of values. One could make the case that, of the five core moral values, *compassion* (for the boss and his family) or *respect* (for the structures and traditions of an organizational chain of command) might have steered her into a different but equally noble course. Had she chosen to argue this way, would she have been succumbing to a temptation to follow (as the West Point Cadet Prayer has it) "the easier wrong" rather than "the harder right"? It's surely not *wrong* to be compassionate or respectful. In fact, she was facing perhaps the most difficult of moral decisions known to humanity: the choice between right and right.

RIGHT VERSUS RIGHT:
A FRAMEWORK FOR DECISION MAKING

The choices where there are equally strong moral arguments for competing sides of a dilemma underlie much of the decision making that results
in morally courageous actions. The second and third steps listed above—
knocking down the "right-versus-wrong" arguments and investigating
any possibility of an alternative "right" choice that would not require
moral courage for its implementation—are both rooted in core values. It
can properly be said, in fact, that if individuals have no values they will
never face ethical conundrums. Why? Because all ethical issues arise from
one of two sources:

- **Right versus wrong.** Ethical issues emerge when a core moral value
  has been violated or ignored. When it's clear that *honesty* is a central, shared value and yet someone is found to be acting dishonestly,
  we have no qualms about saying, "That's unethical!" In such cases
  ethics is (as my dictionary describes it) "the discipline dealing with
  what is good and bad or right and wrong."
- **Right versus right.** Ethical issues also emerge when two of our core
  values come into conflict with each other. When one of our values
  raises powerful moral arguments for one course of action, while
  another value raises equally powerful arguments for an opposite
  course, we find we can't do both. Yet we must act. In such cases,
  ethics is a matter of right versus right.

Ethics of the first sort is without question important. The world needs
a higher sense of right-doing than it now has. Efforts to clean up bribery,
eliminate lying, enhance accountability, upgrade justice, and introduce
empathy are hugely significant. Hence the prevalence of compliance
programs in corporations, honor codes in schools, oaths of office in government, and promise-keeping programs in private life. What's more,

choosing to do right rather than wrong can require serious measures of moral courage. The gang member who decides to go straight, the teenager who finds a full wallet and convinces his friends to turn it in, the single mother who risks her job by refusing to leave her children home alone when the sitter calls in sick—all are expressing moral courage. So are the raconteur who refuses to recount delicious but damaging gossip, the police officer who passes up the offer of free meals at a local diner, and the journalist who won't make up quotes even when attributing them to unnamed sources.

But the toughest decisions are not right versus wrong but right versus right. Determining which side has the higher claim to rightness often requires some deep ethical reasoning. And implementing our conclusion—standing up for what our reasoning dictates—can make strong demands on our moral courage.

Mike Saklar learned that in the case of the vanishing sponsor.

MORAL COURAGE
AT THE HOMELESS SHELTER

In the late spring of 2001 Mike Saklar was appointed executive director of Siena/Francis House, a twenty-five-year-old community-based homeless shelter in Omaha, Nebraska. Through years of experience working with the homeless and following the research in his field, Saklar had come to recognize that homeless people, however different their family backgrounds and personal characteristics, typically share one attribute: addiction. Part of Saklar's work through the years had been in helping those people resist the aggressive presence of alcohol and drugs on the streets. In that endeavor, he was helped by the mission statement of Siena/Francis House, which, after first committing itself to "get our guests off the streets," next seeks to "encourage sobriety in our recovery program, a traditional 12-step recovery process." Not surprisingly, Saklar was adamant about keeping alcohol and drugs out of any shelter in which he worked.

Like many nonprofit homeless shelters, Siena/Francis House fought hard for its funding. Its best source of revenue was a massive and well-publicized walk for the homeless each spring. Through a long tradition of sponsorships, individual gifts, and donations by walkers and their friends, the shelter funded the better part of its annual budget from that single day's returns. By the time Saklar took over, plans were well in hand for the coming event. Their major corporate sponsor had again signed up. The date for the event had been set for the spring of 2002. The various committees of the shelter's board of directors were busy mapping the route, ensuring security, and preparing public announcements.

Then came the awful news: their sponsor, a company now headquartered in Texas but with deep roots in Omaha, abruptly canceled its sponsorship. The company's name: Enron.

With only weeks to go, the shelter's board met to consider its plight. Given the well-publicized implosion of Enron—a story followed in Omaha with more than usual interest, since Enron began life as the Nebraska-based InterNorth—the board knew there was no going back to that stream. The company's philanthropy had dried up almost overnight, leaving hundreds of other nonprofits stranded as well. But without a sponsor, the shelter's march would bring in only a fraction of the support it needed.

And then, just as quickly as Enron disappeared, a new sponsor appeared on the horizon: the local distributor for a major national brewery. The board learned that the firm would be happy to sponsor the event, but if this sponsorship were like other beer sponsorships at national sporting and entertainment events, the board suspected that the firm would want the name of its beer prominently displayed throughout the day.

What should the board do? Some members saw this offer as a lifesaver, coming from a reputable corporation whose products were perfectly legal and widely used. Others argued that Siena/Francis House could not in good conscience use this occasion—a fund-raiser whose purpose was to help people move toward sobriety—to promote the very products that helped foster their addictions. To which the first group responded that beer, low in alcohol and usually not consumed in vast quantities, was hardly as dangerous as hard liquor or even wine—and that, even if it were, it was better to keep the shelter operating for all its guests than to shut it down because a few might be at risk from beer advertisements. That view prompted replies from the second group that the spectacle of shelter staff and board members sporting beer logos on their T-shirts flew directly in the face of all they had stood for since the inception of the shelter—and that in fact there was no point in keeping the shelter open if it had to compromise on such a deeply held principle.

The challenge the board faced lay in the conflict of two right actions. Board members could make a powerful moral case for accepting the funds, putting forth a compassionate argument for benefiting guests who might otherwise be turned out into the street. But they could also make a powerful moral case for refusing the funds, citing their responsibility to avoid harming those same clients by sending mixed signals and appearing to compromise on this key point.

ANALYZING OUR DILEMMAS: FOUR PARADIGMS

To those struggling to resolve it, the dilemma at Siena/Francis House may well have seemed unusual, even novel—a new addition, apparently, to an infinite universe of moral conundrums, never before experienced by any other group in the world. In fact, as research at the Institute for Global Ethics has shown, there is not an infinite number of dilemmas. Instead, there are four. However complex they may be, humanity's dilemmas appear to fall into a quartet of broad patterns or paradigms:

- Truth versus loyalty
- Individual versus community
- Short term versus long term
- Justice versus mercy

These countervailing vectors explain the tensions that drive our dilemmas. Within these wide-ranging categories (as I explained in an earlier book, *How Good People Make Tough Choices*), "the names used here are less important than the concepts:

- "The point behind the justice-versus-mercy paradigm is that fairness, equity, and even-handed application of the law often conflict with compassion, empathy, and love.
- "Short-term versus long-term, or *now versus then,* reflects the difficulties arising when immediate needs or desires run counter to future goals or prospects.
- "The individual-versus-community paradigm can be restated as *us versus them, self versus others,* or *the smaller versus the larger* group.
- "Truth versus loyalty can be seen as honesty or integrity versus commitment, responsibility, or promise-keeping."

These paradigms are not mutually exclusive boxes. They don't ask us to pick one of the four, squeeze our dilemma into it, and discard the rest. They are better understood as lenses that provide different ways of seeing deeply into our dilemmas. If some of them bring more clarity of thought than others—depending in part on the individuals using them—that only reminds us that they are tools, not restraints. Their usefulness lies in helping us understand why the choice we face is so wrenching—helping us to more readily identify and analyze the deep values-driven forces lined up on each side that pull us in different directions. Sometimes one paradigm alone brings the desired clarity. Sometimes all four apply. Unlike championship dives, however, ethical dilemmas don't appear to have degrees of difficulty based on the number of categories they meet: some of the toughest dilemmas are best explained by a single paradigm, while others lend themselves to rich discussions around all four.

In Mike Saklar's dilemma, the paradigm that most clarifies the opposing forces is probably short term versus long term. It was surely right to hold to the organization's long-term vision and refuse the proffered funding. Yet it was entirely possible that Siena/Francis House would have to close its doors if that stand were taken. Unless it accommodated the short-term needs, in other words, the board might have no long-term prospects at all. So it was also entirely right to honor the needs of the short term and accept the funding. But the long-term downside of that decision might be such a compromising of the mission that, over time, the organization would lose its impact, damage those it sought to serve, surrender its credibility, and ultimately dwindle downward into lack of support, insolvency, and failure.

Other paradigms figure here as well:

- *Individual versus community* pits the needs of a small group of real, identifiable guests (who might be back on the street without funding) against the needs of the community at large (which might be appalled at the apparent abandonment of standards).
- *Truth versus loyalty* sets up a dichotomy between what Saklar and his professional colleagues understood to be a fixed fact—that addiction is at the heart of homelessness—and what others saw as their fidelity and allegiance to this quarter-century-old institution that provided help, however it could, for its guests.
- *Justice versus mercy* arrays the powerful claims of compassion, directed at those most at risk and least able to care for themselves, against the overarching principles and standards under which the organization has been founded and run.

Seen through these lenses, the dilemma becomes at once both easier and tougher. Making it easier is the fact that Saklar's dilemma hasn't come barreling out of nowhere. It is not the moral equivalent of SARS, which baffled the global medical community in the spring of 2003 with its sudden, unrecognizable virulence. It is instead a difficult though perfectly understandable instance amenable to readily applied frameworks of analysis. Applying these paradigms, however, may make it seem momentarily tougher. Thinking through the ethical analysis reveals depths of complexity beneath the surface. What may have looked at first blush like a straightforward decision between right and wrong becomes a world-class right-versus-right dilemma—however much it is dressed in the modest street clothes of a low-budget community organization. The apparent simplicity vanishes as the issue is subjected to proper analysis.

COMING TO CLOSURE: THREE RESOLUTION PRINCIPLES

But analysis is not resolution. Applying the paradigms, while helpful, is not determinative. Another step is needed: the application of decision-making principles to the right-versus-right issues we've identified. The goal is not to determine which side is wrong. By the very nature of a right-versus-right dilemma, neither side is wrong. To seek to make one right appear wrong—so that, by default, we can claim victory for the remaining right— is to fundamentally misunderstand the nature of ethical decision making. Instead, the goal is to seek the higher right—the choice that most satisfies, rationally and intuitively, those who must make the final decision.

Arriving at such conclusions requires a set of resolution principles or guidelines that, when their conditions are satisfied, allow us to say, "This constitutes an ethical course of action." Without such principles, of course, we can still make decisions—by the force of brute human will, or by flipping a coin, or by surrendering to some outside authority (political, religious, familial, financial, or whatever) that makes the choice for us. And while one principle is better than none, we may find ourselves in situations where reasoning based on one principle alone leads us to conclusions that our intuition simply can't abide. In watching thousands of participants make decisions in seminars at the Institute for Global Ethics, we've concluded that most people have more than one principle to which they appeal as the basis for moral choice. The most commonly used principles, we find, are three in number:

- The *ends-based* principle of utilitarianism, which calls on us to do the greatest good for the greatest number. This principle, developed by the English philosopher John Stuart Mill and described by philosophers as a *consequentialist* or *teleological* concept, holds that ethics gets done when whatever I do produces consequences that turn out for the best. It focuses on arriving at good outcomes and results rather than on the motives or rules that guided us in our choices.

- The *rule-based* principle, by contrast, takes no account of consequences. It is commonly associated with the concept of the categorical imperative as articulated by the German philosopher Immanuel Kant. He formulated his principle this way: "I ought never to act except in such a way that I can also will that my maxim should become a universal law." In Kant's view, ethics gets done when whatever I do is something I'd like to see everyone else in the world do in similar circumstances. It asks us, in other words, to imagine that our action will establish a universal standard that will forever rule human decision making—so that everyone from now on will do exactly what we've just done in such situations. Depending not on outcomes, it is instead a deontological principle, from the Greek word *deon,* meaning "duty" or "obligation."

- The *care-based* principle looks at a different determinant for our actions: what would we want others to do to us? It is rooted in the Golden Rule, a compassionate standard of great antiquity that lies at the core of all of the world's great religions, including (though not limited to) the biblical religions of Christianity and Judaism. This principle of reciprocity or reversibility calls on us to imagine that we are in another's shoes, about to be impacted by the very actions we're contemplating. If we cannot confidently say that the action we're taking toward another would be acceptable if taken toward us, then under this standard we're about to do something unethical.

While we've given these principles three brief descriptive names—*ends-based, rule-based,* and *care-based*—there is nothing new about them. Each is drawn directly from the traditions of moral philosophy. Unlike the paradigms, each tends to operate in mutually exclusive ways: one sometimes counters the others, compelling the decision maker to set aside all but the one that creates the most satisfying understanding of what's right.

That conceptual standoff is nicely illustrated in Saklar's dilemma:

- Applying the *ends-based* principle of the greatest good for the greatest number, Saklar and his board would probably argue for accepting the funding from the beer distributor. Admitting that such a course posed a risk to some of their guests at the present time, they could argue that other guests (especially those in the future) would be unaffected by this decision. They might conclude that the money itself—given its ability to create good consequences for real people right now—was far more important than any scruples about its source. Yes, they might admit, some harm could come to a few individuals by this action. But "the greatest good for the greatest number" never promised all good for everyone. Their task is simply to maximize the good, even if some may be harmed.

- Applying the *rule-based* principle, by contrast, brings a strikingly different result. Here the point is to create through real-life decisions the precedent we think should prevail for the future. By Kant's own dictum, consequences are irrelevant: you will never know whether an action was right or not simply by watching how it turned out. Some very wrong motivations can have acceptable consequences, while some of the most principled and selfless actions can produce fatal consequences for those who took them. The focus, then, must be not on the outcomes but on the rightness of the principle itself. Thinking this way, Saklar and his board may conclude that it is right to establish standards governing the kinds of funding their organization will accept; that such standards are only meaningful if they are enforced; that enforcement will at times require them to turn down funds; and that if the standards are right, then no circumstance, however dire, should cause them to set aside their standards in the name of expediency. They might also note, with Kant, the foibles of attempting through mere human reason to foresee all possible consequences. Recognizing that humanity frequently gets things wrong in asserting that "if we do A, B will follow," they might argue that the only safe course of action is to continue adhering to the principles that have so far stood them in good stead.

- Applying the *care-based* principle could lead them to several conclusions, depending on how the principle is interpreted. The most obvious application, perhaps, is to ask Saklar how he would feel if he were one of the guests at Siena/Francis House who was deprived of a place to live because the board had refused the necessary funding. But a moment's reflection reveals the obvious point that the phrase "do to others as you would have them do to you" leaves open the possibility of a number of other "others." What if the "others" were not deprived guests but recovering addicts at a delicate balance point, suddenly spiraled backward into addiction by what strikes them as the hypocrisy of a staff preaching abstinence while advertising alcohol? What if "others" means potential funders, puzzled and confused by the seeming contradictions between this organization's professions and its practices? If "others" means "guests who may get bounced," the care-based principle will lead Saklar and his board to accept the funding. If "others" means "guests who may abandon hope of sobriety"—or potential contributors, or other homeless shelter executives, or city officials, all of whom are watching with interest—the care-based decision may well be to refuse the funding.

The above sketch, of course, simply addresses the most obvious vectors of moral reasoning under each of these principles. A fuller discussion may well elicit alternative arguments. Ends-based thinking may decide that since the greatest good must be applied not only to the short term but to the long term, the money must be refused so that future generations can still benefit from the high standards of the organization. Rule-based thinking, by contrast, may conclude that the highest principle to follow is compassion for those around you right now—that if you are not addressing the needs of those whose circumstances demand immediate response, how can you pretend to address some vague and distanced needs in a future whose consequences you cannot know? Whichever approach is taken, one point is clear: the application of these three principles does not automatically produce an answer. In this case, it would probably appear that ends-based thinking is pulling us one way and rule-based thinking another—and that the care-based principle may permit us to support either choice.

Does that fact invalidate these principles? Not at all. Ethics, after all, is not a hard science, where a word like *pi* can have an unambiguous meaning as "the ratio of the circumference of a circle to its diameter"— even though the ratio itself is a transcendental number that begins as 3.14159265 and continues without conclusion. Ethics instead inhabits the realm of the humanities, where the very language we use to comprehend the world shifts and adjusts with what the American poet Wallace Stevens called "ambiguous undulations." Try defining *truth,* or *right,* or *good* with anything like the clarity of *pi,* and the challenge of ethics becomes clear. Not surprisingly, then, the principles we use to define ethics may also blur into one another along their edges, leaving us hesitant to declare a fixed conclusion. But in the real world, such conclusions are necessary. Saklar simply didn't have the luxury of endless analysis or perpetual discussion. He and his board needed to make a decision, and they needed to make it immediately.

To the great surprise of some of their constituents, and after much debate, a deeply divided board concluded that its only right course of action was to decline the funding from the beer distributor. It would seem that the rule-based arguments prevailed: they felt they had to live by a principle they would want everyone else to follow, regardless of the immediate consequences. And so, with no prospect of sponsorship in hand, they bid their potential funder farewell in a salient act of moral courage.

Why? Because in the welter of right-versus-right arguments, with an array of values rising and setting on the horizon of their extended discourse, two of the five core values began to stand out: (1) the responsibility that required them to be unwaveringly protective of their guests and the challenges they faced and (2) the intellectual honesty that required them to remain true to their founding mission. Yes, compassion mattered. Yes, it was important to respect their guests' needs for shelter. Yes, they had to be fair and equitable to all concerned, particularly to those who had already supported them and expected them to continue going strong. But for them, at this moment, the highest form of responsibility and truth-telling lay in remaining true to the obligations of their founding principles. Give up those values, they felt, and there was no real substance left to sustain the organization.

What happened next may seem even more extraordinary. As though to reinforce the rightness of their determination not to rely on a merely consequentialist philosophy, they got a phone call a week later. It was from a local business leader. He had seen a small news item, buried deep in the local paper, about the board's decision to forgo funding on a matter of principle. Saying he was proud of their action, he agreed to sponsor the entire event.

Moral courage? Certainly. But would we think so had the outcome been different? What if, as a result of their decision, Siena/Francis House no longer existed? What if no new sponsor had come forth? Would we then say, "That was a bad decision" rather than "That was courageous"? We would only be inclined to say that, I think, if we were to take an outcomes-based view of ethics. If consequence were the sole determinant of rightness—if, in other words, the only ethical principle we espoused was the utilitarian—we would attribute moral courage only to people whose situations come out for the best.

But is that really how moral courage works?

Is It Only Moral Courage
When It Turns Out Right?

The belief that courage depends on consequences has at least three flaws:

- It puts moral courage at the mercy of history, leaving us unwilling to identify an act as courageous until every attributed outcome has been analyzed.
- It flies in the face of our intuition that moral courage can be expressed even when things turn out badly.
- It causes us to refuse to recognize as morally courageous those actions that produce outcomes we don't like.

The stories of three people illustrate these flaws: the towering nineteenth-century orator Daniel Webster, a twenty-first-century Massachusetts teenager named Amylee Bowman, and the captain of a modern-day Coast Guard cutter in the Mona Passage.

DANIEL WEBSTER

The first flaw of a consequentialist view is that it holds courage hostage to history. Under its influence, we could never know whether an act was truly courageous until the final reckoning of consequences was tallied up—which might be a very long time, well beyond an individual's lifetime. Consider the courage of Daniel Webster.

Was Webster courageous only because the Compromise of 1850, which his legendary powers of elocution were instrumental in passing through the United States Senate, helped hold together the Union at a perilous juncture? The conclusion of the Mexican War had introduced vast new territories—California, New Mexico, Utah—into the United States. But would these new states be free or slaveholding? Sensing a congressional battle over slavery that might shatter the Union, Webster and Senator Henry Clay fashioned an omnibus compromise bill containing something for both sides. As John F. Kennedy argues in *Profiles in Courage*, Webster then had to weigh the competing rights of condemning slavery (a stand upon which his reputation was built) and of preventing secession, which he ultimately saw as even more important than his antislavery views. His constituents abandoned him. His friends turned against him. His fellow senators reviled him. Noting that Webster's famous "Seventh of March" speech on the Senate floor in 1850 "resulted in his political crucifixion, and, for half a century or more, his historical condemnation," Kennedy remarked that "few politicians have had the distinction of being scourged by such talented constituents." The list of his disparagers included Longfellow, Emerson, Whittier, James Russell Lowell, William Cullen Bryant, Horace Mann, Theodore Parker, Charles Sumner, and William H. Seward. He died a disappointed and embittered man.

But his actions, Kennedy argues, may well have stabilized a perilous situation between North and South. It may have shifted the balance of power just enough so that the unionist North prevailed against the secessionist South in the Civil War. Had the reverse happened—had his arguments strengthened the slave-trading economic engines of the South enough to allow them to divide the United States into two separate entities—would we have to recalibrate our views, declaring foolish what Kennedy has urged us to deem courageous? What if today's descendants of Southern slaves were to be convinced that Webster played traitor to the antislavery cause? Would he still be considered morally courageous, or would he be dismissed as woefully misguided? But what if historians in the future should resurrect him by arguing that he was right after all? Would he suddenly become morally courageous after decades of being simply extreme?

If consequentialism were to prevail, we would have to take all these factors into account. And since history is never finished, moral courage would always be resigned to a kind of purgatory of relativism, awaiting a judgment that by its very nature could never be final. Yet Webster himself understood that something other than a consequentialist outlook was shaping his sense of duty. "I shall stand by the Union," he said in his last words to the Senate, "with absolute disregard of personal consequences. What are personal consequences . . . in comparison with the good or evil which may befall a great country in a crisis like this? . . . Let the consequences be what they will, I am careless." In that, Webster was in exact alignment with the arch-nonconsequentialist Kant, who wrote that "what is essentially good in . . . action consists in the mental disposition, *let the consequences be what they may*" (italics added).

AMYLEE BOWMAN

The second flaw in a consequentialist theory of courage is more intuitional. There are simply too many cases where actions are heroic and courageous even though the upshot is disappointment, failure, or death. That point is obvious in the context of *physical* rather than *moral* courage. Tales of military courage abound where soldiers give their lives to defend what later prove to be lost causes. The medieval defeat of Scottish leader William Wallace, the fall of the Alamo in Texas in 1836, the charge of the Light Brigade in the Crimea in 1854, and a vast litany of twentieth-century battlefield tales remind us that physical courage exists in spite of its outcomes. In a similar way we honor the firefighters and police officers who rushed into the World Trade Center in New York on September 11, 2001. When we proclaim that they behaved with immense physical courage, we take no account of whether their actions succeeded or failed, or whether they lived or died. Either way, we say, they showed immense courage.

So it is with moral courage. Bold actions in support of values and conscience do not cease to be regarded as morally courageous simply because they lead to failure. The puzzling case of Amylee Bowman of New Bedford, Massachusetts, suggests as much. In November 2001, as a result of information she provided, police foiled an alleged Columbinelike plot by five teenagers to take over New Bedford High, kill students and staff, and ultimately destroy themselves. In the heightened post–9/11 security climate, however, and because of her earlier insider involvement with the plotting teenagers, the seventeen-year-old senior was treated not as a hero but as a coconspirator. She was sentenced to probation and suspended from high school just a few credits short of her diploma. She was expelled from the JROTC program at her school, under which she had planned to enlist in the military two weeks after graduation and receive substantial educational scholarships. Dashed, too, were her hopes of becoming a Massachusetts State Trooper.

To some, she's a criminal who participated in a murderous plan. "This is the young lady who revealed the plot, and we're clearly in her debt for that," Assistant District Attorney Raymond P. Veary Jr. said after her sentencing in November 2002. "But she also played a more active role [in the conspiracy] than we first believed."

To others, she's the whistle-blower who saved the school. In March 2003 *Teen People* chose her as one of "Twenty Teens Who Will Change the World," and she later joined a national speaking tour against gun violence.

Wherever the truth lies, she apparently summoned up enough moral courage to stand up against her friends—a complex decision for a teen—when what started as fantasy talk began to turn real.

"I said, 'Are you guys really going to go through with this? The cops are all over it,'" Ms. Bowman said after court yesterday, recalling a conversation with her friends last year.

"They said, 'Yeah. Without a doubt.'"

". . . I looked them in their eyes and I could see the seriousness there," she said.

So she sought out adults in the school to tell. Noting that "I should never have let myself even joke about killing people," she says that "I know where my fault is in this, and I take responsibility for it. . . . But if every kid who comes forward gets prosecuted, kids are going to stop coming forward."

Bowman's case raises an important point: moral courage can be expressed by people who are not morally flawless. Of Daniel Webster, John Kennedy notes, "the flaw in the granite was the failure of his moral senses to develop as acutely as his other faculties"—a comment related to Webster's blithely untroubled engagement in improper financial dealings. Kennedy describes another of his heroes, the pugnacious Thomas Hart Benton, as a man of "great ego" that made him "thin-skinned mentally as well as physically." None of these flaws, however, tempers the moral courage that rose into view at the moment it was most needed. And no such flaws need temper our view of Amylee Bowman, who at the right moment, whatever her past, had the moral courage to take responsibility and tell the truth—apparently as a result, she has said, of her feeling a sense of caring and compassion for one of her teachers, whom she felt moved to protect. The larger point, as each of these stories suggests, is that public success is not the inevitable outcome of morally courageous action.

THE CAPTAIN'S DILEMMA

The third difficulty with a consequentialist theory of moral courage has to do with sentiment. It is quite possible to understand rationally that a courageous, right decision has been made, yet to rebel emotionally against its outcome and long for a happier ending. Under the sway of consequentialist theory, we may find ourselves denying the courageous nature of an action if it leads to results we can't abide.

That was the struggle Chuck found himself facing as captain of a U.S. Coast Guard cutter. In the mid-1990s—before the threat of international terrorism reached its post–9/11 pitch, and before the more recent flare-up of public concern about illegal immigration across the U.S.-Mexico border—his ship was charged with patrolling the Mona Passage, an eighty-mile-wide strait connecting the North Atlantic with the Caribbean Sea. Separating the Commonwealth of Puerto Rico (a U.S. territory) from the Dominican Republic, it effectively divides one of the planet's poorest countries from the richest nation in the world. Not surprisingly, the demographic pressures across that passage are intense. By mid-1992 it had become a favored crossing point for refugees and drug runners, as well as for families sundered by their breadwinners' search for work and seeking to reunite.

The cutter was based in San Juan, on the busy north side of Puerto Rico, where most of the island's population lived, including Chuck and his wife. Although not Latino themselves, they had grown very fond of their life on the island, where they fit in well with the affectionate, outgoing, family-based culture they found there. Most of his crew were of Puerto Rican descent. So while English was legally the language of the ship, in practice the conversation on board was entirely in Spanish, which Chuck spoke well.

While on patrol one day, he told me, an Immigration and Naturalization Service plane flying surveillance out ahead of the cutter spotted a small boat crossing toward the deserted jungles of the southern Puerto Rican coast. Over the radio came a request to intercept the boat, which was still some miles ahead. As the cutter closed in, Chuck picked it up in his binoculars. It was indeed a tiny vessel, with only a small outboard motor to take it through that dangerously rough stretch of water. He could also see that it was crammed to the gunwales—not with terrorists or drug dealers, but with grandparents and infants.

But where was it headed? Swinging his binoculars to the shore, he picked up an isolated beach. It was filled with brightly dressed people carrying picnic hampers and waving banners—one of which, he remembers, said, "Welcome Home, Grandma!" in Spanish. Those on the shore, he knew, were families of workers already established in Puerto Rico, about to be reunited with their elderly and their young in the boat. Chuck found his heart going out to them. They were desperate to get together. And he knew from experience that these new arrivals would hardly con-

stitute a drain on the economy of Puerto Rico or the United States. As
illegal aliens, they would drop out of sight in or near San Juan. Few would
have any reason to want to get from Puerto Rico to the mainland.

Yet his constitutional duty was clear. Despite their circumstances,
it was his job to prevent individuals from illegally entering the United
States. His task was to intercept them and return them to the Dominican
Republic.

Chuck's cutter was closing in rapidly. But the tiny boat, with a good
lead on them, was now not far from the beach. Then, with the cutter in
hot pursuit, the boat crossed a sandbar too shallow for the cutter. Had he
wanted to, Chuck told me, he could have abandoned the chase right
there. As a captain at sea, he knew that his word was law, and that no military tribunal would have condemned him for turning back. But he also
knew he had one more option. The cutter carried a shallow-draft inflatable equipped with a seventy-five-horse outboard. If deployed quickly, it
could cross the sandbar and possibly catch the small boat. But the catch
would have to be completed before the passengers made it to dry land.
Once ashore, U.S. law would protect them from being rounded up and
returned by the Coast Guard.

So they lowered the inflatable. But Chuck knew that giving chase so
close to land might cause some of the small boat's passengers to panic.
Given the clarity of these tropical waters—where a sandy bottom can
look deceptively shallow—they might try to leap out and wade ashore,
drowning in the surf while their boat was still dangerously far from the
beach. So Chuck gave careful instructions to the seaman he put in charge
of the inflatable. The Coast Guard, Chuck reminded him, has a duty to
enforce the law. He was to make every effort to catch that boat. But if he
saw the passengers trying to scramble out, he was to pull back—because
above all the Coast Guard has an obligation to save life, not endanger it.

The seaman saluted, fired up the outboard, and headed out with his
small crew. Chuck said he knew that if the seaman gave that inflatable anything but a full throttle, he probably wouldn't catch the small
boat. But he was a dutiful sailor. Whatever he may have been feeling, he

rammed the throttle all the way up. And in full view of the family members waiting on the shore he caught the boat—in water so shallow, Chuck estimated, that its passengers could have waded ashore, if they had only known. But they didn't. The inflatable returned to the cutter, the small boat in tow and all its occupants aboard.

That homeward journey, steaming from the Mona Passage back around to San Juan harbor where the refugees would be processed for repatriation, Chuck recalled as "the longest two hours of my life." There was not a word spoken, he said, and "there was not a dry eye anywhere on that ship."

"We all knew," he said, "that we'd done the right thing. And we all knew we'd done something terribly wrong."

In this justice-versus-mercy dilemma, where does Chuck's moral duty lie? Is it right to round up the intruders in the name of the law or extend compassion to families? Ends-based thinkers, seeing few large consequences here, might argue that the utilitarian principle of the greatest good for the greatest number allows Chuck to look the other way. Who would be harmed, after all, if these few people reached shore safely? Rule-based thinkers, by contrast, would argue that Chuck's duty required him to intercept the boat, since he must operate on a principle that he would want all other Coast Guard officers to follow regardless of circumstances. Care-based thinkers, focusing on the Golden Rule, would urge Chuck to do what they would want the Coast Guard to do if they were in that small boat—or, on the other hand, to do what they would want that captain to do if they were taxpayers or low-skilled workers already legally in Puerto Rico.

In the end, Chuck opted for the rule-based principle. The values that took precedence were fairness and responsibility rather than compassion for those in need. That choice may strike ends-based thinkers as harsh and inappropriate—to the point that they may deny that Chuck, although he was adhering to an overriding principle in a harrowing and emotional situation, was exhibiting any moral courage at all. But he was. You may disagree with the outcome. And a different officer, unwilling to tolerate that outcome, might have taken a different (though not unethical) way out of this right-versus-right dilemma. But surely, dry eyes or not, moral courage was on display in the cutter that day. The point is that there are cases in which, even though we don't like the outcome, we're forced to admit that the decision was morally courageous.

CONSCIENCE, NOT CONSEQUENCE

Reflecting on the stories of moral courage in this chapter, three points emerge:

- Moral courage typically involves an adherence to one or two core values. In the stories examined here, the five core values all played a role. For Dolores it was honesty and fairness. Mike Saklar and his board appeared to focus on responsibility and honesty. Daniel Webster held to truth-telling and a respect for the ideal of the union. For Amylee Bowman compassion drove her into truth-telling. For Chuck the overriding concerns were fairness and responsibility. In each case, had some other set of values prevailed, the consequences could well have been different.

- Moral courage, therefore, depends on an ability to elevate one or more key values above others. That may come naturally, with such a clear sense of rightness as to require little thought. At the other extreme, it may require an anguished and sleepless right-versus-right analysis that finally leads to a choice of the higher right. Whatever the modality, we typically ascribe moral courage to those who adhere so unswervingly to a clear set of values that they are neither lured by unethical, right-versus-wrong temptations nor dragged back to some value they regard as a lesser right.

- It would seem, then, that much of what we choose to regard as morally courageous owes more to Kant than to Mill. Moral courage, it appears, is less consequentialist than deontological—determined not so much by the outcomes of the actions as by the duty or obligation we feel toward a particular core value, despite the possible consequences.

This last point bears emphasizing. Again and again, the morally courageous experiences cited in this book tend toward a rule-based commitment to a value rather than an ends-based weighing of the consequences. In that way, Webster's ringing affirmation—"I shall stand by the Union with absolute disregard of personal consequences"—resembles one of history's most famous battle cries of moral courage: "Here I stand. I can do no otherwise; so help me God! Amen!" Those words, attributed to Martin Luther after he nailed his ninety-five theses to the church door at Wittenberg in 1517, are similarly void of any consequentialist considerations. Luther had no idea of outcomes—either that he would be excommunicated and plunged into hiding or that he would begin the Reformation. In fact, historians remind us, those famous words may be a misrepresentation of his summary comment at the Imperial Diet of Worms in 1521. Asked to recant, he told the emperor, "I cannot and I will not recant anything, for to go against conscience is neither right nor safe. God help me. Amen." In either formulation, the words carry his conviction that conscience rather than consequence must be the prevailing consideration. That commitment to core principles remains to this day a defining characteristic of moral courage.

But if a focus on consequences is not the principle that drives moral courage forward, does that mean courageous individuals are heedless of consequences? Do they not assess danger, analyze threats, and contemplate risk on the basis of probable outcomes? Indeed they do. Crucial to any expression of moral courage is an awareness of risk and its consequences—the subject of the next chapter.

Moral Courage Checklist
Step 3: Acting on Conscience

If it's already clear from step 2 that the five core values are in operation in my situation, the next step is to see how one or more of these values can direct my decision making.

The first step is to **focus** on one or two key values. Sometimes that happens almost automatically, when the values seem obvious. At other times it will involve a right-versus-right analysis.

In either case, it's important, as a second step, to **dismantle** the right-versus-wrong arguments that might lure us into inaction. Often the simple articulation of a wrong course of action makes it clear that we must strive to avoid it—even though it may seem tempting.

The third step may be more subtle. It requires us to **recognize** that no higher right value ought to draw us into a different course. Here our weighing may present powerful moral arguments that, if followed, could themselves produce right outcomes—but which, as we examine the situation, would not call upon us to express much moral courage.

In the end, then, the test may be to ask, What course of action will arise when I give the highest weight to principles and conscience rather than to outcomes and consequences? You may not always decide to follow that rule-based course—and your decision to go with a more ends-based or care-based approach may, in a given circumstance, be absolutely right. But it's when the rule-based course is followed that we're usually most comfortable saying, "That's morally courageous."

CHAPTER FIVE

The Second Circle:
Recognizing the Risks

Gloucester, 'tis true that we are in great danger;
The greater therefore should our courage be.

—William Shakespeare

Where there's no danger, there's no courage. That statement is so axiomatic that it hardly needs saying. When no threat hovers darkly on the horizon and no storm troubles the placid seas, what's the risk in setting forth on the voyage? But if physical courage is (as I quoted General William T. Sherman saying in chapter 1) "a perfect sensibility of the measure of danger and a mental willingness to endure it," then courage doesn't arise in the absence of risk. Anyone can "endure" security and well-being. The real challenges—the ones that force our endurance to grow from mere perseverance into true courage—arise in the face of hazard.

So it is with moral courage, where danger is endured for the sake of an overarching commitment to conscience, principles, or core values. Here, too, the key lies in properly assessing the "measure" of peril. Underestimate the danger, and our moral courage will be written off as imprudence. It will be seen as pointless self-sacrifice, doomed from the outset because we never understood the difficulties we would encounter. But overestimate the danger by inflating mundane annoyances into fantasies of fright—and then riding bravely out against them in battles we're sure to win—and the world will credit us with nothing more than bluster, bravura, and rant. Our courage will be relegated to the imaginary realm of "the lunatic, the lover, and the poet," for whom, as Duke Theseus observes in Shakespeare's *A Midsummer Night's Dream,*

> *. . . in the night, imagining some fear,*
> *How easy is a bush suppos'd a bear!*

A proper assessment of risk, in other words, is an essential component of moral courage. But risk involves, as my *Webster's* puts it, "exposure to loss, injury, disadvantage, or destruction." Measuring such exposure is an inherently subjective process. In the insurance business, where risk is the defining element of the work, actuarial calculations can minimize subjectivity, replacing human judgment with formulas that pool and calibrate risk. In mountain climbing, where risk can be mitigated somewhat by pinpoint weather reporting and Global Positioning Systems, the subjective element remains in the wisdom and experience of the climbers. So it is in ethical dilemmas, where the moral risk to the decision maker can be reduced, though not eliminated, by thoughtful reasoning and accurate analysis of the facts. But whatever the situation, risk must be present before we're willing to say, "That was a courageous act!"

Any assessment of danger rests heavily on an understanding of outcomes. Risk, after all, doesn't inhabit the past or the present. It lies in the future, where something either will or won't happen. To examine risk, then, is to examine possible consequences. In the previous chapter, I argued that the ethical principle upon which moral courage usually stands is the Kantian standard of the categorical imperative. That philosophy is a deliberately nonconsequentialist view of the world. Under its rubric, ethics gets done not when good consequences follow and things turn out well, but when fundamental laws are applied universally regardless of the consequences. Yet here, in assessing risk, the consequences *must* be taken into account. Every calculation of moral risk is, in some way, an estimate of consequences apt to flow from a range of alternative actions. If there are no bad consequences in sight, there is no need to put moral courage into practice.

As the following examples suggest, then, there is a distinction to be made between *expressing moral courage* (a nonconsequentialist act) and *assessing moral risks* (a consequentialist process). Some consequences, as for Dorothy Ehrlich, are immediate and physical, though they require moral courage. Some are intermediate and financial, as for Hector. And some, as for Hans Vogel, are long-term and world-shaping.

FREE SPEECH AND FIREBOMBS

"I'm not a particularly brave person," says Dorothy Ehrlich, "but I have a fairly high tolerance for threats."

Given her position, that's not surprising. As the head of the American Civil Liberties Union of Northern California for twenty-five years—the first woman to occupy that post—she has lived her life on the cutting edge of controversial campaigns to protect free speech, oppose censorship, and support individual freedoms. Threats, she says, come with the territory: hardly a month goes by without a staff member in her organization receiving some kind of message of intimidation. For the most part, she says, "I don't take most threats literally. I think sometimes people need to say these things just to vent."

So when on March 1, 1989, she found herself having just seconds to choose between her principles and a credible death threat, even she was surprised by the intensity of the fear she felt. She was sitting, she recalls, in a studio at KPFA Radio, a listener-supported station in Berkeley, California, known for its passionate concern for free speech and cultural diversity. With the talk-show host and two other guests, she was discussing a firebombing the day before at Cody's Books, a landmark independent bookstore on nearby Telegraph Avenue. Why the bombing? Because Cody's had chosen to display a new and highly popular novel, Salman Rushdie's *The Satanic Verses,* in its window.

Keeping a book on display does not ordinarily require moral courage. But two weeks earlier, on February 14, the supreme religious leader of Iran, Ayatollah Ruholla Khomeini, issued a fatwa. That now-infamous Islamic legal ruling called on Muslims around the world to hunt down and kill Rushdie, both because of the book's blasphemous characterization of the prophet Muhammad and because of Rushdie's own criticisms of the Islamic faith in which he had been raised. Ten days later, on February 24, the ayatollah upped the ante by offering a bounty of $3 million to the killer, an act that sent the Indian-born Rushdie into hiding in Britain.

By the end of February, fearing reprisals from angry Muslims, bookstores across the United States already had started pulling Rushdie's novel from their displays. Cody's Books owner Andy Ross remembers that "America's largest chains, including Barnes & Noble, B. Dalton [Bookseller], and Waldenbooks, removed *The Satanic Verses* from their shelves nationwide," and that "over 1,500 bookstores stopped selling [it]." Cody's, with a defiance befitting its independent spirit, kept the book prominently on display in its front window—through which, on February 28, someone threw a pipe bomb.

The next day, with the Bay Area abuzz with the news, Ehrlich agreed to go on air and, as she had done so often, make her case for freedom of speech. "The notion that a bookstore would be subject to harassment" simply for displaying a book, she says, was "something the ACLU has spoken out on regularly." To her, it was yet another example of the ACLU's core principle that "controversial ideas should be protected." Walking into KPFA's beige stucco building that day was for her almost as routine as going to work. It was just another step in defending the nation's civil liberties, this time on a live, call-in program where listeners could share their concerns and ask their most pressing questions.

But they were not far into the program when the switchboard downstairs relayed an urgent message. They had received word that a bomb had been planted in the building. Taking a quick break, the host conferred with his guests.

"We had a matter of seconds to decide whether to go off the air," Ehrlich recalls. "I remember being extremely frightened—feeling that the room was getting extremely small." To have gone off the air, she knew, would have been "a complete surrender." But given the explosion at Cody's, they had to admit that this threat might not be hollow.

In those few seconds, she says, they agreed to stay on the air. Coming back after the break, they continued their discussion. No bomb was ever found at the studio, nothing more happened at Cody's, and the bomber was never apprehended. "There were a few days of enormous concern," she recalls, "and then it all died away."

Yet at the time, Ehrlich recalls, both the danger and the courage to surmount it were not merely imaginary. To "stand up against intimidation," she says, can be "a very real danger." But for her the greater danger—for the community as well as for the individual—would have been to fail to take that stand. "If people think they are able to shut down speakers" by their threats, she concludes, the voices of oppression and intimidation "really *do* win." For her, courage entails "the notion that you have to be willing to take a risk to protect the values you stand for."

What was that risk? Surely it was physical. So wasn't this a case of physical rather than moral courage? After all, it was not simply reputation but perhaps life itself that was at stake. And as she said, that feeling of being "very claustrophobic" in that tiny studio produced in her "a physical sense of fear." What did she mean, I asked her, about not being particularly brave?

"When I compare myself to others who have exhibited some kind of bravery," she says, she realizes that "there are people who have really paid the price for their convictions." Her life seems tame by comparison to that of an ACLU colleague in Oklahoma, she says, who lost her house when it was firebombed by people who were "less hospitable to civil liberties." But even when the action is physical, Ehrlich comes back to the

moral imperative that drives it—to what she variously calls "convictions," "principles," or "the values you stand for."

What drove her forward, then, was not physical courage but moral
courage. That sense of an overarching principle was, for her, the element
of conscience that impelled her to overcome fear. The fright was intense.
It was also, in those split seconds, laden with consequence—a fleeting but
chilling recognition of what might happen if a bomb really were to
explode in their midst. But the action that followed—the willingness to
keep going—appears to have been rooted not in consequence but in principle. It was not that an alternative set of consequences swept in to drive
her decision: she did not, apparently, reason her way forward through an
examination of the good that might flow from her being bombed. She
never consciously weighed the threat of death against, for instance, the
benefits of a tragic martyrdom—the encouraging example her death
might set, the useful social outrage that might flow from it, the deepened
public interest it might engender in the ideals of the ACLU. None of this
seemed to have crossed her mind.

What impelled her decision, instead, was a fixed conviction, developed over long years and grooved to an almost intuitional reflex, that the
principle of free speech must be upheld at every turn. That conviction no
doubt owed a great deal to her understanding of consequences. She knew
well the outcomes that resulted from the moral courage of those who had
come before. Had there been time or inclination to repeat them, she had
plenty of examples to add to the one about her colleague's house in Oklahoma. She knew well the horrors experienced by people around the
world who spoke out about the right to hold controversial ideas and talk
truth to tyranny. She also knew that these people, even when they paid
the ultimate price, were no less morally courageous for having died.

The preparation for this instant of choice, in other words, lay in long
years of assessing perils, threats, and dangers. It lay in a deep and nuanced
understanding of the consequences that might flow from taking those
risks. But when the moment came to decide, the determinant of her
action was her recognition that if free speech is to be protected, you must

stand up against intimidation at every point. Her courage, in other words, was shaped by risk. But the decision to act was rooted in principle.

The Governor's Request

For Hector, too, the courage grew out of risk—though unlike Dorothy Ehrlich, he had time to walk in the woods and reconsider his initial, gut-level response. During the recession of the early 1980s, he was appointed director of a powerful state government department overseeing employment and job-training issues. Shortly after he took office, a series of plant closings in the steel and automotive sectors sent workers across his state reeling into unemployment.

Hector and his staff responded with a job-search program that won high praise from union, management, and government executives. Central to its success were workshops that helped laid-off employees assess their interests, inventory their skills, find needed training, and seek new work.

For Hector, the goal was more than simply economic. Born to Mexican parents and raised in a small city in Mexico, he remembered learning early in life the strength of family ties, the dignity of even the most basic work, and "our responsibility to each other as people." He also knew that many of those losing their jobs were from longtime union families who "generation after generation" had come to think of themselves as "part of a family that's going to take care of you."

All of that was now being shattered. Hector held no animosity for the corporations. He knew that as they struggled to survive in a slackening economy, they had to be free to downsize their operations. He also recognized that the real challenge lay in the minds of the dismissed workers— what he called "the illusion that the plant will reopen or that you'll find something identical." He had seen firsthand the price of that illusion in anxiety, depression, high blood pressure, alcoholism, and family abuse. So for him the job-search program was no mere bureaucratic response. It was a mission.

As his programs gained credibility around the state, the governor's office took increasing interest. One day, as election time came around, Hector had a visit from one of the governor's top aides. The aide told him that a longtime state senator, a good friend of Hector and a key ally of the governor, was facing stiff opposition from a challenger. One way the governor could show support and also steer some welcome state resources toward the senator's home territory would be for Hector to schedule a major job-search conference in the senator's district and conduct it himself. Would Hector help in this way?

Hector could see the logic of the governor's plan. "It sounded," he said, "like a simple request." But that senator's district didn't fit the profile of places where the workshop was likely to be beneficial. In Hector's eyes, it was the "wrong intervention" for that location, which had been so "bombarded" by plant closings that there were few options left for work of any kind. Such a conference, he feared, would have given "false hope" to local workers, who even with new skills might find only dead ends in their job searches. Despite the fact that the conversation with the aide "happened so quickly," he recalls that he had no doubt about his decision.

"No, I can't do that," he told the aide, explaining why.

"Do you know the implications of your response?" he recalls the aide saying. "Do you realize the consequences of what you're doing?"

Hector did indeed know. The sole supporter of his wife and young son, he had few accumulated assets. His family lived paycheck to paycheck. As a political appointee, he could be fired that very day. And with that firing might well go his potential for appointment to other government positions. With it, in other words, might go his career.

But even at that stage, he says, "my life was all about giving to others." He knew the governor's plan would have resulted in "a terrible abuse" and "a misuse of public office." So while he didn't have much time to think, he says, in a way he didn't need it.

"It was so clearly wrong," he says, "that I couldn't do it." There was no extended examination of pros and cons, no careful weighing of the consequences, no dwelling on an impossible string of "what ifs." Yes, there was a massive risk. Yes, he could see it. And yes, he would still refuse to bend his principles.

That evening, he and his family left for a brief holiday in the mountains. He didn't tell them what had transpired. But out there "with my family and the trees," he says, he reexamined his choice. And in the end, he felt sure his all-in-a-moment decision had been right. What occurred to him was that his expression of moral courage was "a moment of legacy for my son"—whether or not his son knew.

When I asked Hector about the legacy left to him by his own parents, he traced it back to a strong, loving mother who fought courageously for her family—and to a quieter, affectionate father who, though a labor arbitrator in a country where corruption was endemic, had such a strong sense of honor that he never took bribes. His family "knew great pain in life," but they also knew "the power of innocence." Hector was given, he says, "an instinct to help others" and what he remembers as a spiritual (though not necessarily religious) sensitivity.

What, then, are the qualities that accounted for his moral courage? Hector sees three things:

- A sense of responsibility
- The ability to know right from wrong
- A spiritual base

When I asked him whether moral courage could be taught, he hesitated.

"I don't think so," he finally replied. "But we should nurture it in our children. You can't teach your children values and then do the wrong thing. You live it—you express it. And we can all get tune-ups!"

I asked Hector what happened after he declined the governor's request. Did he lose his job? No. In fact, he was promoted several times in the coming years. But he never felt particularly close to the administration after that. "I couldn't be a buddy," he recalled. And even as he made his decision, he sensed that looming divide. The risk of losing such a welcome sense of camaraderie, in fact, was part of what made his decision so tough.

"I think we all want to be part of the clan," he concluded.

As for lessons learned, he recalls a conversation years later with a wise mentor. It followed a highly visible and widely reported incident of ethical challenge and commitment in Hector's life. When it was all over, he had survived—and while part of him wanted to set the record straight, another part of him simply wanted to move on and never look back.

His friend, counseling the latter, made a point Hector never forgot.

"People will not remember the incident," his friend said. "They'll remember how you handled it." It is as though he had said that while the consequences won't be part of your legacy, the principle upon which you stood will be.

RISKING GERMANY'S FUTURE

But what if you've had years to contemplate the risk—and to recognize that the stakes might involve the future of a nation? That's where Hans Vogel found himself on November 23, 1940, as the Portuguese steamer *Nyassa* lay at the Quai da Fondacao in the port of Lisbon, making ready for a voyage to New York. Scheduled for departure at 4:00 P.M., it was receiving the finishing touches of a repainting. It was also receiving a steady stream of passengers and their families, clogging the docks and bidding farewells that, given the wartime uncertainties, were more than usually tearful.

Among them was Hans Vogel, the little-known chairman of the German Social Democratic Party—the Sozialdemocratische Partei Deutschlands, or SPD. Established in 1875, it became the largest party in the Weimar Republic. By the end of the twentieth century, it would be the party of Chancellor Gerhard Schröder, who followed in the illustrious footsteps of SPD chancellors Willy Brandt and Helmut Schmidt. But in 1940, it was a party in tatters. Seven years earlier, Vogel and his ninety-three SPD colleagues in the Reichstag had voted against Hitler's Enabling Act, a courageous move in treacherous times. Six weeks later, Vogel began his life in exile, first in Prague and then in Paris.

With the fall of Paris to the Nazis on June 14, 1940, Vogel and his wife, along with their nineteen-year-old son, Ernst, found themselves swept into a calamitous river of refugees surging south across Europe seeking passage to safer countries. For many of them, Britain was the logical destination. Vogel had visited London in 1939, shortly after the death of the SPD's formidable chairman, Otto Wels. There, he found European opposition to the Third Reich beginning to coalesce. His enthusiastic reception by well-regarded British political figures gave him needed confidence in his role as Wels's successor. After his visit, when he was back in France and once again on the run from the Nazis, the British Labour Party invited him and his colleagues to emigrate to England. But their escape route across the Channel was cut off, and by September 1940 the Luftwaffe had set in motion its relentless blitz against London.

For many of Vogel's SPD colleagues, however, it was America—distant, secure, still neutral, and willing to supply visas—that had become the longed-for goal. And by 1940, the *Nyassa* was not simply a ship: she was a lifeline for anti-Nazi refugees. That November afternoon, it was to New York and not London that the Vogels were sending the youngest of their three children. As it turned out, that was the last Hans Vogel would see of his son.

It didn't have to be that way. The three of them together could have made the trip to New York. Six weeks before, as they had boarded the train in a torrential Marseilles rain for the French border town of Cerbère, that had been the plan. What made it possible was the elder Vogel's possession of a rare and valuable document: a visa to the United States.

But his visa brought Hans Vogel no joy. In diligent diary entries that recorded this period of his family's trials, young Ernst wrote from Marseilles, "I felt the expressive silence. . . . To have purchased a ticket to

Cerbère meant complete capitulation before Hitler." For as long as Ernst could remember, his family had been entirely wrapped up in the fortunes of the SPD. Exile had only made the party more prominent in their lives. Through publishing, meetings, and letter writing, Hans and his colleagues had managed to keep the organization together. Yet so many of those colleagues had been tortured and murdered by the Nazis that the remainder felt themselves at times to be the last remnant of this once-proud party. Was this, in fact, the end of the SPD? Could it hold together until Hitler was stopped, order restored, and Germany once again in need of democratic leadership? Or were they foolish even to imagine such an eventuality, given the relentless victories that the führer's forces were notching up each day?

As Vogel's biographer Francine Kiefer puts it, "the choice between the United States and England was the greatest moral dilemma of Hans Vogel's political career, and also of his personal life. At its most basic, it was a weighing of two factors: personal safety for himself and his family versus the survival of his political party." At that time, she notes, the United States was almost magnetic for Vogel's colleagues, who flocked there to settle down after years of turmoil. But the more Vogel pondered his options, the more he felt that London had to be his next destination. New York was seductive, but his visitor status would preclude him not only from working but from political activity. A charity case in a nation with no significant labor party, he would effectively have brought his political life to a close by joining Ernst on the *Nyassa*. And that, he knew, might have spelled the end for the SPD.

Ernst, ever the insightful chronicler, understood the tension. In his father's mind, he could see that "the USA . . . sinks like a stone and England rises to the surface. . . . To go to the USA under the conditions that have already been indicated would be an enormous mistake." Then he added a comment that, within the next month, would become a point of major argument between a father wanting to keep his family together and a son seeking the promise of a new life. "I have already let father know that I shall go to the USA," he wrote, "no matter what."

But deciding to go to the United States was one thing. Getting a visa was something else. It took two months of persistent cables, letters, and calls before the U.S. consulate in Lisbon granted Ernst a visa. And it was not until November 16—seven days before Ernst was to leave—that Hans and his wife, Dina, finally got their visas to England. "Exasperated and impatient," writes Kiefer, "Hans did not handle this ticklish situation with grace. . . . 'Father is extremely nervous and the littlest thing makes him angry and irate,' wrote Ernst. . . . And although Ernst had made up his mind to go to America, his father had reopened the discussion, suggesting his son first accompany them to London." The resulting family blowup was settled the next morning when Hans, knocking on his son's door, offered reconciliation.

For his parents, despite their visas, getting to London was even more vexing. It was not until the morning of December 28 that Hans Vogel and his wife touched down at an airport near Bristol, passengers on a Royal Air Force Liberator bomber. The next day, the Luftwaffe launched its massive holiday bombing campaign in London.

What was it that inspired that act of courage? It surely was not the prospect of a safe and happy life: Vogel's letters from his years in London speak of exhausting work, depression, betrayal by SPD colleagues, and an intense sense of separation from his family. On May 17, 1945—just days after Germany's unconditional surrender should have buoyed him with elation—Vogel writes to his two older children in a darkly retrospective mood:

> . . . I am constantly asking myself the meaning of life. Would it really have been a loss for mankind if, in these years of war, my life had been extinguished through some kind of incident? It may have been sad for next of kin and a few friends. If it had happened right at the start of the war, not even a rooster would have crowed about it. Sooner or later life must come to a close, and this life can hardly offer any more joy. . . . But as long as we are given life, we must try to use it to the full advantage of mankind.

Earlier, in 1941, he had written to Ernst about the difficulties he was facing in London. "Those eight years in Czechoslovakia and France do not offset what I have experienced here in just this one year," he told him. "But we must hold out. Our time will yet come."

These twin convictions—that life is to be used to "the full advantage of mankind" and that we must "hold out" and hope that "our time will yet come"—seem to have undergirded his moral courage. Ever alert to risk and threats, Hans Vogel faced a full array of them in the course of his career, from the external threats of brutality and murder to the covert dissensions and defections that nearly destroyed the SPD during his years of exile. Yet his convictions that he was working for something beyond himself and that he must never give up hope apparently gave him the courage to keep moving forward while so many of his colleagues were turning aside.

While postwar papers from Bolivia to Berlin reported that he might become Germany's next chancellor and urgently sought interviews with him in London, Hans Vogel did not live to see his party reclaim its place in his country's political future. Following emergency stomach surgery, he died in London on October 6, 1945. "Ironically," writes Kiefer, "it is the very day on which his party meets for the first time in post-war Germany—a meeting he was supposed to have led."

As these three experiences suggest, moral risk is the harbinger of moral courage. To face down its dangers is to express a principled fortitude. But what about the outcomes? Had Dorothy Ehrlich's radio studio been bombed, had Hector lost his job, had the SPD faded into oblivion after the war, would these three examples still have earned their place in the registry of morally courageous deeds? Indeed they would. But would we *know* about these stories? Perhaps not. And that raises a caveat about the way we record history. Ask historians to ply their trade in the crowded waters of the past, and they're apt to focus on individuals who stood out and achieved some notoriety during their lifetimes. Ask the public to identify examples of heroic characters, and they're apt to point to people who against tough odds accomplished towering deeds rather than those who failed valiantly. Ask people to share their personal stories of moral courage, and they are apt to single out experiences that ended on a positive note. The very process whereby we learn about the values that shape courageous individuals, in other words, has its own built-in subjectivity. The streams feeding the reservoirs of historical commentary have their own screens and settling pools, and not everything makes it past the filters. What passes, typically, are those things that speak of personal success or social progress.

But a moment's reflection should convince us that moral courage is not merely the defining feature of a success cult. True, the three examples above are all from people who have "made it" in their cultures—people of stature and influence, highly placed on the ladder of accomplishment, and articulate enough to narrate their tales and comment on their motivations. But risk and principle are not confined to publicly acclaimed leaders. Sometimes the most telling stories are from those at the other end of the spectrum.

CRAFTSMANSHIP IN THE AIR-CONDITIONING TRADE

"I am in the heating and air-conditioning business," writes Albert Slottje from Bellevue, Nebraska. "As such, I have daily contact with at least three of the five basic values: fairness, honesty, and responsibility."

He goes on to explain a situation so specific to his craft that most people would not even recognize it as involving moral courage.

"I don't know how many times," Slottje writes, "I have popped a ceiling tile, looking for equipment or piping to equipment, and wondered, 'Who was the S.O.B. that put this in like that?' "

He explains that "there are many things that make a job look professional," like running pipes with right-angle bends "square with the world" rather than along "as-the-crow-flies" diagonals. There is one thing, however, that even a professional can't detect once the system is installed: the proper de-burring of cut copper piping. He explains that when copper pipe is trimmed to length with a pipe cutter, the sharp cutting wheel slicing into the soft copper raises a burr on the inside of the pipe that in effect reduces its diameter. Unless that burr is removed—a quick operation involving a couple of twists of a triangular de-burring blade inserted into the end of the pipe—it can cause a degradation in performance of up to 15 percent. Once the pipe is soldered, the flaw is invisible and the pipe can't be readily disconnected for inspection. Only when the unit "isn't quite working up to snuff," he says, does a mechanic begin to suspect a de-burring problem.

But if de-burring is so simple, why not do it routinely? For Slottje, such routine is fundamental to craftsmanship. In the press of circumstances, however, it's not hard to imagine a harried installer trying to complete a job on deadline by cutting corners in undetectable ways. The pride in vocation, the commitment to craftsmanship, the desire to protect reputation—these may all be running in the background of thought. But if the foreground provides an overwhelming sense of hazard—*the owners are moving in tomorrow, it's ninety-six degrees outside, and I've promised to get this done on time*—the temptation simply to get it done may override the will to do it right. Adhering to the hidden details of craftsmanship in the face of the larger pressures for speed and economy can take real moral courage. So, too, it can take courage to correct a mistake—whether you're installing air-conditioning or financing an initial public offering.

Gary learned that lesson as an untested rookie on Wall Street.

THE $30 MILLION CALL

"Jack, this is Gary. I screwed up the numbers."

When your cell phone rings during dinner at a New York restaurant, that's not the kind of news you want to get—especially when "the numbers" relate to your decision, earlier that day, to put $30 million into a new venture, and when the call is from a young man you recently hired into your principal-investing firm.

Gary knew all of that when he made the call. But in an odd way, placing the call wasn't what required moral courage. That came later, as he spent the rest of the night wondering whether he'd done the right thing during this frantic, unforeseen twenty-four-hour period that would change his life.

Gary had joined Jack's Wall Street firm in 2001 as a newly minted MBA from a prestigious business school. By early 2002, he was hard at work on a complex deal that would knit together a large public company out of a number of smaller distribution networks. The dozen partners in this twenty-five-person firm, which managed some $2 billion in investors' assets, had offered to put up $60 million to make this new venture work. But as the negotiations dragged on and became more entangled, the partners backed away, setting Gary to work on other, more promising deals.

So when Gary arrived at work early that October morning, he was stunned to discover that his firm had been reapproached by the new venture, which had managed on its own to put together a $300 million initial public offering. It was going public the next day. Did the partners want to take a position in the new venture for $30 million? If so, they had to make a decision by 3:30 that afternoon. The partners needed to know whether it was a good opportunity. And since Gary had tracked the negotiations so closely six months earlier, they were depending on him to tell them.

Gary yanked out his files on the negotiations and began working through the numbers. By midmorning, his printer was spewing out spreadsheets, charts, graphs, tables, and bullet points. And at 3:00, he recalls, "I sat down and walked everyone through the numbers." On paper, it looked good. Yet the partners were evenly split: half wanted to go for it, while the others demurred—not because they didn't think this was a good opportunity, but because they worried about doing things on a "rush basis." What if in their haste they overlooked something? What if some crucial fact was incorrect, some vital number wrong? Was this, they asked, the way they ought to do business? If they made a mistake, they could attempt to rectify it by selling their shares in the public markets in the following days—although, since their stake in the new company was so large, any sale would probably be at a discounted price and produce a meaningful loss. In any case, such activity would be viewed as unprofessional by their colleagues in the field, and as wobbling and indecisive by their investors.

So they talked it through until they reached a consensus. And with three minutes to go before the offering was priced, they phoned in their $30 million offer.

That night, as Gary returned to the spreadsheets, he began to notice that something wasn't right. "I kept looking at it, and looking at it, and looking at it," he said, "and finally I concluded that I had screwed up." While it was not a major, glaring error, it was, he said, "a material mistake."

That's when he called Jack, the firm's senior partner. A man of few words, Jack asked how serious the mistake was. Gary told him that it certainly made him less confident in what he had previously told the partners. Jack asked him to pull together the details and said they'd look at it in the morning.

And that's when Gary began asking himself more questions. Oddly enough, the decision to call Jack right away caused him no difficulty. Maybe, he says, it was just the leftover momentum of that pell-mell day, during which everything had happened without pause or reflection. "I don't think I took a lot of time thinking about what I should do," he told me. "I was surprised with myself, frankly, that I *didn't* have the inclination to hide." For whatever reason, alerting the partners simply seemed the right thing to do.

But when he put the phone down, the second-guessing started. Maybe, he told himself, nobody ever would have caught this mistake. Clearly none of the partners had noticed anything amiss when he made his presentation. Why would they pick up on it later? And would it really make that much difference? He was pretty sure the new venture would succeed despite his recalculation. If it didn't, he knew his numbers would be reexamined. But even so, "somebody would have only a 25 percent chance" of finding the mistake, he felt.

So had he blown his future by blurting out his error? This had been his first big opportunity to help steer investments for his firm. Is this how he wanted to begin, with a reputation for making mistakes? "I would clearly have caught it if I'd had more time," he told me. But time or no time, "I get paid too much to make this kind of mistake." Besides, he explained, in his business "more than half your pay is decided at 'bonus time' in December" as the partners look back over your work. That left only two months to create a more favorable impression.

He had to ask himself whether his impulse to call the boss—which had been just that, an impulse—had been courageous, or whether he had made a mountain out of a molehill. He knew himself to be conscientious—sometimes too much so. "I hold myself to an unfairly high standard in my work product," he said. Had that thirst for perfection led him to wreck his career? He knew his profession well enough to know that many other young fast-track MBAs would never have done what he did. They would have let the mistake slip past unheralded. And who would have blamed them? "Look," he told me, reaching for a metaphor from football, "if a field-goal kicker misses a fifty-five-yard game-winning kick, nobody blames him." But he well might blame himself, since achieving difficult goals is "what you're trained to do." Everyone in the firm knew it had been a blazing sprint to the finish that day and that he had pulled together all kinds of information rapidly and coherently. Had he not spoken up, he was sure he would not have been condemned very harshly had the mistake later surfaced.

And then he made perhaps the key point: "If I'd had more time," he said reflectively, "I might have tried to cover it up."

But time is what he did not have. He was operating on intuition rather than rationality. Fortunately, those intuitions channeled him along the course of his inner values—his sense of integrity, his responsibility to the others in the firm, and, yes, his responsibility to his own work ethic. So he spent the whole next day, he said, "eating crow." The partners, while worried, understood the unusual pressure he had been facing. The new venture got off to a good start. And when he sat down with the partners for his year-end review, one of the glowingly positive statements it contained was that he was willing to own up to his mistakes.

The result? "It was a godsend for my career here," he says. "It's definitely given me more confidence" in making the tough moral calls in the gray areas. In the future, he says, "I'd react the same way again."

And the new venture? It became a stunning success, outperforming everyone's fondest expectations.

But the risk was substantial. Had Gary's résumé been tagged for a $30 million loss—or, worse, for failing to speak up about what he knew—his run on Wall Street well could have been over. When I asked what gave him the courage to speak up, Gary recalled a course he'd had in business school on moral leadership. It examined, he said, the "gray areas" in business, using cases from fiction and from real life. And while it convinced him that there was ample right on both sides of a tough dilemma, it also made him more resolute in finding the highest right rather than settling for a more convenient compromise.

In that sense, Gary had been in training for years for this decision. It's the kind of training that can happen in schools, at home, or—as Peter learned—in organizations like the Boy Scouts.

BACK TALK IN THE BOY SCOUTS

When Peter was sixteen years old, his Boy Scout troop went on a fifty-mile hike in Oregon. It included an overnight at a campground where the adults leading the trip had parked their cars. Coming in from a long hike and preparing for a rafting trip the next day, the group stopped for dinner at a restaurant. When the boys finished eating, the Scoutmaster, Tad, asked them to wait outside to be driven down the highway to the campground a quarter-mile away. They were happy to oblige: Tad was a tough and caring man, impatient with back talk but dedicated to Scouting, for whom the boys had great respect.

But as the adults lingered over after-dinner beers, three of the boys tired of waiting and walked back to the campground. When the adults caught up with them, Tad berated them vociferously, asking them to consider how he would feel if he'd had to call a parent to say that a Scout had been hit by a car on the highway.

That's when Peter, to the shock of his peers, blurted out, "Well, how would you feel if you'd had to call to say there'd been an accident in the van and the driver had been drinking alcohol?"

In the stunned silence that followed, Tad was clearly furious. Rather than expressing his anger, however, he let Peter know they'd talk about it in the morning. He later told Peter's parents that after spending most of that night struggling mentally with himself over what had happened, he concluded that Peter had been right and the adults had been wrong, and that he would not conduct himself that way again when leading the Scout troop. The next morning, Tad apologized to Peter for his behavior.

Did it take moral courage on Peter's part to speak up? His friends thought so, finding such an outburst to be out of character for Peter. But what if Peter was simply swept away by an angry emotion, blurting out something not only unwise but disrespectful? Perhaps he was. Yet the driving force behind his outburst appears to have been less a youthful brashness than a feeling for the core values of fairness and respect—a sense of moral outrage at the injustice of being berated, coupled with an unwillingness to tolerate the lack of respect the adults were showing the boys. Without those values, would he have spoken up at all? The risk was clear: by speaking out, he was provoking the anger of someone he respected and perhaps doing irreparable damage to a relationship that made Scouting so rewarding for him. On the other hand, the pressure of conscience proved irresistible. In the event, he couldn't hold his peace.

And did it take moral courage on Tad's part to apologize? Unquestionably. Apologies, it seems, almost always require moral courage for their implementation. Many are the instances where reason leads inexorably to the need to say, "I'm sorry," and where emotion even prepares the way and senses the occasion—only to see the intended apology collapse into inaction for lack of the moral courage to carry it through. In Tad's case, however, the peril was more subtle. The risk lay not in giving offense or in terminating an enjoyable activity as a Scout leader. It lay in damaging one's own pride, undermining one's own self-esteem, and shattering confidence in one's own leadership skills. Easier, certainly, to say nothing—except that candor and compassion, having driven Tad to come to terms with his own failings, now required him to put into practice at dawn what he'd seen in the dark hours of the night.

As it happens, the story has a coda. When Peter later became an Eagle Scout, he asked Tad to speak at his Eagle Court of Honor ceremony. Before the assembled Scouts, parents, and guests, Tad had the courage to recount how Peter once had the courage to speak up when Tad had done wrong, helping him mend his ways. Tad's actions illustrate another telling aspect of moral courage: its contagious nature. Moral courage, it seems, begets and replicates itself. Peter's mother put it best: "When people live in a morally courageous way, it not only [elevates] their own experience [but] also touches others who witnessed the event or heard about it."

AMBIGUITY, EXPOSURE, AND LOSS: THE ELEMENTS OF MORAL RISK

As the experiences recounted in this chapter suggest, expressing moral courage means enduring moral risk. While that risk comes in myriad forms, facing it frequently involves a willingness to tolerate three things: ambiguity, exposure, and loss.

Ambiguity

Among the most noticeable attributes of situations calling for moral courage are perplexity, obscurity, and lack of clarity. From Dorothy Ehrlich's gut-wrenching moment of panic in the radio studio to Albert Slottje's unseen but suspected cause for a degradation of air-conditioning performance, confusion reigns in large and small ways. Was it right for Hans Vogel to go to the United States or to London? The signals were conflicting and puzzling. Was Gary putting his job on the line by speaking up about his $30 million mistake? Who could say? Would Hector hold his job in government or Peter his place in the Boy Scout troop? Neither could be certain.

A moment's reflection makes it plain why this should be the case: instances requiring moral courage often arise out of ethical dilemmas that demand a wrenching moral choice between two rights. Why should we expect that the moral courage to *implement* a decision should be any less roiled by ambiguity than the moral reasoning that *produced* the decision?

But what about right-versus-wrong situations? What happens when moral courage is expressed by standing up for what's obviously right instead of tolerating what's patently wrong? What's so ambiguous about that? Here it helps to draw a distinction between actions that are *morally courageous* and those that are *persistently firm*. Merely manifesting a fixedness of purpose, however unyielding it may be, is not the same as expressing moral courage. Admirable though it is, we don't call it *courage* unless it entails risk—unless, that is, there's some real ambiguity as to the situation and its outcome. The young Abe Lincoln's fabled walk to return two cents to a woman who had overpaid at his country store would, if true, have demanded little moral courage from a man of his integrity. It was so clearly the right thing to do and so obviously devoid of real risk as to be a matter more of dogged determination than of moral courage. It evidenced, rather than tested, his integrity.

But what about the young police officer who watches his superiors plant drugs in a suspect's pocket as they arrest him? A clear wrong has been done. But the risk of speaking out and shattering the code of loyalty may be so great as to plunge the young officer into a wrenching internal debate: *Do I take this stand or let someone else do it? Do I take it forcefully or quietly? Do I do it now or later?* To the extent that these are real choices—to the extent, in other words, that they involve genuine risks to the reputation, efficacy, and future of the officer—they may require significant moral courage. Even if the officer knows *what* to do, the confusion persists as he or she struggles to know *how* to do it.

One quality of those expressing moral courage, then, is a tolerance for ambiguity. That may sound strange, since (as I've argued above) bold decisions almost always entail a certainty of principle. While that's true at the point of final outcomes, it is anything but true at the stage of assessing the risks along the way. In moral decision making, those who can't tolerate ambiguity will tend to be risk averse—and, as a result, will tend to avoid situations where moral courage is required. By contrast, those who have confidence in their ability to cut through ambiguity—along with a track record of reading the faint signals, penetrating the obtuse, and getting it right—may well be prepared to make the monumentally courageous decisions. That confidence grows by experience: as Aristotle would say, you learn to be confident by doing confidence-building acts. While going to London was by no means the first morally courageous stand Hans Vogel ever made, it may have been his most important—and one for which his whole life experience had prepared him.

Exposure

If ambiguity fogs the decision-making windshield, the second challenge—a fear of exposure—can grind the whole vehicle to a halt. The word *exposure* is common in the financial world, indicating the extent of liability of an insurer to potential claims or of an investor to potential devaluations. Here it means not a monetary risk but a danger of being open, unprotected, and vulnerable—not physically or financially, but morally and mentally. Whistle-blowing, for example, is all about exposure—bringing to light issues that an organization desperately wants to hide, and in the process exposing oneself to the wrath of the antagonists. So, too, the morally courageous actions recounted in this chapter touch on questions of exposure—to a reputed bomb at the radio studio, for instance, or the shame of joblessness, or the legacy of failing to hold together a dying political party. Again and again, it seems, morally courageous action takes place only when some fear of exposure is put down.

But there is another, more subtle kind of exposure. It has to do with a fear of prominence. Expressing moral courage is not simply a *trait* of leadership; it is often the thing that *creates* leaders. Put a group of relative strangers together around a restaurant table. Provide them with an obstreperous and incompetent waiter. Then notice that the guest who first gets up to speak to the manager has become the de facto leader of the group. That may require (to use our earlier distinction) less courage than persistence. But it does require a willingness to accept the exposure that prominence brings.

It may seem odd to talk about a fear of prominence in an age of telegenic egos scrambling for media exposure. But the unwillingness to become a public figure, to accept the responsibility that prominence brings, and to weather the batterings that notoriety provokes is, I suspect, a more significant detriment to the expression of moral courage than we may imagine. Ask eclectic groups of U.S. citizens how many of them are willing to run for elective office (as I have had frequent occasion to do), and the refusal is nearly unanimous. Part of their negativity lies in a perception of the degrading atmosphere of personal attack that so pervades today's campaigning. But part of it reflects a more basic problem: an intolerance for exposure and an unwillingness to take on a leadership role that would thrust them into the limelight.

T. S. Eliot, in creating the character of J. Alfred Prufrock, identified that tendency of our age in 1917. "Do I dare," his character asks, "[d]isturb the universe?" Prufrock dreads encounters with those, especially women, who could see right through him, "as if a magic lantern threw the nerves in patterns on a screen." So he settles into an unhappy and uncourageous role out of sight—"a pair of ragged claws," as he imagines, "[s]cuttling across the floors of silent seas." And in one of the sharpest poetic commentaries ever penned about the distinction between leadership and management, Eliot distinguishes his character from Hamlet, who, though a classic antihero plagued with indecision, was nevertheless forced to play out his role as a leader. Prufrock can't even bring himself to do that:

> No! I am not Prince Hamlet, nor was meant to be;
> Am an attendant lord, one that will do
> To swell a progress, start a scene or two,
> Advise the prince; not doubt, an easy tool,
> Deferential, glad to be of use,
> Politic, cautious, and meticulous;
> Full of high sentence, but a bit obtuse;
> At times, indeed, almost ridiculous—
> Almost, at times, the Fool.

What Prufrock lacks is not physical courage—this is not a poem about bravery under fire or while daring the elements—but the moral courage to seize the moment, "[t]o have bitten off the matter with a smile" and "squeezed the universe into a ball." He has occasion to act, since he seems to move in the right London circles, but in the end the fear of exposure is too overwhelming:

> I have seen the moment of my greatness flicker,
> And I have seen the eternal Footman hold my coat, and snicker,
> And in short, I was afraid.

A lack of moral courage can, of course, always be explained that way: "in short, I was afraid." It can be addressed, however, in proportion as we know what engenders the fear. Developing a tolerance for exposure and prominence, like developing a tolerance for ambiguity, is a key to building a capacity for morally courageous action.

Loss

Perhaps the most obvious of these three challenges, however, is the fear of losing something essential, important, or desirable. Jobs and careers spring easily to mind. How many morally courageous acts have failed to materialize because individuals chose to cling to their personal security? How many bureaucracies have sunk into inertia because civil servants were unwilling to risk their positions by speaking out? How many lives have been lost in battle because soldiers knew things their officers did not, but dared not breach the hierarchy by raising a warning? How many employees—at Arthur Andersen, Christie's, Elf Aquitaine, Enron, Global Crossing, Royal Ahold, Talisman, Tyco, WorldCom, and a host of other global firms that have endured moral implosions in the opening years of this century—had to choose between paying their bills and sounding the alarms?

Put that way, it sounds as though moral courage has failed unless, on every occasion, you've scaled the ramparts and waved the flag. But in most circumstances where moral courage is an option, the stakes are more than simply personal. Most of us have responsibilities for others. And if responsibility is one of the core ethical values that shape our decisions, then moral courage will require us at times to act boldly in defense of those obligations. Children at college, mortgages to pay, parents to support—these are not insignificant responsibilities. They involve promises, explicit or implied, made along the way to those closest to you. An intriguing movie about corporate malfeasance may reduce these issues to an apparent black-and-white choice, where the only moral option is to speak truth bluntly to power. In real life, it is rarely that simple—in part because of ambiguity and the fear of exposure but also because of the economic stability we stand to lose.

Loss, too, can be more than financial. What was it Peter stood to lose by speaking up to his Scout leader? The answers are legion: the opportunity to experience the outdoors, to test himself physically and emotionally, to build friendships, to learn leadership, to discover ways to subsist on little, to pay attention to the struggles and triumphs of his fellow Scouts, to understand endurance—in short, to move from the inward-looking and egocentric habits of boyhood to the outward and sociocentric habits of adulthood. Peter stood to lose the one thing that, as a sixteen-year-old, would perhaps have been foremost in his mind: growing up. Seen from outside and through the lens of our own adulthood, Peter's experience may strike us as a pleasant tale of secondary intensity, with a foregone conclusion and a nice outcome. We may forget what it's like to be sixteen, when a fear of this sort of loss can be gripping, authentic, and life-defining.

Part of every decision about moral courage, then, involves some form of that starkly famous military question: is this the hill you want to die on? Is this issue in fact the big one? If you must hazard all—house, family, children, job, career, financial future—is this the mast on which to nail your colors? Perhaps, instead, this issue is simply an overture to something bigger, for which you must husband your resources. Should Dorothy Ehrlich have fled the radio station immediately in order to be there the following day when, with the studio possibly in smoking ruins, she could focus her oratorical outrage for a far more important audience than the relatively few radio listeners she reached that day? Or perhaps, conversely, the issue is so monumental that any effort to resist it would be crushed instantly, producing no useful result. Instead of fleeing into exile in Czechoslovakia and Paris, Hans Vogel could have stood and fought against Hitler's minions, as some of his colleagues did. But they tragically perished within hours, while he survived to provide crucial leadership a decade later.

These three challenges—of ambiguity, of exposure, and of loss—may not be the only fears confronting those who would be courageous. But they are, I think, the big ones, and they seem to appear in this ascending order of significance. It is easier to accommodate confusion than exposure—and certainly less difficult to tolerate either of those than to endure significant loss. But if moral courage is to be met, the leader must:

- *Penetrate* the mists of confusion, complexity, and uncertainty;
- Accept the *prominence* and public exposure that often accompanies courageous action; and
- Willingly risk the loss of *prosperity* or reputation that this action may bring.

Penetration, prominence, and prosperity. These three *P*s help clarify the nature of the risks leaders take as they engage in morally courageous acts. But what gives them the will to act—the ability to endure that risk? That's the subject of the next chapter.

Moral Courage Checklist
Step 4: Understand the Risks

Understanding risk involves the contemplation of possible outcomes. Unlike the nonconsequentialist, rule-based application of principles examined in step 3, the assessment of risk requires an ends-based, consequentialist approach. Have I adequately assessed the dangers involved both in acting and in failing to act? Am I clear on the moral hazards, even if the situation involves physical hazard as well?

   Do I have a clear picture of the three principal challenges—involving ambiguity, exposure, and loss—inherent in any situation demanding moral courage?

➤

- **Ambiguity.** Am I willing to face up to the ambiguity and confusion that surrounds this problem? Can I penetrate its mysteries without being baffled, duped, or mentally overwhelmed? If I fear I could be wrong about the facts, does that prevent me from moving forward? Or do I have that tolerance for ambiguity, that confidence in my ability to figure things out, which is essential to moral courage? Can I distinguish *persistent firmness* in the face of wrongdoing from true moral courage in the face of right-versus-right dilemmas?

- **Exposure.** Do I recognize the fear of exposure that can inhibit moral courage? Am I willing to make myself vulnerable for the sake of achieving some higher good? Do I acknowledge that by acting with moral courage, I may be thrust into a highly visible leadership role—whether I want it or not? Or am I hoping I can hide and still make a difference? Have I got the focus and stamina to weather the exposure that frequently accompanies morally courageous acts?

- **Loss.** Do I grasp the peril to my income and position—as well as to personal relationships and public reputation—that may be involved here? Is this the hill I want to die on? Have I underestimated the risk, so that I might lose everything to no avail and be accused of foolishness? Or have I overestimated the risk, so that what I think to be courageous has very little risk at all, leaving me open to charges of mere bluster and bravado? Do I understand that moral courage shines most brightly when the stakes are highest?

CHAPTER SIX

The Third Circle:
Enduring the Hardship

*Never give in—never, never, never, never, in nothing great or
small, large or petty, never give in except to convictions of honour
and good sense.*
                                        —Winston Churchill

In the southwestern corner of the Yukon Territory stands Mount Logan,
the largest (though not the tallest) mountain in the world. If you could
uproot it and dump it into the sea, it would displace more water than any
other mountain. At 19,850 feet, it is Canada's highest peak, rising more
than two miles above its surroundings, visible for more than 250 miles,
and second only to Alaska's 20,320-foot Mount McKinley among the
highest peaks in North America.

It's also a mountain famous for weather. Fierce north coastal snow-
storms, brewed in the North Pacific not far away across a thin wedge of
Alaska, can whip up sudden, blinding, tent-shredding winds. Less than
four hundred miles below the Arctic Circle, it can chalk up temperatures
of minus seventy degrees Fahrenheit. Even in the summer, with daylight
around the clock, it can be twenty-seven below zero.

Tom Armstrong Jr. knows that firsthand. That was the thermometer
reading one July morning in 1983 when he and four friends crawled out

of their tents and prepared to make the final six-hour push to reach the peak. A seasoned climber, trim and boyish-looking, Armstrong is now an executive with L. L. Bean. At that time, he taught at Holderness School, a private school in New Hampshire. So cold weather was nothing new to him. Nor was hiking and guiding, which he did regularly with his students.

Altitude, however, was something else. The evening before, he and his friends had pitched their camp at nineteen thousand feet, on a six-mile plateau at the other end of which rose the small spike of the summit. They had hauled in four or five days of food, Armstrong recalls, "so that if a storm came in we could hunker down," wait it out, and keep going. As deputy leader of the expedition, Armstrong felt that they had planned for every eventuality. They had readied their packs the night before. They had stayed up late melting enough snow for water. Given the cold and the lack of oxygen, they recognized that their minds weren't working up to full capacity. Still, "we were well positioned," he says, "and feeling pretty good. There was no way we weren't going to get to the summit."

But that morning something was wrong. One of their party, Donny, was clearly very sick. The problem, they recognized, was high-altitude cerebral edema, a potentially fatal buildup of fluid in the brain that can create confusion, disorientation, and loss of coordination. The only safe cure was to get him down below fourteen thousand feet, quickly.

There was one other expedition on the mountain, a party of Canadians who had reached the summit the day before. They were camped just below Armstrong's team, on their way down. When the American team failed to break camp early, the Canadian team sensed something was wrong and waited to see what was up.

Armstrong knew that short-landing, short-takeoff aircraft had touched down on that plateau in the past. So, working with the Canadians, they agreed to call for help. Stringing out the antenna of their small single-sideband radio, and matching up a Rube Goldberg array of crystals and batteries from both teams, they managed to contact their glacier pilot, who agreed to pick up Donny high on the Logan plateau. Then they set to work packing out a runway with their snowshoes, marking the edges with ski poles and tying a ribbon of tape to one of them as a wind sock.

It was a clear morning, but as they worked the wind picked up and the temperature began falling. About two hours later, they heard the plane approaching. Reestablishing radio contact, they started talking the pilot in, telling him what the wind gusts were doing. He was making his final approach, Armstrong recalls, when "at the last second the wind came up and the entire plateau turned into a whiteout—just blowing snow. And all we heard was 'Abort! Abort rescue! You're on your own. Good luck.' " Low on fuel, he could not afford to circle and wait for the snow squall to clear.

At that, the Canadians offered to take Donny down with them so that the American party could continue to the summit. Armstrong's team began weighing its options. There was no way they could take Donny down themselves and then return to make the summit: they simply wouldn't have had the strength. And there was no way they could leave Donny at their camp, race for the summit, and then return and move him downhill, since he might not last twenty-four hours at that altitude. Nor did Armstrong like the idea of splitting up their team, sending two down with Donny and letting the other two go for the summit. "My sense was that if we split up we'd be weaker if something were to happen," he said. "So we needed to stay together."

That left them two choices. They could accept the Canadians' offer, relinquish Donny, and do what they all longed to do: make the summit. Or they could stay with Donny themselves, move him down the mountain, and give up the goal of their twenty-one-day trek when it was just hours away. Some of the team were for letting the Canadians help. Armstrong and team leader Mike Perry, on the other hand, felt that Donny's safety was not a responsibility they could hand off. While Donny "wasn't a litter-case at this point," said Armstrong, "he could have been forty-five minutes later." Besides, at any moment the weather could change, forcing the entire team to hunker down and wait it out. Could Donny survive that wait? Did they want the Canadians to have to assume *that* kind of responsibility?

It would take continuing physical courage to push on to the summit. But it would take greater moral courage to turn back just as they were about to reach their goal. Yet that's what they did. Thanking the Canadians, they committed themselves to getting Donny back to safety.

To get down, however, they first had to cross a ridge nearly a thousand feet higher than the plateau—with obvious danger to Donny, who though he was still able to walk was by now barely capable of following instructions. So Armstrong put Donny on a rope in front of him. He didn't use the usual fifty-foot length that gives one climber a chance to arrest the fall of the other if one goes into a crevasse. Instead, to give him more control over Donny's movements, he put him on a ten-foot rope, risking both their lives should one of them fall. With the other team members staying behind to prepare the gear for the descent, the two of them painstakingly climbed the ridge and then began belaying their way down the other side.

The others figured they would catch up with the pair, Armstrong recalls, but "it turned out Donny just kept going, so I just kept going." They went all that night, "one foot in front of the other," until they reached the base camp at about twelve thousand feet, and all night long Donny's condition kept improving. At the base camp, the pilot flew back up, landed on the glacier, and slammed the door open without even turning off the engine. "We literally just picked Donny up like a sack of potatoes and threw him in the back," Armstrong recalls. The pilot pulled the plane around and took off. Donny was safe. And at that moment a storm blew up, stranding Armstrong's team at the base camp. It was another three days before the plane could ferry them out.

Sitting in his office in Freeport, Maine, on a sunny December morning, I asked Armstrong to describe the decision making that led to that choice. Was it quick and intuitive, or deliberate and reasoned? At that altitude, he chuckles, "your mental capacity is about half-mast." But "we wanted to do the best due diligence you can at nineteen thousand feet and twenty-seven below zero," he recalls, so they "weighed lots of options." In the end, the gut seemed to get the better of reason. Intuition told them to stick by the time-seasoned principle of mountaineering, which says (as Armstrong puts it), "you take care of your own," and "you get your teammate out."

Yet in mountaineering, as in any sport, there's a competing principle: you fight to win, you do your utmost to reach your goal, and you don't let anything turn you back. Armstrong knows that, too. He's seen plenty of it in his years as an athlete and a coach. And it worries him.

"What's happening in mountaineering—and maybe in sports in general—is that it's the fastest, the highest, the strongest, the most successful who get the rewards," he notes. "It's almost like the summit—the reward, the gold medal, winning the play-off—is out of proportion to the ethics that the sport was really premised on." There are instances, he says, "where people are on their way to the summit of Everest and another party is in trouble, and they just literally walk by them because that's a different group from theirs."

So what was it, I ask, that gave him the moral courage to choose the caretaking principle over the winning principle? He points to his leadership experience as a teacher and guide at his school in New Hampshire, where, he says, "you would never leave a student exposed like that." As coaches, he says, "we would never strive to win a game by any means. Standing on the summit is not the most important thing. It's how you got there as a team."

To this day, he says, the people he chooses to make up a team for an outdoor activity are those who see it from this perspective—people who are "competitive with themselves, but not with each other," as opposed to those who are "driven at all cost" and put everything else behind the desire to succeed. There was one member of the Mount Logan team, he recalls, who was "pretty adamant that we go to the summit and not take Donny down." Armstrong had met him on Mount McKinley, and he was a good, strong climber. "But he was the one person none of us knew very well. Our way of thinking as one team, healthy or sick, was very different from his perspective."

Does Armstrong have any regrets? None at all, he says. "To this day I think it was the right call, because if that storm had come in twenty-four hours earlier, or if we had been slower on the descent, we would have been in a major storm coming down the mountain. For me it was a gut instinct that that was the right thing to do. It wasn't even really a question. The only thing we didn't do was the last six hours of the summit, and I can live with that. I've been higher."

W H A T   M A K E S   M O R A L   C O U R A G E
P O S S I B L E ?

What gave Tom Armstrong the capacity to endure the hardship and push through the danger? Why, when some were urging him to compromise on his fundamental principle of mountaineering—*you take care of your own*—was he willing to act with moral courage?

Think back to the elements of our Moral Courage Checklist. One step calls on us to distinguish moral from physical courage. No one can dispute the tremendous physical courage required on that July night, as Armstrong sidestepped Donny down to twelve thousand feet on a short rope. But the driver of that action was a decision based on principle. To interpret this experience as simply another adventure in physical courage is to miss the dominant moral values that determined that choice.

A second step asks us to identify the particular moral values being put into practice. First among them, apparently, was a strong sense of responsibility. With that, however, came a sense of compassion. Without using the term *Golden Rule,* Armstrong explains it this way:

I think that had I been in his shoes and then been left with some strangers when I was feeling very, you know, at death's door—were

I coherently to come back, get clear, and suddenly say, "I don't know any of these people. What am I doing here? Where are we? Where's Mike? Where's Pat?"—it would be a very terrible experience. I think we were trying to put ourselves in his shoes.

A succeeding step entails an assessment of risk, including the fear of ambiguity, exposure, and loss. The ambiguity was obvious. Donny was suffering but was not immobilized. The weather was threatening but not yet that bad. The Canadians were strong and willing but Donny was not their responsibility. Perhaps most important, the ultimate purpose of the trip was in plain sight at the end of the plateau but was squarely in conflict with a moral principle. Obvious, too, was the exposure—both to a public disappointment at turning back that would be reawakened in these team members whenever mountaineering tales were being swapped and to the possible remorse at making a bad and unprofessional decision should something go wrong. Fear of loss was also evident: loss of life should Donny not survive, but also a loss of self-regard should a core value be violated so profoundly as to cause that loss of life.

The final step calls on us to find the most important principle to uphold—not necessarily because we think it will produce the best outcomes, but because it's the right thing to do regardless of the consequences. In this case, through the fogged mentality of thin air and bitter cold, one principle remained clear: you get your teammate out.

Armstrong passed through each of these steps. He knew it was an issue of moral courage. He understood that the ethical values of responsibility and compassion were at stake. He spent time with his colleagues assessing the risks. And he identified the principle that should rise above all others. But people can do all that and still not have the courage to act. What gave him the capacity to endure the hazards for the sake of principle?

Recall his telling comment, *I've been higher.* In those three words Armstrong identified a central motivator for his willingness to act: his experience. With years in the trenches as a coach and guide, with decades of testing himself in tough conditions and forcing himself onward to reach his goals, he knew what reaching the summit meant—and what it did not mean. His was a balanced view of goal-seeking, conditioned by the wisdom that comes from a lifetime of experience at both winning and losing. Ultimately, he was free to express moral courage because he had learned to trust in the fact that doing the right thing leads to rewards different from and greater than those that come from simply pushing onward through self-will and blind determination. He had learned, over the years, one of the most powerful lessons of life, which is that the keystone of ethical living is trust.

A sense of trust is vital to morally courageous decision making. If you can't trust that some powerful benefit will flow from holding to a principle in the face of danger, what will inspire you to take a morally courageous stand? To understand why individuals engage their moral courage by being willing to endure the hardships of principled decision making, we need a fuller understanding of the nature of trust.

AN ANATOMY OF TRUST

Trust is defined by the *Oxford English Dictionary* as "confidence in or reliance on some quality or attribute of a person or thing, or the truth of a statement." The definition makes a useful delineation between *confidence* and *reliance:*

- *Confidence,* involving a mentally engaged investment of faith that things are or will be right, is what you hope to have in your bank, your alma mater, and your marriage partner.
- *Reliance,* which suggests a more rote, unexamined acceptance that nothing will go wrong, is what you need to have in your car, your dry cleaner, and the lad who mows your lawn.

Journalists dealing with their sources and investors dealing with their brokers need both: a sense of confidence in the information they're receiving and a sense of reliance on those sources to tell them when news breaks or markets change.

Trust comprises two subsidiary concepts:

- *Trustfulness,* whereby an individual expresses a sense of confidence in others, and
- *Trustworthiness,* wherein an individual acts so as to engender trust and merit the confidence of others.

When *trust* is used in an organizational context, it almost always takes on the primary meaning of *trustworthiness*—inspiring customers, vendors, regulators, the media, and the public to feel confident in and rely on a person, a team, an organization, a product, or a service. It is widely recognized, however, that one of the best ways to create trustworthiness is to act with *trustfulness*—first extending a sense of trust to others, so that they will trust you.

This sense of reciprocity is suggested by the adjective *mutual,* so often applied to trust. "Trust inevitably requires some sense of mutuality, or reciprocal loyalty," writes British business economist and philosopher Charles Handy. Or, as Canadian author John Dalla Costa puts it, "Dignity extended to employees and customers by the company creates the foundation for trust to be exchanged."

Lest all this sound too coldly rational, American business consultants Robert K. Cooper and Ayman Sawaf put trustfulness at the center of their version of "emotional intelligence." Trust, they write in *Executive EQ: Emotional Intelligence in Leadership & Organizations,* is

> an emotional strength that begins with the feeling of self-worth and purpose that we're called on to extend outward to others, like the radius of a circle, eventually reaching everyone on our team, and in our department, division, or entire company. The warm, solid gut feeling you get from trust—from counting on yourself and in trusting and being trusted by others—is one of the great enablers of life.

These comments on trust, while useful in a business setting, miss the mark in our discussion of moral courage for one particular reason: they tend to focus on persons rather than ideas. Those who are morally courageous, as we have seen, tend to be so because they trust that if a principle is upheld, right will be done and (hopefully) good will result. Their confidence does not especially lie in others. They don't put their faith in personalities but look instead to overarching ideals and values. Nor are they particularly concerned about winning praise, promotion, or profit through expressions of trustfulness. More Kantian than utilitarian, they tend to invest themselves in trust not for what it *does* but for what it *is.* For them the principle trumps the transaction. They may be trustworthy, but more important they are trustful.

The term *trust* occupies the same orbit as a number of other ethical concepts, including *credibility* and *teamwork.* Another term often used as a kind of overarching, umbrella concept is *integrity.* Stephen Carter, devoting a book by that name to the topic, notes that "integrity . . . creates the trust that we need for ordinary social and political discourse." Carter quotes business guru Warren Bennis's comment that integrity is "the basis of trust."

For our purposes, then, we can recognize three aspects of the trustfulness that enables us to express moral courage:

- *Confidence,* including aspects of faith, belief, and reliance;
- The qualities or *attributes* in which one has such confidence; and
- An active *application* of those attributes to self and others.

If, under that second point, the confidence is not to reside in other people, in what will it inhere? What are the qualities and attributes in which, when leaders trust them, make possible morally courageous decisions?

Business consultants James M. Kouzes and Barry Z. Posner, in their book *Credibility: Why Leaders Gain and Lose It, Why People Demand It,* pose four questions to measure one's own trustworthiness as a leader:

1. Is my behavior predictable or erratic?
2. Do I communicate clearly or carelessly?
3. Do I treat promises seriously or lightly?
4. Am I forthright or dishonest?

Trustworthy behavior, then, is *predictable, clear, honorable,* and *honest.* John Gardner, whose leadership experience includes serving six U.S. presidents, founding Common Cause, and heading the Carnegie Corporation, bolsters the first of these with the words *steadiness* and *reliability.* He also adds *fairness,* which he says must apply both in open dealings and "in the backroom" when no one is looking.

Bolstering the fourth of these attributes—honesty—Kouzes and Posner write:

> Of all the attributes of credibility . . . there is one that is unquestionably of greatest importance. The dimension of honesty accounts for more of the variance in believability than all of the other factors combined. Being seen as someone who can be trusted, who has high integrity, and who is honest and truthful is essential.

British investment banker and consultant Elaine Sternberg, in *Just Business,* summarizes some of these ideas in the third term—honorable—when she speaks of "ordinary decency," which for her goes beyond what she calls "niceness" to include "the conditions of trust necessary both for taking a long-term view and for surviving over time; it consists of honesty, fairness, the absence of coercion and physical violence and the presumption of legality."

Among the most expansive lists, however, is the one that grows out of Charlotte M. Roberts's work as coauthor of *The Fifth Discipline Fieldbook.* Creating something called the Trust Survey, she asks twenty-one yes/no questions to help identify various aspects of trust. Among the attributes it tests for are *consistency, promise-keeping, caring, honesty,* and *openness.*

Yet another route to the attributes is taken by Stephen Carter. Writing about integrity, he finds that it "requires three steps: (1) *discerning* what is right and what is wrong; (2) *acting* on what you have discerned, even at personal cost; and (3) *saying openly* that you are acting on your understanding of right and wrong."

Carter's emphasis on right and wrong is instructive. Throughout the literature on trust, there is an implicit assumption that trust is an ethical concept, and that it inhabits a realm of shared core values. That, in fact, is one of the twelve key findings in James C. Collins and Jerry I. Porras's groundbreaking book *Built to Last: Successful Habits of Visionary Companies.* Based on extensive research into "visionary companies"— those founded before 1950 and still the premier institution in their industries—the authors picked out "core values" as a crucial factor in their success:

> Contrary to business school doctrine, "maximizing shareholder wealth" or "profit maximization" has not been the dominant driving force or primary objective through the history of visionary companies. Visionary companies pursue a cluster of objectives, of which making money is only one—and not necessarily the primary one. Yes, they seek profits, but they're equally guided by a core ideology—core values and sense of purpose beyond just making money. Yet, paradoxically, the visionary companies make more money than the more purely profit-driven comparison companies.

Those core values, Collins and Porras find, are nearly immutable. "A visionary company," they write, "almost religiously preserves its core ideology—changing it seldom, if ever. Core values in a visionary company form a rock-solid foundation and do not drift with the trends of the day."

FOUR SOURCES OF ENDURANCE

As the above discussion indicates, a range of attributes are bundled together in our understanding of the word *trust.* In the context of moral courage, four of them stand out as the deepest sources of our willingness to trust:

- *Experience,* through which we rely on what we've done and, by extension, what we can do;
- *Character,* encouraging us to trust in who we are rather than what we've done, and giving us comfort that the values and virtues we've always expressed will be there in the future;
- *Faith,* which causes us to trust that whatever we worship as an authority beyond ourselves will sustain us as we move forward; and
- *Intuition,* leading us to act according to a gut feeling, with the confidence that if our intuitions have been right in the past they will probably be right in the future.

Looking back over Tom Armstrong's story, it's clear that he was able to trust his intuition as well as his character. But the point that rings most loudly through his story is experience, summed up in his phrase "I've been higher." Only someone with years of mountaineering would have been able to say that—and to feel the importance of it so clearly that he could cheerfully turn away from his goal and head back down the mountain confident that he had chosen the higher right. As the following examples demonstrate, the capacity to endure the hardship associated with moral courage often partakes of a combination of these attributes—although, as in Armstrong's case, one attribute frequently stands out above the others. That same attribute—experience—stands out in the curious encounter of another Mainer, Martha Kirkpatrick, with a tiny endangered seabird.

T R U S T I N G   O U R   E X P E R I E N C E :
T H E   P I P I N G   P L O V E R

On a late March afternoon in 1996, Martha Kirkpatrick returned to her office at the state capital in Augusta, Maine, to a flurry of urgent phone messages. As director of the Bureau of Land and Water Quality for the Maine Department of Environmental Protection (DEP), she'd been tied up in a morning meeting. Now, it seemed, there was a tempest brewing in the coastal town of Wells, famed for its sandy beaches and the summer tourism it supported.

The town had submitted paperwork for a permit to reconstruct and fortify a seawall on a frontal dune on Drake's Island, which had been hammered by winter storms and needed repairs to survive the following winter. Kirkpatrick's office had approved the project. But it appeared that the form her office had asked the town to submit was outdated, not taking into account some recent changes to the law. The remedy, ordinarily, would have comprised an apology, a resubmission, and a go-ahead. But this, she knew, was no ordinary project. This one involved a small, sandy-colored shorebird known as the piping plover.

Once numbering in the thousands, the plover—a quick-darting beach-runner resembling a sandpiper—had been nearly decimated in the nineteenth century by excessive hunting for the millinery trade. Following the Migratory Bird Treaty Act in 1918 and the plover's subsequent listing under the Endangered Species Act of 1986, the population began increasing, although by 1996 there were only sixty nesting pairs in Maine. In early April each year, these migratory birds returned to Drake's Island just as beachfront communities stirred to life, with caretakers and town crews at last able to repair damage from winter storms and brace for summer tourists. As their hammers rang and shovels crunched, the plovers began their own construction work, building their open, vulnerable nests on the beach and launching the hazardous breeding season they share each year with human and animal populations.

Historically, Kirkpatrick knew, the townspeople of Wells had not smiled on these tiny creatures. Their protected status interfered with humanity's enjoyment of the beaches that were so central to the town's livelihood. By 1996, although some progress had been made, there were still, she told me, "real tensions over the issue." Coupled with the usual concerns that arise around the protection of sand dunes, and multiplied by the impression that, as she said, "the press never had a good word to say about the DEP," this petty confusion over paperwork had outsize implications.

At issue was a question of timing. The paperwork was for a permit-by-rule—a decision by her department to allow the construction work to go forward. In signing off on the project, her department had agreed with town officials and the Maine Audubon Society on a key point: the work had to be finished by the coming Saturday, March 30. After that, the plovers would be returning. And by the time they left in the fall, it would be too late to complete the work before winter weather set in. Sitting at her desk that afternoon, Kirkpatrick knew there was still time to courier a new form to Wells and have it returned. There was just one major glitch: the permit-by-rule process required a fourteen-day period for agency comment and public review. After that, March 30 would be well past.

Blame? Kirkpatrick could see little to fault here beyond her own office. The town officials had brought the matter to her attention, discovering it when they submitted similar paperwork for a different project and noticed a discrepancy in the forms. Their lawyers were reluctant to move forward with the project, noting properly that because a new form had been published, the old one was null and void. "So in effect," Kirkpatrick recalls, "the town had no permit. If we waited fourteen days, either the nests would be endangered or the project would be put off for a year, potentially creating a safety hazard over the winter."

As she saw it, she had two choices. She could stick by the letter of the regulations by blocking the project, protecting her agency from any legal challenge but potentially endangering the public with a hazardous

Moral Courage:
Is It Masculine or Feminine?

Do men and women have different views of moral courage? Popular stereotypes about *morality* and *courage* see women as keepers of the moral flame and men as heroic conquerors. That distinction suggests that definitions of moral courage emphasizing the former term (*moral* courage) would be favored by women, where conceptions focused on the latter (moral *courage*) would be more suited to men. In fact, the picture is more complicated.

In her groundbreaking 1982 book, *In a Different Voice,* Harvard University educational psychologist Carol Gilligan commented on the first term, *morality.* Men, she noted, tend toward an "ethic of justice," in which morality consists of rights, fair treatment, a hierarchical chain of command, and a dilemma-resolution process that is "formal and abstract." Women, by contrast, tend toward an "ethic of care" that emphasizes responsibilities, help for others, a resolution process that is "contextual and narrative," and "the premise of non-violence—that no one should be hurt." What constitutes a moral act, then, may depend on the gender of the actor, although Gilligan is quick to point out that women normally express many masculine qualities and vice versa.

Building on Gilligan's work two decades later, Mary Beth Rose of the University of Illinois at Chicago focused on the courage side of the equation. In *Gender and Heroism in Early Modern English Literature,* she argues that over the course of the seventeenth century the portrayal of heroism in English literature moves from a masculine "heroics of action" to a feminine "alternative heroics of endurance."

Today, she notes, the popular view of the hero still evokes images of "socially or morally elevated protagonists waging war and managing politics: courageous, superior, noteworthy individuals creating or redefining the public sphere," which, as she says, "points to a tradition of heroism as distinctly masculine." But an alternative view—heroism as "the patient suffering of error, misfortune, disaster, and malevolence"—takes hold over the seventeenth century, "idealized in a newly and self-consciously constructed heroism of endurance that privileges the private life and pointedly rejects war."

Why the change? She traces it to a decline in a warrior mentality, the growth of a middle class, a new social mobility, the nation-state's increasing "monopoly on violence" with the growth of standing armies, and "the triumph of Protestantism, with its emphasis on interiority and the capacities and obligations of the individual self." Whatever the cause, it is clear that by the beginning of the eighteenth century "the heroics of endurance is open to women as well as men."

For both scholars, it would seem that our clichés of courage—driven so deeply into the language that they show up in terms like *manly* (meaning "courageous") and *sissy* (from *sister* and meaning "a coward")—reflect a fundamental gender bias. Yet the more modern term *moral courage* (which first appears in English early in the nineteenth century) seems to blend a feminine sense of values with a masculine sense of valor. By the twentieth century, the term fully embraced both the courage of action and the courage of endurance. As the examples in this book suggest, women and men are by now equally adept at expressing (or failing to express) moral courage.

seawall during the coming winter. Or she could issue a letter authorizing the work. The former course was in some ways simpler and more direct. While she would be opening her department to criticism over the pettiness of bureaucracy and the entanglements of red tape, she would at least be obeying the law, which, as a state official, she was sworn to do. It was, however, the more timid approach.

If, on the other hand, she approved a project in fact that had already been approved in substance, she would have been taking a bolder stand. But by doing so, she says, she would have been "authorizing the town to do something that someone could charge—and I would have to agree—was not strictly legal." She further notes that "if the thing had gone awry—the contractor had made mistakes, etc.—and people were looking to place blame, we were vulnerable to criticism for not doing things by the book." She was, she remembers, very conscious of the "potential perception of bypassing the procedural requirements when they became 'inconvenient,' which is just the kind of thing the cynics accused us of doing and that legislators were on the watch for."

Weighing her options in the short time she had, she found that "the 'front-page test' helped me make a decision: If this hits the front page, what decision would I feel the most right about explaining, in light of all the circumstances?" Exercising the courage of that conclusion, she faxed the town a letter that authorized them to proceed with the work.

The thing that gave her the courage to move forward—the thing she found herself trusting in most deeply—was the experience she brought to her position. This was not the first glitch she had encountered involving mishandled paperwork. She also understood that the revisions in the law that made the new form necessary were unrelated to the issue in Wells—meaning that information from the old form could essentially be copied onto the new one with no changes or additions. She had a pretty good reading on the motivation of the legislature, too, as well as on the position of the governor who had appointed her. Finally, her years of legal work had developed in her an ability to discriminate between major and minor issues. Trusting her experience, she felt reasonably confident that the situation would turn out right if she issued the approval.

And so it did. The repairs were completed without a hitch, and in subsequent years the population of piping plovers continued to rise. To this day, however, Kirkpatrick sees this situation as unique to her experience—the only time she can recall that the *right* thing to do was, technically, the *illegal* thing to do.

Thinking back on it, she also notes that "it's a good illustration of how quickly these things can hit us and won't wait for lengthy deliberation." That's another valuable reminder of the importance of trusting our experience. The more we learn from our experience, the more we exercise the mental muscles that make it easier to express moral courage. We build what I've earlier described as Ethical Fitness®—a term so apposite and clear that our institute had to register it. Like physical fitness, it refers to getting in shape to tackle the tough ethical dilemmas as they arise. That same fitness applies to our ability to express moral courage. The more we exercise our moral courage, the more readily we make courageous decisions. Of all the reasons that people come to trust themselves to be courageous, *experience* is surely a central one.

TRUSTING OUR CHARACTER: THE VELVET REVOLUTION

Šimon Pánek isn't sure where the courage came from. "There was no time to think about it," he says, "no time to feel fear." That Monday morning in 1989, when somebody overturned a garbage can at a gathering of a thousand of his fellow students at Charles University in Prague, Pánek simply clambered up on top and started speaking.

All he meant to do was read a statement protesting his nation's oppressive Communist government. He was simply demanding academic freedom and calling for an investigation of the police brutality that had erupted at a street demonstration the previous Friday, November 17, at which a student was reported (erroneously, it later turned out) to have been killed. But when Pánek climbed back down, his life had changed. He had been chosen to represent the university's natural sciences division in the massive, high-energy, and illegal protest movement that had begun with a student march and would later be called the Velvet Revolution. By the next day, November 21, he had been elected cochair of the central strike committee, which a few days later would coordinate a gathering of 750,000 protesters in Letna Park, a prelude to a general strike so popular that workers' unions and even some policemen joined in. For the next six weeks, until the Velvet Revolution ended on December 29 with the formation of a new government under President Václav Havel, Pánek recalls that he "never went home."

Instead, he and his fellow students traveled the Czech countryside with pamphlets and posters. They visited factories and farms and—when authorities prevented them from entering—met with predawn commuters at railway stations. Their purpose, he says, was "to fight the information war against the Communist papers" and tell people what was really happening. It was heady, edgy, exhausting, and compelling.

It was also, at times, frightening. By Tuesday night, he says, with 250,000 protesters assembling in Wenceslas Square, "we got scared." The reason: following the imposition of Stalin-like rule in 1948, the Communists had established armed militias in factories across the country, trained and ready to be called up on just such occasions. If they were mobilized, Pánek and his colleagues realized, the results would be horrendous—and they, the student protesters who had implored the citizenry to turn out and protest, would be partly responsible. They drew some comfort from the fact that the workers in Prague were already "angry against the government, just fed up," and that the city's trained militia were little more than "a funny group of old guys" who, in the end, refused to march against the demonstrators. But rumors were spreading of a ten-thousand-strong band of militia converging on Prague from other parts of the country. Frightened, the students sent delegations to the American and the Soviet embassies. While the Americans didn't let the students in, the Russians assigned top-level people to meet with them. The students were assured that, despite the threat of violence, "nothing would happen."

Remarkably, nothing did. The protests took place, but nobody died and the government was replaced. To this day, writes former U.S. ambassador to Czechoslovakia William H. Luers, historians marvel at the "almost miraculous disappearance" of the Communist governments in Eastern Europe in 1989. "Many in Prague," Luers observes, "find their own revolution so mystifyingly beautiful that they attribute it to astrological forces, to the recently canonized Bohemian princess St. Agnes, or to the return of Rabbi Loew's golem." In fact, there were tectonic forces at work far beyond Prague, shaping those events in a clearly political mold. Poland's uprising, Mikhail Gorbachev's perestroika and glasnost, the opening of the Berlin Wall eight days before the Velvet Revolution began—the momentum was all toward democracy and freedom, and nowhere was it felt more swiftly and irreversibly than in Czechoslovakia.

The forces shaping Pánek's own moral courage, however, were more personal. Before he was born, his father had spent eleven years in jail, first for resisting the 1948 Communist putsch and later for smuggling in and distributing uncensored stories from the Reuters news service. Released from jail and working as a translator in Berlin, he was a man Pánek remembers as "educated, calm, very wise, speaking very little," and "very modest in his way of living." His son recalls him contentedly eating beans and bread and saying, " 'That was enough for me before [in prison], and it's enough for me now.' " Pánek's stepfather, too, spent a year in jail for cooperating with Václav Havel's Charter 77 movement and for printing and distributing anticommunist pamphlets. So "we were not scared of prison," Pánek says about himself and his fellow students, because "our parents had been in prison."

Pánek also traces his willingness to fight the Communists to his own "romantic and adventurous character." The year before the uprising, in 1988, his love of travel and excitement had led him to organize a relief convoy to help the victims of the earthquake in Armenia. Working with the Soviet embassy and Czech television, he assembled a convoy of one hundred trucks to move donated clothes, sleeping bags, and food from central Prague to the airport, where they were ferried to Armenia. "That feeling that one can do these things quite easily was very strong with me," he says. "From that moment on I knew that I would like to help people in the crisis regions." But he confesses that part of the motivation was that "it was adventure—and I was twenty years old, looking for adventure."

That spirit eventually led him away from politics. As a well-known student member of Havel's team, he helped negotiate the terms under which parliament freed itself from Communist domination. Although that body eventually included ten student members, Pánek chose not to be one of them. Why not? I asked him. Again, it was his love of adventure—his need, as he said, to travel and get out of Prague regularly to maintain his peace of mind—as well as a "special feeling that politics was not for me," since "I might not be able to keep my principles." And while he worked for President Havel part-time for several years, he eventually stepped down from that position as well, feeling that it, too, was out of character.

Since then, his life has been devoted to helping run People in Need, a nongovernmental organization he cofounded with Czech television that has delivered relief aid to Sarajevo, Kosovo, Afghanistan, Chechnya, Iraq, and other trouble spots over the past decade. As a relief worker, he admits, he is sometimes "a little bit scared." He is often in places where there are hardly any other foreigners and where long hours for reflection can raise doubts in a character that thrives on action. On gray winter days in such places, he says, when "you have two hours to have breakfast and check the mail—this requires more courage than to step on the top of a garbage can."

What does he think constitutes moral courage? For him it is closely allied to responsibility—the value that figures most frequently in our nearly two-hour conversation. What's most important, he says, is "the courage to be responsible for things, even if things go wrong." He worries that Czechs in general have "a national habit just to sit and wait to see how things will go. The courage to step forward and say, 'Okay, I'll start it'— that's something that is missing from the Czech life."

What principles motivate him? He lists a few key ones:

- "Collective work"
- "Don't be scared"
- "Always take the responsibility"
- "Money and property is nothing that will make you happy"

Expanding on that last point, he notes that the problem with life in modern Prague is that "we concentrate on the form of things, not the substance of things." If there were "young people listening," he tells me with a smile, they need to know that "happiness is not about the most powerful vacuum cleaner."

What drove Pánek to take his morally courageous stand in the Velvet Revolution, then, was not a complex sequence of analysis. Looking back, he says, "I don't see any big decision-making process" that was needed in order "to collect my courage." Nor was it mere impulse. In one sense, of course, he came suddenly to his position as a student leader. In another sense, his character led him to it rather naturally. His background gave him some context for his acts, and the same quietness he attributes to his father seemed evident in his own demeanor. There's nothing impulsive, either, about the planning he does for his relief work. He told me about the logistical efforts involved in moving thirty thousand displaced Afghans back to their homes during the war against the Taliban, sometimes driving his convoy of trucks down riverbeds to avoid minefields on the nearby roads.

He seems, instead, to trust most readily in his own adventurous spirit and engaging, helpful character. Part of his trust, to be sure, is rooted in experience—his success with the Armenian relief effort, for example, which gave him "that feeling that one can do these things quite easily." Untroubled by ego, happier in nature than in cities, he also shies away from grand gestures, intellectual wrestling, or hyperbole. What makes his courage possible, it seems, is a trust in the few simple principles he's seen operate in his own character. In the end, he trusts in principles of character that, as he says, make you "feel good because you are doing good things."

Trusting Our Faith: The Watergate Plumbers

In the flat light of a Thanksgiving afternoon in 1973, a thirty-four-year-old lawyer stood on the lawn outside the House of Burgesses, once the home of the colonial legislature in Williamsburg, Virginia. With him were his wife and two young children. Behind him was a tumultuous year in which he had been sworn in as undersecretary of the U.S. Department of Transportation and feted by President Richard M. Nixon at a candle-lit, seven-course White House dinner—only to resign three months later, a casualty of the widening Watergate investigation. Ahead of him, though he did not know it that November day, was a six-month jail sentence and disbarment from the legal profession. And all around him were agonizing decisions, as he sought to hold together the shards of a once-stellar career.

Egil Krogh—his friends call him Bud—had joined the Nixon administration in 1968. A devoted team player, he became codirector of the White House Special Investigations Unit (colloquially known as the White House Plumbers) in 1971. Its official task was to protect national security, which President Nixon felt had been severely compromised by the publication of the Pentagon Papers that were leaked to the press by Dr. Daniel Ellsberg. The Plumbers were organized to stop such leaks, fast.

The work of the Plumbers has, of course, become a matter of history. Working with G. Gordon Liddy and E. Howard Hunt, Krogh helped orchestrate a break-in at the Los Angeles office of Ellsberg's psychiatrist, Dr. Lewis Fielding. The plan: locate the files on Ellsberg, find out whether he had any relationship with the Soviets, and dig up anything else that would aid in discrediting him.

It was a surprising place for Krogh to find himself. Brought up as a student of the Bible in a faith-based household and known to his colleagues as a straight arrow, Krogh admits that he became deeply entranced by the aura of authority surrounding the president. Writing about the experience several decades later, Krogh notes, "I came to equate the President's interests (as I perceived them) with the country's interests. The President's view of what was critical to serve the national security interest became my view. Loyalty to the President was primary. Loyalty to spiritual and moral principles, to the U.S. Constitution, and to the law became secondary."

As the Watergate investigation ground onward, Krogh found himself facing, and ducking, a second challenge. Asked under oath in 1972 about his role in the break-in, he lied to protect the confidentiality of the Plumbers' activities. Now, a year later, he was working with his lawyer to plan his defense. But facing "sharper and sharper pangs of conscience, and a growing sense of despair with my legal defense," he remembers that he had reached "the lowest point of the lowest period of my life" as he stood at Williamsburg that day.

Yet on that afternoon, he recalls experiencing what he would later describe as "a feeling of extraordinary peace and clarity and certainty" that welled up inside him. It was accompanied by "an extremely bright, all-encompassing glow" as the setting sun shone through the windows of the House of Burgesses and out onto the lawn where he was standing. "That afternoon in Williamsburg, I felt the fear, anguish and despair that had attended the intense investigations, indictments, public notoriety and legal maneuverings over the previous six months begin to dissolve," he writes.

In the prior two months, driven by fear, he writes that he had for the first time "genuinely opened my heart in prayer. I asked God for guidance and comfort. I simply didn't know what to do. I was open." In those months, too, he had come to feel "increasingly uncomfortable with the soundness of my 'national security' defense"—an argument he had used with himself to justify not only the break-in but also the lying under oath. Standing there in the light, he recalls, "the answer came as a steady stream of ideas which flooded my consciousness and fell into place like the tumblers of a precision lock."

"Just look at this," came the thought which seemed to come from a mind outside and yet still inside myself. "Just look at the rights you and your family are enjoying right now. These rights emanate from the founding ideas of this country that are protecting you. You're under indictment in both federal and state courts. You're publicly identified with a profoundly serious crime. Yet just look, just look at what you're enjoying. You're able to travel wherever you want. To speak with whomever you wish. To pray freely in any church. Talk to the press. Now, what are you standing for in the defense you're putting forward to the charges against you?"

The answer came again in a stream of thought. "You're standing for the right of a person in government, serving a President at the seat of highest power, to make a judgment based on his personal, subjective sense of the national security interest to strip away from another American his constitutional, Fourth Amendment right to be free from an unauthorized search. How can you continue to enjoy all of these wonderful rights, guaranteed to you and your family by the Constitution you were sworn to uphold, while defending conduct that abolished a similar right for another?" The answer came immediately. "You can't do it anymore. You must stop defending yourself. If you defend further, if you continue to justify violating rights you're continuing to enjoy, you're a hypocrite. Even worse, you're a traitor to the fundamental American idea of the right of an individual to be free from unwarranted government intrusion in his life."

. . . I walked over to where Suzanne was standing. She looked at me quizzically as I had been quiet for a while.

"Well, Sue," I said, "the answer has just come. I think it's time to plead guilty. . . ."

Three days later, he and his lawyer walked into the K Street office of Leon Jaworski, the special prosecutor for Watergate and related crimes, and began the process of entering his guilty plea. In a twelve-page "Statement of Defendant on the Offense and His Role" that Krogh submitted to the court on January 3, 1974, he addressed the ways in which his ethics— his understanding of what was right—had been overshadowed by his commitment to what he thought of as "national security."

While I early concluded that the [break-in] had been a mistake, it is only recently that I have come to regard it as unlawful. I see now that the key is the effect that the term "national security" had on my judgment. The very words served to block critical analysis. It seemed at least presumptuous if not unpatriotic to inquire into just what the significance of national security was . . .

The discrediting of Dr. Ellsberg, which today strikes me as repulsive and an inconceivable national security goal, at the time would have appeared a means of blocking the possibility that he would become such a popular figure that others possessed of classified information would be encouraged to emulate him. More broadly, it would serve to diminish any influence he might have in mobilizing opposition to the course of ending the Vietnam War that had been set by the President. And that course was the very definition of national security. Freedom of the President to pursue his planned course was the ultimate national security objective.

. . . I can recollect that I would have accepted the rationalization I have just described. The invocation of national security stopped me from asking the question, "Is this the right thing to do?"

Is this the right thing to do? That question, had it been asked at the time, could have forestalled the need for Krogh ever to plead guilty. It could have led him, early on, to a clearer sense of ethics, which, to use his own terms, might have provided him with a "critical analysis" rather than a "rationalization" of his actions. That might not have prevented the need for moral courage: he might have had to take a stand against White House wrongdoing and resign his post then and there. Would the young Bud Krogh's resignation have helped fast-forward the agonizingly slow pace of the Watergate revelations that led to President Nixon's own resignation? One can only speculate, because at that point such moral courage wasn't in operation.

But was it true moral courage that arose in the wake of his epiphany at Williamsburg, or merely a will for self-preservation? Certainly a criminal sentence, if it ever came, would be reduced if he cooperated. But given the snakes-and-ladders convolutions of high-stakes government trials, there was still a real chance that, if he stuck to his defense, he could walk away undamaged. That approach, as he had come to realize, might not be the most ethical one. But it might save his career, salvage his pride, and feed his family. A guilty plea, by contrast, would take real moral courage—not only by that term's core definition as *the courage to be moral,* but by Krogh's willingness to put at risk all these temporal and personal benefits for the sake of a higher principle.

But can one make a morally courageous decision in the face of such egregious wrongdoing as he had committed? Indeed one can. Moral courage is not reserved for those who, having led impeccably ethical lives, earn the right to base their decisions on a core of moral values. If values are (as the common analogy suggests) the compass points of our lives, nothing prevents us from suddenly picking up a compass and finding our way out of a morass in which we've been wandering for years. It may be difficult to *commit* to doing right after a long immersion in wrong. Once the commitment is made, however, there is no reason that the compass points of, say, responsibility or fairness should provide any less direction to the former wrongdoer than to the long-standing right-doer. The North Star can guide a boat damaged and disoriented by a three-day storm just as much as a ship setting out from a calm harbor.

But assuming Krogh could spot that star, how did he know he could depend on it? What drove his decision? The real question is, In what did he put his trust? He certainly could not claim to trust his experience. His short, meteoric career had never brought him remotely close to such an awesome and frightening situation, where he found himself indicted by federal and state courts and pursued by the likes of the redoubtable Leon Jaworski. Nor was he able to trust (as he came to realize) in his character. The more he compared the moral tenor of his upbringing with the actions he had taken, the more disconnected they became for him. What evidence did he have, after all, that if he simply let his character be his guide he would be led to make sound, positive, and strategically safe decisions? That hadn't happened so far. Why should it happen now? Nor, finally, was he trusting simply in his human intuition. For months he had been searching for answers—asking himself, in a sense, what his gut told him would be the right course of action. Yet for months he had had no clear sense of direction: his gut had not spoken.

His trust, instead, fell to a power beyond himself, which he later described as "thought which seemed to come from a mind outside and yet still inside myself." Using the term common to the Christianity of the founding fathers and to the public religion of the nation, he described that power as "God." How people describe that power, and the particular role they ascribe to it in times of moral courage, is the subject for another book. For our purposes, it is enough to note that the trust underlying Krogh's decision—as in many examples of moral courage—came principally from his faith rather than his experience, character, or intuition.

In the end, that trust carried him through—though not, perhaps, in the way he would have hoped. He understood the risks, and out of a sense of faith he endured them for the sake of a principle. In that way he expressed true moral courage. He recalls the result, however, with some irony. "Exactly one year after dining at The White House with the President, I entered a maximum security jail in Rockville, Maryland where, sitting on a cold metal bench, I dined on cold hot dogs off a stainless steel plate, and finally felt free and at peace." Now a successful lawyer in Seattle after reinstatement to the bar, Krogh is spending much of his energy helping others recognize and avoid the ethical pitfalls of excessive loyalty that he encountered.

TRUSTING OUR INTUITIONS: THE DOWRY REBEL

On balance around the world, girls outnumber boys at birth. In India, however, women account for only 49.4 percent of the total population. Behind that apparently benign statistic lies a host of grisly social trends—as Nisha Sharma well knows.

Before May 11, 2003, the twenty-one-year-old computer student from New Delhi was among the millions of young Indian women seeking a proper, family-arranged marriage. Her father, Dev Dutt Sharma, placed the customary ads in several English-language newspapers. Not long afterward, he came to terms with the family of the prospective groom, twenty-five-year-old Munish Dalal, a computer instructor. The agreement included a dowry, paid by the bride's parents to the groom and his family, that everyone agreed was fair. It included two home theater sets, two cooking ranges, two televisions, two air conditioners—one each for the groom and his brother—and a car.

Ms. Sharma did not object. Nor did her father, who owns several car-battery factories and was relieved to have everything wrapped up. "Getting his daughter married is the primary duty of a father," he told the BBC. Never mind that the 1961 Dowry Prohibition Act, which made the paying and accepting of dowries illegal, had been strengthened twice in the mid-1980s. Prosecutions under the law were still few and far between, and the ancient tradition of providing a dowry was still the common practice.

By the spring of 2003, however, India's antidowry movement was expanding rapidly, and for good reason. According to antidowry activists and women's groups, the institution of dowry is directly or indirectly responsible for tens of thousands of female deaths each year. The problem begins with abortion and infanticide, practices that reflect a strong parental preference for sons rather than daughters. The practices are chillingly effective. A 2003 report by *India Together* notes that "today in Punjab and Haryana, the number of females in proportion to males in the 0–6 age group has dropped below 800:1000," which the report attributes to "sex-selective foeticide." Part of the reason: fear of the high costs of marrying off daughters. So pervasive are these sex-selection practices that it is now illegal in India for doctors to perform tests to determine the gender of unborn babies.

But the problem doesn't stop in infancy. Paying the dowry brings no assurance for the bride. Official Indian government statistics indicate that nearly seven thousand brides were killed by their husbands and in-laws in 2001—most burned alive to simulate cooking accidents—

many as a result of allegations of inadequate dowry payments, and usually with the intention of leaving the groom free to pursue another marriage with a larger dowry. The numbers are widely assumed to be grossly underreported, and in certain areas, New Delhi among them, instances of violence and death from dowry disputes were reported to be rising rapidly in the early years of the twenty-first century.

All of that lay in the background as Ms. Sharma, wearing the traditional red wedding dress of a Hindu bride and adorned with intricate patterns painted in henna on her hands and feet, prepared for the ceremony that Sunday night. But suddenly, with two thousand guests gathered under the wedding tent and the Hindu priest standing ready, a violent scuffle broke out. The groom's family, unsatisfied with the dowry already provided, was demanding an additional $25,000 in rupees from her father, payable on the spot. When he demurred, they shoved him and spat on him.

What happened next launched a new chapter in the history of dowry in India—and launched Ms. Sharma into popular acclaim across India. Picking up her cell phone, she called the police. After some hesitation, they arrested her groom-to-be and his mother under the antidowry laws. The wedding was called off. And Ms. Sharma rocketed into national stardom, winning admiration from politicians, women's organizations, and the public. "Bravo, We're Proud of You," wrote a major Hindu daily, *Rashtriya Sahara*. The *Asian Age* newspaper wrote, "She is being hailed as a New Age woman and seen as a role model to many." But perhaps the headline in the *Times of India* put it best: "It Takes Guts to Send Your Groom Packing."

But what kind of guts? Was Ms. Sharma's phone call simply an Indian version of Paddy Chayefsky's famous rant "I'm mad as hell, and I'm not going to take it anymore"? Or was it, by contrast, a lifesaving escape—a last-minute revelation of the pervasiveness of greed in the groom's family, leading her to realize that she herself could become a victim of bride-burning? Whatever drove her decision, it seemed largely an act of impulse. It was no doubt fed by a concern for the plight of women in her culture and by a growing insistence that educated females ought to speak out and stand up for their rights. At the time, however, her courage appeared to be impelled by rage at the aggressors and by an almost instinctual desire to defend her family. Given her age and position, she was not acting out of deep experience. There was no indication that faith was driving her decision to act. And while the suddenness of her action may have been driven by her character, it seems that at that point her impulse took over. Sending her groom packing, she also sent packing any arguments about consequences—the "what-ifs" about parental wrath, social standing, or her own future marriageability that might have caused a less impulsive woman to leave the phone untouched. That her weapon of choice in defeating such an antique and discriminatory tradition was a cell phone—the quintessential symbol of the freedom, immediacy, and equalizing force of modern communications technology—made the moment all the more emblematic. As she said to a *New York Times* reporter a few days after her decision, "I'm feeling proud of myself."

Did her impulses prove sound? Her father was initially worried. "People say now it will be very difficult to marry my daughter again," he lamented. In the five days following the would-be wedding, however, Ms. Sharma said she had received as many as twenty-five marriage proposals—some by cell phone and e-mail. Over the following summer she was swamped with awards and invitations to speak. The following November, in a simple Vedic ceremony with seventy-five guests at her parents' suburban home, she married a groom who neither asked for nor received any dowry. "She said she wants to leave the past behind and start afresh," said her father, indicating that for the near future, at least, this icon of the women's movement would not be talking to the media. Given the limelight surrounding her, that decision, too, may have required moral courage.

COURAGE AND TRUST

As the above examples suggest, moral courage and trust are closely linked. You don't get the former without the latter. Moral courage doesn't arise, apparently, in the lives of those who are convinced that everything is futile, that there's no hope and nothing left to believe in. It arises instead out of a confidence that goodness will flow—in some way, however small—from taking a bold stand. It may not arrive immediately. It may not come personally to the one taking the stand. And it may show itself in unforeseen ways. But it comes about because the actor trusted something. Tom Armstrong on Mount Logan and Martha Kirkpatrick on the Maine coast trusted their experience. Šimon Pánek in the Velvet Revolution believed in his own strong character. Bud Krogh in Watergate turned to his religious faith. Nisha Sharma trusted her gut. These four sources of trust account for a wide array of morally courageous actions.

Yet as these examples also demonstrate, these four categories are not discrete pigeonholes, each claiming the sole right to label and file away an experience. They are more usefully thought of as filters on the lens of our perspective, each throwing one source of trust into sharp relief and subduing the other three. That doesn't mean the other three sources aren't present: Tom Armstrong, for all that he relied on his experience, also exhibited sharp intuition and strong character. It appears, in fact, that we can profitably change filters as we examine an experience or stack up multiple filters to create a compound picture. The point of the exercise is not to categorize morally courageous experiences into the hard-edged boxes of a mutually exclusive taxonomy. It is to understand that although these categories are overlapping and fluid, our willingness to express moral courage can often be explained by our affinity for a particular source of trust that rises above the rest and shapes our action.

This exercise also gives us a powerful tool for strengthening our moral courage. Just as an analysis of core values helps strengthen our first-circle capacity to understand the principles that are at stake, and an examination of risks and consequences improves our second-circle ability to understand the dangers facing us, so this exercise sharpens our third-circle willingness to endure the hardships attendant upon our stand. Understanding the sources of our trust, we can strengthen them by:

1. Expanding the range and depth of our *experience* so that new activities begin to fall into patterns we recognize as familiar, manageable, and less threatening;

2. Building and enhancing our sense of our own *character,* shaping it so that our actions will be consistent, responsible, and appropriate to the circumstance;

3. Maturing our *faith* in a power beyond ourselves until we recognize its presence as a reliable and accessible guide to our actions, attitudes, and choices; and

4. Grooving our *intuitions* through practice, so that the spontaneity of our gut impulse grows increasingly sure-footed and reliable.

The methodologies for developing these sources of trust are manifold. Experiential education, world travel, extreme sports, and what used to be called "the school of hard knocks" may help expand our experience. Character education, moral reasoning, and working in sound ethical environments will strengthen our character. Faith has numerous avenues for its expansion, from formal religious practice to personal adventures in spiritual awareness. And intuition, often thought of as the purview of the arts, is also a requirement for good craftsmanship, athletics, management, and parenting, and can be developed through those channels. Not everyone will choose to develop all four. Some may focus almost exclusively on one. But I suspect that the most well-rounded actors—those most capable of expressing moral courage—will have in their quiver more than one of these arrows, to be drawn out depending on the occasion.

Our three interlocking circles of principles, risk, and endurance, then, lead us to the center point of moral courage. But expressing moral courage is a bit like purifying alcohol. You can make it 90 percent pure with little difficulty. Moving to 95 percent is more difficult: the alcohol seems to want to reach out and suck in all the stray moisture it can find. And as you push toward 100 percent, it is as though every water molecule in the universe rushes in to prevent it from reaching full purity. What challenges this purity—what keeps us from expressing moral courage—is the topic of the next chapter.

Moral Courage Checklist
Step 5: Endure the Hardship

What if I've understood the distinction between physical and moral courage, identified the core values that are in play, assessed the risk, and spotted the principle that most needs upholding? Do I have the confidence to endure the hardship that moral courage entails? What moves me from contemplation to action?

The key quality is trust. By expressing it, I build a reputation for *trustworthiness*. But to put it into practice requires *trustfulness*. That raises a defining question: What do I trust? What are the sources of my confidence? Four of them are worth watching for:

1. **Experience.** Can I rely on what I've done in the past, taking it as a predictor of what I can do in the future? Have I "been there, done that" enough to have confidence in my background, training, talents, skills, and abilities?

2. **Character.** Can I trust who I am rather than what I've done? Will the values and virtues that make up my inner being—the ones that have sustained me in the past—be there again for me this time? ➤

3. **Faith.** Is there something beyond myself, some higher power in which I can trust to bring me through? Have I built a relationship with a source of spiritual insight that, having got me this far, will see me through to the best conclusion this time around?

4. **Intuition.** Is my instinct for what's right telling me what to do? Is there a gut feeling that steps naturally out onto the stage even if my reason wants to hang back in the wings?

These four sources aren't mutually exclusive. My willingness to endure may be founded on several of these, though one of them usually takes prominence. But I'll be better equipped to express moral courage if I have more than one of them in my quiver. Expanding my range of experience, enhancing my moral character, maturing and deepening my faith, and grooving my intuitions through practice all make me more comfortable in deciding to persist in my expression of moral courage.

CHAPTER SEVEN

Fakes, Frauds, and Foibles: What Moral Courage Isn't

Courage is a moral quality; it is not a chance gift of nature like an aptitude for games. It is a cold choice between two alternatives, the fixed resolve not to quit; an act of renunciation which must be made not once but many times.

—Charles McMoran Wilson

One autumn day I meticulously painted dozens of small-paned sash windows in the living room of an eighteenth-century New England house we owned. When I was done, I stepped back to survey my handiwork and called my wife in to have a look.

"What's that?" she said, pointing to the one tiny blob of paint that had oozed over onto the glass. It didn't matter that every other pane was picture-perfect. She had zeroed in, quite rightly, on my one mistake. Considering all my brushstrokes and the large number of panes, my margin of error was well below 1 percent. But that wasn't good enough. Chagrined, I set to work to repair the blunder and win her compliments.

There are some areas of our lives where just getting close is good enough. Sweeping up the shop floor after every saw cut rather than at the end of the project, while it may be neat, is inefficient. So is reparking the car because it ended up ten rather than five inches from the curb, or phoning back your friend to correct a wrong but insignificant detail in an

anecdote you've just related ("his new tie was green, not blue"), or fault-
ing the checkout lady's grammar when there's a line behind you at the
supermarket. Some games aren't worth the candle, and an obstinate sense
of precision can sometimes be worse than a tolerance of petty mistakes.

But there are other arenas where the only satisfactory standard is perfection. Drawing sash is one of them. So is space flight. In September
1999 that lesson came home to flight controllers for the Mars Climate
Orbiter. They had launched the spacecraft nine months earlier from Cape
Canaveral. Now, at two o'clock in the morning on September 23, they
were watching their screens intently from the control center at the Jet
Propulsion Laboratory in Pasadena, California. They were looking for
signs that the vehicle was firing its main engine to thrust itself into orbit
around the red planet. Five minutes into the burn, they confirmed its disappearance, right on schedule, behind the planet.

They never heard from it again. It never reemerged into view. Long
after the radio transmissions should have begun streaming earthward, all
was silence. A day later, after straining for any signals from the Deep
Space Network of antennas 230 feet in diameter, the search was abandoned. The orbiter was officially declared lost.

What happened on the far side of Mars that day? Piecing together the
data, NASA scientists suspected that the engine had pushed the vehicle
into orbit only thirty-seven miles above the planet's surface rather than
the intended ninety-three miles. At that relatively low altitude the atmosphere around Mars, thin though it is, was dense enough to tear apart the
unshielded orbiter.

Prior to the launch NASA engineers, not realizing that a small but key
set of parameters was stated in English instead of metric units, misinter-
preted the technical specifications provided by their colleagues at Lock-
heed Martin Corporation. As a result, the $125 million Mars Climate
Orbiter, after traveling 416 million miles, missed its target by less than
sixty miles. That's a margin of error of about 0.000014 percent. In most
quarters that would be regarded as stellar. At NASA it was disastrous.

A simple mistake? Yes and no. "People sometimes make errors," said

Dr. Edward Weiler, NASA's associate administrator for Space Science, six days later. "The problem here was not the error, it was the failure of NASA's systems engineering, and the checks and balances in our processes to detect the error. That's why we lost the spacecraft."

In hindsight, his comments have a sobering prescience. Less than four years later, on February 1, 2003, the space shuttle *Columbia* disintegrated in the skies over Texas, killing her seven-member crew and launching an anguished search for clues. The immediate cause, apparently, was a piece of rigid foam that broke loose during launch, hit the wing, and damaged the protective tiles meant to form the heat shield during reentry. Like the tiny mix-up in the numbers by the Mars Climate Orbiter team, the chunk of foam was so small that it almost escaped notice in the videos of the launch. Although it damaged only a small fraction of the wing, that was all it took to create disaster.

But there was a cause deeper and more fundamental than the damaged tiles. When the *Columbia* Accident Investigation Board issued its final report in August of 2003, it also commented on the very phenomenon that Dr. Weiler, four years earlier, had identified when he spoke of problems with NASA's "systems" and "processes." Reporting on the *Columbia* accident, the board determined that "NASA's organizational culture and structure had as much to do with this accident as the external tank foam." It further defined "organizational culture" as "the values, norms, beliefs, and practices that govern how an institution functions," including "the assumptions the employees make as they carry out their work." The report went on to note that NASA's "broken safety culture" itself had suppressed the willingness of employees to come forward, share their concerns, and speak up about potential problems.

So where in *Columbia*'s saga were the named villains? From the investigation board's perspective, that was the wrong question. Perhaps anticipating objections from those who wanted identifiable officials to condemn, the board noted that its focus on "the context in which decision making occurred" (which is yet another definition of *culture*) was not to be interpreted as a statement that individuals need not be held "responsible and accountable. To the contrary, individuals always must assume responsibility for their actions. . . . [But] NASA's problems cannot be solved simply by retirements, resignations, or transferring personnel."

That conclusion will baffle some readers. After all, our age is enthralled with technology and personality. We've been taught by magazines like *Wired* and *People* to look to one or the other as the cause of every problem. In Wall Street scandals, for example, blame typically gets fixed on a few high-flying personalities playing fast and loose with complex financial technologies. If organizational culture is mentioned at all, it usually plays only a minor role.

That's not to say that individuals aren't important. In a damaged organizational culture, they play a crucial role, usually in proportion to their moral courage. It should come as no surprise, in fact, to learn that organizational culture—often simply defined as *the way we do things around here*—plays a vital role in the expression (or lack of expression) of moral courage.

In part that's because organizational culture is central to survival. An organizational culture can shape decision making so deeply that executives sometimes mistake the cultural influence for their own thinking. When a bad culture creates bad decisions, and when those choices are leveraged by large-scale technologies like the *Columbia,* the result can be a world-class calamity of a kind unknown to earlier, less technological generations. On the other hand, when a culture is fundamentally ethical—when it holds in high regard such values as honesty, fairness, respect, responsibility, and compassion—the result is a climate of integrity that creates trust. With that in place, the culture tends to promote sound decisions.

But culture, as the NASA report implicitly recognized, is more than the sum of the employees currently passing through it. Organizational culture reaches back to individuals long gone, reflecting their traditions, histories, and decisions. It can reinforce and refine their values or it can reverse and remove them. Even when it does the latter—even when the end result is a clearly unethical organizational culture—individual employees can still express high ethical values and standards. In such situations, however, most employees learn to go along, to get out, or to stand up. The first invites fatal compromise. The second leaves problems unaddressed. The third requires moral courage.

The moral lessons from the NASA examples are manifold:

- Being nearly right can be entirely wrong. Sometimes you can miss by a hair and still fail egregiously.
- In an era of worldshrink and technobulge, tiny errors can have such enormous consequences that it is patently unethical to allow them to be overlooked.
- Some blunders can be corrected, while others can't. There are times when you've simply got to get it right the first time.
- Organizational culture is as important as bad data or damaged tiles. Get it wrong and you can wreck a $125 million project in minutes—or kill famous astronauts in real time on global television.

But perhaps the key moral lesson is that a dysfunctional culture creates barriers to communication that require moral courage to surmount. Had NASA's channels of communication been open, speaking up would have been less a matter of moral courage than of routine responsibility. Those who raised their concerns would not have met with what the investigation board described as a culture "clearly overconfident" in its own rightness and unwilling to listen. They would have been heard. As it was, NASA employees apparently felt that their reputations and even their careers were on the line if they exposed problems for the sake of principles.

Moral courage, then, has a defining role when organizational cultures are in disrepair. And that leads to a conundrum. We want employees with moral courage. Yet we must strive to create organizations where moral courage is not needed. If that sounds like a paradox, think about Bud.

THE PARADOX OF
MORAL COURAGE

Voluble and savvy, with a grizzled exterior hiding a puff-pastry heart and a seasoned hand, Bud manages top-level teams of analysts and report writers in a large organization. He understands his people well. He knows who's got great hunches and a lucid literary style but can't self-start. He knows who can give you the skinny on anyone who ever supported the company line on policy X (whatever that was) but is a lousy judge of character. He knows who got promoted before he or she was ready and won't ever quite catch up. He also knows who's been diligent but self-effacing and may therefore be passed over for promotion.

This last group concerns Bud deeply. As a manager of his organization's thoughtware, he sees who's goofing off and who's wound up tight, who's logging the bare minimum and who's doing the work of two people. So when it comes time for review panels to consider promotions, he's sometimes in a hard place. Others on the panels—his friends and peers— may see only the résumé, the portfolio of writing, the prior recommendations. Bud, on the other hand, may have known an individual over many years. Yes, there may be flaws. But this may still be an extraordinary employee well worth retaining.

When his colleagues lobby to pass over someone, the easiest thing would be to go with the flow. He could salve his conscience by entering a modest demurral and then letting the candidate be swept aside. The harder thing is to stand up for the candidate, set himself directly athwart the current of peer opinion, fight the process to a standstill, and labor for what he feels is right. The hardest thing, in other words, is to express moral courage. But that means cashing in his political chits and spending down his reservoirs of goodwill. Do that too often and he risks his reputation. Do it too forcefully and he may risk his career.

Bud is deeply committed to his work. But his conversation betrays a needling frustration over the culture of his organization. He tells me he's being called on to take these morally courageous stands more frequently these days. He knows something is amiss.

What he's facing is the paradox of moral courage. He's savvy about that. He understands that moral courage may in fact be the essential characteristic of leadership. He knows leadership has many other attributes—energy, humility, discipline, articulation, and creativity among them. Without the catalyst of moral courage, however, he's seen those grand qualities languish. His efforts to cultivate leadership put moral courage at the top of his wish list of qualities for future executives in his organization.

Yet he's coming to suspect that one mark of a healthy organizational culture is that moral courage, unlike vitamins, has no minimum daily requirement: you shouldn't have to use it every hour just to survive. He sees that the optimum culture will be the one in which the core business of the organization gets transacted daily in ways that don't make bravery essential. Of course risk taking is crucial for leadership. But it shouldn't be required in every meeting. When it is, the warning flags should go up.

What happens when culture trumps courage? That's the story of Enron, where a fast-moving, underhanded culture made it difficult for managers and board members to offer even the most routine suggestions for course correction without needing exceptional moral courage. That was the story at the *New York Times* in the spring of 2003, where journalists and editors felt uncomfortable speaking up even when they sensed something amiss in the plagiarisms and fictions of their young colleague Jayson Blair. And that's the story of NASA, where the now-famous "broken safety culture" would have taken towering courage to address from within. Get these cultures right, and the requirement for moral courage as a vital component of everyday living would recede, corrections would be made, and disasters would be averted.

Successful organizations, in other words, must require moral courage in their leaders and then work assiduously to make sure it's rarely needed. When even the most routine decisions—like promoting employees or outing plagiarists—put moral courage into play, that's a sure sign of something out of whack in the culture.

CHALLENGES TO
MORAL COURAGE

A rotting culture, then, is one of the great inhibitors of moral courage. Not surprisingly, there are others. In his *Profiles in Courage*, then-senator John F. Kennedy addresses three "terrible pressures" that, he says, "discourage acts of political courage" and "drive a Senator to abandon or subdue his conscience." The first form of pressure, he says, is that "Americans want to be liked—and Senators are no exception. . . . Realizing that the path of the conscientious insurgent must frequently be a lonely one, we are anxious to get along with our fellow legislators, our fellow members of the club." Getting along, he says, "means more than just good fellowship—it includes the use of compromise," which he understands to be at the heart of the legislative enterprise. "All legislation," he quotes Henry Clay as saying,

> is founded upon the principle of human concession. . . . Let him who elevates himself above humanity . . . say, if he pleases, "I never will compromise"; but let no one who is not above the frailties of our common nature disdain compromise.

Compromise is necessary because, as Kennedy notes, there are "few if any issues where all the truth and all the right and all the angels are on one side."

Kennedy's second "pressure" centers on the overwhelming desire to be reelected and to subdue conscience to that goal whenever necessary. "It should not automatically be assumed that this is a wholly selfish motive," he writes, "for Senators who go down to defeat in a vain defense of a single principle will not be on hand to fight for that or any other principle in the future." With a curiously nonjudgmental tone, he cites "the advice allegedly given during the 1920 campaign by former Senator Ashurst of Arizona to his colleague Mark Smith":

Mark, the great trouble with you is that you refuse to be a demagogue. You will not submerge your principles in order to get yourself elected. *You must learn that there are times when a man in public life is compelled to rise above his principles.* [Italics in original]

The third pressure discouraging courage, says Kennedy, is "the pressure of [the] constituency, the interest groups, the organized letter writers, the economic blocs and even the average voter. . . . If we tell our constituents frankly that we can do nothing, they feel we are unsympathetic or inadequate. If we try and fail—usually meeting a counteraction from other Senators representing other interests—they say we are like all the rest of the politicians. All we can do is retreat into the Cloakroom and weep on the shoulder of a sympathetic colleague—or go home and snarl at our wives."

Kennedy's recognition that moral arguments reside on each side of most issues, and that hardly a case exists where "all the angels are on one side," strikes a chord familiar to those who understand that the toughest decisions are those pitting right against right. Kennedy's praise of compromise, however, will probably sit better with ends-based thinkers, comfortable with a utilitarian philosophy, than with rule-based thinkers dedicated to adhering to duty without concern for the consequences. A compromise may result from any of Kennedy's three pressures: the desire to be liked, the need to garner votes for the next election, or the difficulties of balancing intransigent demands from constituents. But the end result will appear the same: a surrender of principle for the sake of expediency. That helps explain, perhaps, why the legislative process and its demands for what Kennedy calls "the fine art of conciliating, balancing, and interpreting" draws to it those who pay more attention to a consequentialist philosophy, emphasizing the results obtained, than to a deontological philosophy focusing on the principles upheld. If philosophers were canonized, the patron saint of legislators would be John Stuart Mill rather than Immanuel Kant.

Kennedy's taxonomy of the three pressures, then, helps us understand

what the challenges are and how they show themselves. It doesn't, however, indicate why they arise or what their antidote may be. For that it's
helpful to return to our three intersecting circles—principles, danger,
and endurance—and examine the three most powerful contraries to
moral courage:

- *Timidity,* occurring when principle and risk are present but the will
  to endure is missing;
- *Foolhardiness,* occasioned when endurance and principle coincide
  without due regard to the dangers involved; and
- *Physical courage,* arising when risk and endurance come together
  without regard to moral principle.

As figure 8 suggests, these contrary attributes arise when only two of
the three elements of moral courage are present.

Figure 8. Moral Courage and Its Contraries

To see how these three play out in real life, consider the experiences of a French figure-skating judge, an English explorer, and an American high-school student.

TIMIDITY AT THE OLYMPICS

The contrary quality that has the poorest disguise—the one most people would take to be the polar opposite of moral courage—is the kind of timidity that, while aware of moral principle and well apprised of the risks, refuses to endure the danger. That was the sad case of Marie Reine Le Gougne, the French skating judge suspended during the pairs figure-skating scandal that rocked the 2002 Winter Olympic Games in Salt Lake City. Voting with the majority in a 5–4 decision to give the gold medal to the Russian pair Elena Berezhnaya and Anton Sikharulidze—whose technically flawed performance seemed clearly inferior to the near-perfect skating of Canadians Jamie Salé and David Pelletier—she was almost immediately overcome with pangs of conscience. A stylish woman at the pinnacle of her judging career, she burst into tears during a postcompetition review with her fellow judges the following day, complaining of pressure placed on her to swing her vote to the Russians.

By the time the International Olympic Committee and the International Skating Union (ISU) had awarded an almost unprecedented second gold medal to the Canadians, Le Gougne had already checked out of her Salt Lake City hotel, heading home in disgrace. The ISU later suspended her for three years for misconduct by awarding first place to the Russian pair "upon the instruction of Mr. Didier Gailhaguet, the President of the Fédération Française des Sports de Glace, although in her own opinion the pair Salé/Pelletier from Canada presented a better performance." The ISU also suspended Gailhaguet for three years and specifically "excluded him for participation in any capacity within the ISU in the 2006 Olympic Winter Games."

Where did Le Gougne's courage fail? Probably not through ignorance of the dangers: she must have known the risks in conspiring to "fix" an Olympic match. Nor was she entirely devoid of moral principle: her conscience brought her to tears, observers noted, within moments of her vote, finally causing her to go public in a move that put her principles above her own career. What was missing, at that key moment early on, was her ability to endure hardship. She lacked the fortitude to take tough and courageous action against those pressuring her. Did she trade votes in hopes of getting herself elected to a seat on the ISU's prestigious technical committee? Was she voting for Russia in return for Russia's vote when France's skaters competed later? Was she afraid to stand up to the pressure from Gailhaguet, whose organization nominated her as a judge for the pairs event? Whatever the reason, the timidity is clear: what could have been moral courage became, instead, an expression of cowardice by virtue of a failure to act.

Could a different ethical climate have saved her? If she had understood more fully the irresponsibility of vote-rigging—and if her colleagues had actively upheld a tradition of ethical concern—she might never have been tempted. But no such tradition was in place. In fact, when the U.S. Figure Skating Association proposed a lifetime ban for any official guilty of an ethics violation, the proposal was scrapped because the sport had no formal ethics guidelines on which to base such expulsions. Those guidelines are now in place: six months after this incident, the International Skating Union finally closed the barn door after the judge had fled, adopting a fifteen-point code of ethics that alerts members to pitfalls and conflicts of interest.

FOOLHARDINESS AT THE SOUTH POLE

If moral timidity spelled the downfall of Marie Reine Le Gougne, the same cannot be said of the tragic hero of a different kind of ice. On January 4, 1911, as the brief Antarctic summer lengthened that continent's still-frozen days, Robert Falcon Scott reached Ross Island on the sailing vessel *Terra Nova* on what was, in his mind, the start of a race to claim the South Pole for Britain. His former fellow officer on an earlier voyage to the pole, Ernest Henry Shackleton, had set out for the pole in 1908. Each faced extreme danger. The way each handled risk illustrates a central point about moral courage.

Though Shackleton never made it, his leadership skills and friendly, outgoing personality probably saved not only his life but the lives of his men. "By January 9, 1909," writes Dennis Perkins, coauthor of *Leading at the Edge: Leadership Lessons from the Extraordinary Saga of Shackleton's Antarctic Expedition,* Shackleton and his men "were 97 miles shy of the South Pole and desperately short of rations. In a typical act of generosity, Shackleton gave one of his last biscuits to a companion, Frank Wild, and then made the painful decision to turn around. He later explained to his wife, 'I thought you'd prefer a live donkey to a dead lion.' "

Though he was pilloried back home as unpatriotic for failing to claim the pole for Britain, there is little in Shackleton's story that strikes a modern reader as timidity. It seems more appropriate to describe his decision as an act of wisdom. Having measured the extent of the danger—from frostbite, starvation, and sheer cold—he concluded that saving his men's lives was of more importance than pushing on to a goal they might well reach but from which they would almost certainly never return.

Writing about Shackleton's later venture—a trans-Antarctic expedition of 634 days that involved a crushed ship, a mutiny, an eight-hundred-mile sail in a tiny boat to South Georgia Island, and a treacherous crossing of glaciers—Perkins applauds "the extraordinary leadership and teamwork" exhibited by Shackleton and his men. Not only did every one of them survive, "they all survived with a unique level of caring and camaraderie." And, it might be added, with an exceptional sense of courage that knew when to push on boldly and when to back off without cowardice.

Not so for Scott. Born in comfortable circumstances in Plymouth, England, he was charming but detached, physically strong but personally reserved. As he began his final push for the pole in 1911, Scott knew that a young Norwegian named Roald Amundsen was also in the race. What Scott did not know was that, even as he was setting out, Amundsen and his team had already returned to their base camp, having claimed the pole for Norway.

But the pressure was on. On January 3, 1912, writes Perkins,

> Scott made a last minute decision. Although plans for the polar assault had been based on a team of four, Scott announced that he would take one extra man on the final leg of the journey to the Pole. The sleds were equipped with supplies for four men and the tents were designed to accommodate four, so this change complicated their movement. They had also brought only four sets of skis, so the entire polar party was restricted to a walking pace.
>
> Scott and his men arrived at the South Pole on 17 January 1912—35 days after Amundsen. Finding the Norwegian tent, Scott wrote: "Great God! This is an awful place, and terrible enough for us to have labored to it without the reward of priority. . . . Now for the run home and a desperate struggle. I wonder if we can do it. . . ."
>
> They could not. One member died a month later after sinking into a coma. The next month, a second man—Titus Oates—stepped out into a blizzard never to return. Suffering from severe frostbite, Oates apparently sacrificed his life rather than slow his comrades.
>
> On 19 March a blizzard again enveloped the remaining three members of the Terra Nova expedition. . . . They had only enough food for two days. Scott's last entry on March 29 reads: "We shall stick it out to the end . . . and the end cannot be far. . . ."
>
> Eight months later, expedition survivors came upon the tent of the polar party. When Scott and his two companions were finally found, they were carrying 35 pounds of geological specimens. The weight of those specimens, symbolic of Scott's dedication to science, was not the main cause of his tragic death. But they symbol-

ize the inherent contradiction of trying to run a race while carrying rocks.

Courage? Perhaps it was more like foolhardiness. Being stung by the lash of competition, ill-prepared by temperament, caught short by poor planning and bad decisions, battered by brutal and unforeseen weather—there are abundant excuses for Scott's failure. But chief among them was that, unlike Shackleton, he failed to respect the extent of the risk facing him. He died with his principles intact and not a doubt in the world about his endurance. But he misread the danger.

RAW COURAGE IN THE WOODS

Nearly a century later, Jenny didn't misread the danger. She first saw it, she remembers, in the eyes of a fellow student standing tensely beside his pickup truck along the country road that day. His weapon of choice, gripped firmly and held almost out of sight behind his pant leg, was a baseball bat. He was ready, if necessary, to enter forcibly into the melee that threatened to erupt among the hundred teenagers gathered in a muddy, out-of-the-way pasture for a face-off that Thursday afternoon.

A high-school senior and member of her student council, Jenny lived in a small town near "the city," which, in her rural state, meant a large town of perhaps thirty-five thousand people. For as long as anyone could remember, her school had been locked in athletic rivalry with the city high school. For the most part, it was a playful and healthy competition, which Jenny and her friends took with a grain of salt. They all had friends in the city school. So although they cheered their respective teams passionately and relentlessly from opposite sides of the field or court, the friends reunited after the games for food and conversation.

But one day, Jenny recalls, she heard that a boy from the city had insulted her classmate Max. While Max was not part of her circle of friends, she knew him as a friendly kid. He moved in a slightly rowdy cluster of boys whose lives were tied more to their pickup trucks and their after-school jobs than to the school or its extracurricular activities. Put in perspective, she recalls, the insult was nothing earthshaking: it had something to do with the muddy appearance of Max's truck. But in the mind of a high-schooler striving to maintain his sense of self-respect among the faint and nuanced signals of status in a community of teenagers, the insult cut deeply. Lashing back in kind, Max escalated the situation to the point where the boys challenged each other to a fight. They would battle it out in one-on-one, hand-to-hand combat in the pasture after school the next Thursday.

Max's friends tried to talk him out of the fight. But Max wouldn't hear of it: his honor was at stake because he had been disrespected. As word of the planned fight spread secretly through both schools—consciously held below the radar of each administration's early-warning systems—some students dismissed the encounter as silly, self-serving, puerile, and indulgent. Others, intrigued by a spectacle that pushed the envelope of obedience and legality, promised to be there. Still others, like Jenny, were swept into the current as observers, dismayed by the pending personal violence but helpless to avoid the most talked-about happening of the season.

That Thursday afternoon, as students from each school piled into cars and trucks and made their way to the pasture, Jenny was among them. As the fight began, with the combatants warily circling each other, she found herself playing the part of the loyal fan and cheering Max on. Then the harsh incongruity hit her. This wasn't just another game. Maybe those other kids she didn't recognize weren't just friendly rivals. Maybe someone really could get hurt. At that moment, she said, she was absolutely overcome with fear. Turning away, she hid behind a friend and started crying.

That's when she noticed the baseball bat—and found herself contemplating the potential enormity of the situation. What if the private matchup exploded beyond the bounds of the two fighters? What if the city students attacked her friends? What if years of rivalry had produced not managed competition but nursed grudges, ready to explode into the open? What if, at the end of the afternoon, someone lay dying?

Fortunately, that never happened. The two fighters got bruised and bloodied before the crowd dispersed into the twilight. And for the next few days, cars from both sides prowled at each other's schools and out by the pasture, looking for another fight. But the momentum died away. The baseball bat was never used. And the wounded honor (such as it was) began to heal.

Was courage on display in the pasture that day? Yes, if by courage we mean the raw, basic bravery that faces threats of physical harm and toughs it out even at risk of bodily pain and suffering. Max knew the danger he faced from his antagonist. And he was willing to endure it. But wasn't he enduring it for the sake of a principle—his sense of honor? Shouldn't that elevate this instance to the status of moral courage?

Some might think so. But as I listen to the way people use the term *moral courage,* I find an emphasis on the term *moral* that focuses not just on the broadly mental nature of courage but more on the way in which it is driven by and supports a higher set of specifically moral values. Moral courage, for most people, is a kind of courage that is right, proper, and virtuous. It is, in other words, courage in the service of not just any principle but of a particularly elevated principle.

That distinction, I think, keeps us from naturally ascribing moral courage to the hijackers who flew planes into the World Trade Center on September 11, 2001. Courage they indeed had, but not in the service of what, in the democratic cultures of the developed world, would be called a high principle. To argue otherwise—to agree with Islamic radicals that the murder of three thousand unarmed noncombatants is perfectly justified—is to sustain a kind of moral relativism that can also condone the genocides of Adolf Hitler, Slobodan Milošević, and Saddam Hussein. They, too, had courage, but not what would widely be defined as *moral courage.*

HONOR AND MORAL COURAGE

But Max was fighting for his honor. Is honor not an elevated principle? At times, yes. There is nothing ignoble about the idea that students should respect one another, right down to the level of their pickup trucks. But honor (to use a distinction raised in chapter 3) is an operational value— useful not so much as an end in itself as for attaining or characterizing higher, more intrinsic values. My dictionary, noting this distinction by defining *honor* in terms of other values, describes it as "that which rightfully attracts esteem, respect, or consideration, as dignity, courage, fidelity; esp[ecially] excellence in character; high moral worth; nobleness." It is, in other words, an instrumental virtue that carries us toward the terminal end-state values that most matter. But because *honor* stands in contrast to terms that help describe what Max was feeling—*contempt, disdain, scorn, disgrace, ignominy,* and *shame*—was not Max right to defend it?

Yes and no. Perhaps without knowing it, Max and his opponent were lapsing back into that classic and antique expression of courage known as the duel. Defined as a "prearranged armed fight with deadly weapons, usually swords or pistols, between two persons concerned with a point of honor," dueling traces its roots to the Middle Ages. In that period various forms of "trial by combat" or "wager of battle" developed, consisting of fights held under judicial supervision, often with the belief that God would cause the evildoer to lose and the righteous to win. By A.D. 887 such spectacles had become so popular that Pope Stephen VI prohibited them. The practice flourished, however, on an individual level as a means of settling slander, libel, and nasty slurs against a gentleman's character.

By 1410 the practice was so brisk that a manual on dueling was published in Italy. And in 1777 the Code Duello was published in Ireland, quickly setting the European standard for the proper ways to deliver a challenge, employ "seconds" or friends to solicit apologies, negotiate time, place, and weapons, and determine how, if the duel ended with no death, the slight or affront that provoked it was deemed to have been washed away. So important to the United States Navy was this manly tradition of upholding honor that "a copy of the Code Duello was in every midshipman's handbook, and until the Civil War no niggling official rules hampered naval dueling." In a notorious 1804 duel, Aaron Burr gravely wounded Alexander Hamilton. When Hamilton died, Burr not only did not go to prison for this manslaughter but continued as president of the Senate. Andrew Jackson, having slain Charles Dickinson in 1806, went on to become the seventh president of the United States.

By the Civil War, however, dueling was in decline. In the twentieth century it was rendered illegal in most countries, where laws now recognize that killing someone in a duel amounts to willful murder and is punishable as such. Once seen as an essential expression of courage—such that for a gentleman to refuse a challenge was to be branded a coward and suffer a severe loss of reputation—dueling is now broadly rejected as a quaint and curious brutality. Honor is instead protected by lawyers in far less violent ways.

But some wisps of an older conception of honor still remain. Perhaps due to its tradition of dueling, the United States Naval Academy still operates under the motto of "Honor, Courage, Commitment." Yet even today that first term, *honor,* creates some unfortunate pressures. The May 1996 suicide of Admiral Jeremy Mike Boorda, chief of Naval Operations, appears to have been provoked in large part by a journalistic revelation that two of the medals he wore on his uniform may not have been properly earned. Acting out of what he apparently felt to be his highest sense of honor—a desire not to dishonor the military—he took his own life.

Did it require courage for Admiral Boorda to kill himself, or for Aaron Burr and Andrew Jackson to slay their opponents in duels? Did it take courage for terrorists to create the deadly chaos of September 11, or for Max to show up for the fight in the pasture? By most definitions of the term, the uncomfortable answer is probably yes. But was it *moral* courage? Did the overlay of motivation that drove each of them forward—a defense of honor—rise to the level of the highest and best moral values?

Probably not. Risk, yes. Endurance, certainly. But without the highest sense of principle, it's difficult to assign these kinds of acts to the category of *moral* courage. What becomes clear is that adherence to a valuable but secondary principle—an instrumental rather than a terminal value—can lead to a failure of moral courage.

But holding first-order values does not in itself guarantee that moral courage will be expressed. It matters how those values are held. If even the highest intrinsic values are expressed in narrow and tepid ways, that, too, can result in a failure of moral courage—as Elliott found in witnessing a surge of layoffs at his firm.

TEPID ETHICS
IN THE CORNER OFFICE

An executive with a large U.S. firm in the home products industry for more than a decade, Elliott found himself in regular contact with the CEO. Coming from a legal background and working closely on personnel matters, he helped the CEO address the kinds of issues that sometimes propelled once-contented employees along a vector of concern stretching from doubt and skepticism to cynicism, outrage, and even whistle-blowing. He also knew the complex, challenging dilemmas that could face senior management in issues involving the evaluation, reassignment, and termination of employees. And he knew that his own corporation's culture was built more on trust than on confrontation, with managers at every level willing to assume that people were doing their jobs well unless it proved otherwise. Mature, seasoned, and confident, with a national reputation in his field and an accumulated wisdom often sought out by his peers, Elliott was a loyal player—very willing to criticize as needed, but quick to recognize and reward good wherever it appeared.

In his early years at the company—years that coincided with the economic bubble of the 1990s—he'd seen only growth, steady and at times spectacular. The firm had continued its upward trajectory, octopussing itself into a sprawling conglomerate. Some of its mergers and acquisitions, he thought, were better than others. But with revenues flowing in nicely, everything seemed in balance.

And then things changed. Following September 11 the markets tumbled. They failed to rebound in the wake of the collapse of the technology sector, the implosions of Enron and Arthur Andersen, and the state and federal budget crunches—each of which, in its own way, hit the home products industry. His CEO and senior management came face-to-face with an unpleasant reality. Although markets were partly to blame, the challenges facing the company could have been mitigated to a significant extent through better planning, more thoughtful budgeting, and a more realistic setting of revenue targets.

Elliott knew the CEO to be a thoughtful, straightforward individual, willing both to listen carefully and to decide firmly. He also knew him as decent and ethical, committed to building and maintaining the integrity of the firm. So by May of 2002, as it became clear that major layoffs were in order, he found himself sympathizing with the CEO's agonies. He knew that laying off even one employee was not easy. Now, according to the revised plan, top management needed to lay off at least twenty-five hundred.

Not surprisingly, the "watercooler opinion" was abuzz with concern. Whose job was at stake? How would they structure the changes? When would it happen? What criteria would they use? As the weeks passed, the worries shifted toward distrust. Too many good people were being let go. There seemed to be no pattern. Worse still, no coherent message was emerging from the corner office, beyond the CEO's oft-repeated lament that layoffs among people for whom he cared so much were deeply painful.

By July the process had, Elliott told me, "created a ruckus." Morale was declining. Skepticism was building. Characterizing the core responses he was hearing, Elliott felt he could reduce them to one statement: "This process lacks credibility." It came down, he said, to a simple observation that was shockingly visible to everyone in the company: nobody in the CEO's inner circle of top executives had been terminated or transferred. Mayhem was rolling through the ranks. Yet none of those whose own strategic missteps had contributed to the situation had been asked to join the other twenty-five hundred.

Elliott was not part of that small team at the top. But he was close enough to it to sense, as could many others, that some of them should have been asked to leave. And he was wise enough—and privy to enough figures—to know who. Yes, he admitted, the CEO obviously knew things Elliott could not have known. He may have had compelling reasons of his own for preserving that top team. But to thousands of others in the firm, his failure to act, or at least to communicate about his inaction, was deeply disappointing. It provoked a passion in Elliott's usually cool voice as he explained his response. "He fires thousands of others," he told me, "but not one of his own reports. Why? Because he simply lacked the courage to look them in the eye and say, 'You screwed up!'

"There's a great deal of moral *outrage* that I've seen in my years in this job," he said sadly, "but I've also seen an incredible lack of moral *courage*. The CEO had a great deal of morality—and not a lot of courage."

That's a damning conclusion. It's a legacy no executive would want carved in stone: *This was a person of great morality and no courage.* Yet far too frequently that's what appears to be the case. Why? Moral courage combines principle, endurance, and danger. The failure here stemmed not from an unwillingness to endure hardship. As a decisive leader, he had already proved willing to cut sharply and endure the personal and professional hardship of that choice. Nor was it for lack of awareness of the danger. He knew the challenges of cutting too far, too fast, and losing too much of the accumulated wisdom and excellence in his workforce. But neither was it for lack of principles. He labored hard to be fair, respectful, and responsible.

The failure seems to have come, instead, in his inability to express these qualities with sufficient intensity and breadth:

- **Intensity.** Was the CEO resoundingly just and equitable, or just pleasantly fair? Was he notably and proactively respectful of others, or just properly tolerant? Did he go out of his way to be responsible, or was he simply dutiful in fulfilling his obligations?
- **Breadth.** Did he express his moral concern only within a narrow moral boundary—a close-in "perimeter within which we exercise our values," as I described it in chapter 3? Did he, in other words, reserve one application of moral interest for his team of senior executives and another for more distant circles of employees?

Fairness, fully manifested, might have led him to understand that the layoffs should be shared across the firm, not just in the lower ranks. A richer sense of respect might have encouraged him to listen more carefully to the increasing outrage bubbling up from the watercooler and, more important, from those who, like Elliott, were close to him. True responsibility might have caused him to recognize his own personal obligation to make the tough choices, hold the difficult conversations, and reshape the top team. Instead, at least in Elliott's view, he never quite rose to the challenge of the moment. A man of personal boldness and basic morality, he never could bring these two qualities together into moral courage.

Bringing things together, for most of us, involves a process of thought, a willingness to make intelligent connections among ideas, a capacity for reasoning from one idea to the next. That often requires time—or at least focus, concentration, and space for reflection. Had Marie Reine Le Gougne had more time to contemplate the pressures she was facing and the enormity of the risks, would she have made a better decision as a skating judge? Might Max's friends, with more reflection, have been better able to talk him out of his after-school fight? Could Elliott's CEO have made better decisions if he had more leisure? Our gut tells us yes. Time for reflection, we tend to think, is an unconditional good: the more of it the better. Like Stephen Dedalus in James Joyce's novel *A Portrait of the Artist as a Young Man,* we find that growing up is synonymous with learning to value the reflective process. "By thinking of things," the schoolboy Stephen discovers in one of his flashes of insight, "you could understand them."

Or so we believe. Now and again, however, too much thought seems to militate against good decision making—and, at times, against moral courage itself. There are moments when the first intuition is right and further thought only degrades the clarity and confuses the issue. So it was in the tragic case of Rob Viscome, a high-school senior in the upscale Westchester County town of Harrison, New York.

THE DAY NOBODY CALLED 911

Shortly after noon on a sunny April day in 2002, the students at Harrison High School were dismissed early after a power outage sank the building into darkness. A group of teenagers headed for the home of sixteen-year-old Beth Porzio, whose parents were away. Located in an expensive subdivision near the Westchester Country Club, her home was a place they often congregated, since Beth's parents were happy to have them gather at their house—they were usually home—rather than elsewhere. Rob Viscome, who was planning to be Beth's date for the prom, arrived after stopping along the way with a friend, Nicholas Rukaj, to buy some beer. A two-hundred-pound seventeen-year-old with a goatee, Viscome easily passed for an adult and was rarely asked for identification by store owners. In the graduation yearbook for his class, he was voted "Class Partier" and "Most Likely to Extend Weekend" in recognition of his drinking habits.

As the afternoon wore on, some twenty-six teenagers came and went. At about 2:45 P.M., according to police records, an argument broke out between Viscome and Rukaj, which quickly degenerated into scornful comments about each other's lineage. That was a tense topic on both sides. Viscome's father, who was superintendent of Harrison's Water District No. 1, lived with his family in what the local newspaper described as "the working-class section of town known as Silver Lake." Rukaj's father, convicted in the 1996 killings of an ex-lover and her father-in-law, was serving twenty years to life in prison. As the altercation developed, Rukaj's younger brother, Pat, joined the fray and, according to one teen-ager's police interview, "grabbed Viscome by the neck, threw him against the wall, [and] said, 'Don't you ever talk about my Dad.' " The two went outdoors onto the stone patio, where Pat threw one punch. Viscome went down, hitting his head sharply on the stones and lying motionless.

What happened next depends on whom you ask. It was clear, however, that Viscome was seriously hurt, and that all efforts to wake him up failed. It was also clear that, typical of teenagers these days, there were plenty of cell phones at the scene. And it was clear that the words "nine one one"—the general emergency number in the United States used to summon police, fire, or ambulance services—were spoken urgently by more than one of the students there that day.

"I yelled to everybody to call the cops, call 911," Pat Rukaj told the police, "and everyone was yelling 'No' 'cause they don't want cops there and stuff." Miguel Ramos had a different story. He remembers someone telling Ashley Fanelli, who had a cell phone on her belt, to call 911, "and she was like 'No, can't do that.' " Ramos himself, it turns out, also had a phone, but didn't use it to call.

When Beth's older brother arrived and grasped the seriousness of the situation, he took charge, directing everyone to say that Viscome had taken a fall at nearby Pettijohn Park. Several teenagers bundled Viscome into a car—apparently dropping him more than once as they did so—and drove him to a local hospital. Seven days later, never having regained consciousness, he died.

Most would agree that these were not bad kids. Fond of one another, tolerant of one another's foibles, they cared a great deal for their group. And in one matter they had been well drilled, probably since kinder-garten: when something bad happens, call 911. That was, indeed, their first impulse. But in the surge of panic that overcame them—and with the passing moments of reflection enforcing their fear of the danger they faced if caught drinking under the age limit—the right intuition faded, replaced by more self-serving motivations. Getting their injured friend the quick assistance he needed stood second in line to their priority of self-protection.

Why that was so is a question that continues to trouble Harrison residents, as *Rolling Stone* magazine writer John Colapinto concluded in his detailed account of the incident:

> How could these young adults with every advantage have acted so selfishly? Only the teenagers themselves know what was in their heads as Rob Viscome lay dying in front of them. All those who attended the party at the Porzios' declined to speak for this story. The sole insight into their behavior is provided by their police interviews. Those can be chilling. For even as they evoke a scene of muddled panic, another dynamic emerges, one of cold calculation and steely self-interest.
>
> "So," Det. [Neil] Marino asked Pat Rukaj, just hours after the incident, "in spite of the fact that a friend is lying on the ground and having some trouble and needs some medical attention immediately—the more important thing to everybody there was the fact that—" And here Pat cut him off.
>
> "To save their ass," he said.

A profound collapse of moral courage? Yes, but not an unprecedented one. These students were manifesting an "unresponsive bystander" phenomenon—a term coined in response to a number of high-profile urban murders in the 1960s in which numerous bystanders witnessed physical attacks but failed to come to the aid of the victims. Summarizing their research on this phenomenon, Ohio State University professor Bibb Latané and Princeton University professor John M. Darley concluded that "the presence of other people serves to inhibit the impulse to help." They note four main reasons:

> (1) Others serve as an audience to one's actions, inhibiting him from doing foolish things. (2) Others serve as guides to behavior,

and if they are inactive, they will lead the observer to be inactive also. (3) The interactive effect of these two processes will be much greater than either alone; if each bystander sees other bystanders momentarily frozen by audience inhibition, each may be misled into thinking the situation must not be serious. (4) The presence of other people dilutes the responsibility felt by any single bystander, making him feel that it is less necessary for himself to act.

At the Porzios' house that afternoon, no one wanted to look foolish (point #1). Each took his or her cues from the others (#2), who to some degree were "frozen by audience inhibition" (#3). And each felt a diluted sense of responsibility (#4), making it "less necessary . . . to act." It was, in other words, a classic case of culture stifling courage. What any one of these students might have done had he or she been alone became undoable when they were together. And the more they reflected on it, the harder it became to call for help.

GROUPTHINK, DEVIANCY, ALTRUISM: THREE MORE CHALLENGES

Like bystander apathy, three other challenges can pose significant complications to moral courage: the "groupthink" effect that causes a team to make decisions no one of its individuals would have countenanced; the redefining of deviancy as normalcy, leaving no perceived moral wrong that must be courageously righted; and a misplaced sense of altruism that forces others to act with courage.

Groupthink

The teenagers in Harrison, New York, were inhibited from acting, in part, because they were part of a group. Their challenge, however, was not specifically the result of "groupthink" as psychologist Irving Janis defined it. Writing in 1972, Janis described "a mode of thinking that people engage in when they are deeply involved in a cohesive in-group, when the members' strivings for unanimity override their motivation to realistically appraise alternative courses of action." Groupthink typically takes over when a group is under significant pressure to arrive at a decision. Its symptoms include:

- A conviction in the inherent morality of the group, with no interest in exploring the ethics of its actions
- A sense of unanimity, in which group members assume that everyone agrees with the group's decision and in which silence is taken as consent
- An unwillingness to examine alternative points of view or seek expert opinion
- A deliberate refusal to gather information that could be contrary to the group's predilections
- An illusion of invulnerability, producing overly optimistic views that overlook danger and downplay risk
- Pressure to conform, including negative stereotyping of those outside the group and the branding of opposition from within as "disloyalty"
- Collective rationalization, in which the group explains away warnings and failures contrary to its position

It differs from bystander apathy, in part, because of its reflective component: where bystanders fail to act in the moment, groups can fail to act deliberately, over time, and for carefully detailed reasons.

The groupthink phenomenon has been used to explain some key failures in decision making regarding President Truman's decision to drop the atomic bomb on Hiroshima in 1945, the abortive Bay of Pigs invasion in Cuba in 1961, and the destruction of the *Challenger* space shuttle in 1986. The concept also helps us understand some of the most egregious failures of moral courage in the business community in recent years. One of those, involving the sudden and notorious collapse of Enron in 2001, is now widely understood as a failure of corporate governance. It is also a significant example of groupthink inhibiting moral courage.

- **Pressure to conform.** With Enron board members paid as much as $350,000 a year—more than twice the average pay for nonexecutive directors at America's two hundred largest companies—there was ample reason for them to "turn a blind eye to many of the questionable activities undertaken by management."
- **Unwillingness to examine alternatives and gather information.** In February 1999 David Duncan, the Arthur Andersen partner in charge of the audit for Enron, described to the audit committee of the Enron board some of the company's accounting practices as "high risk" and "pushing limits." In spite of similar warnings that persisted through 2001, "not one director on the committee (including a former Stanford accounting professor) objected to the use of these procedures, asked for a second opinion, or demanded a more prudent approach."
- **Illusion of invulnerability.** Most famously, when Enron's chief financial officer, Andrew Fastow, proposed creating and managing some off-balance-sheet partnerships—despite the conflict of interest created by having him work both for Enron and for another entity—the board waived its own code of ethics. That event, as the board later agreed, should have been "a red flag the size of Alaska." A copy of Enron's code of ethics, an elaborate sixty-four-page document, was later said to have been sold on eBay with a description consisting of a single deeply symbolic word: "unopened."

Enron's board, it seems, exhibited the classic symptoms of groupthink. In the driven and highly competitive atmosphere created by chairman Kenneth Lay and CEO Jeffrey Skilling, speaking up against the group's interests would have required significant moral courage—a quality apparently missing around the directors' table.

Deviancy

Another force undercutting moral courage is a tendency to redefine deviant behavior as acceptable. The phenomenon was made popular by sociologist and New York senator Daniel Patrick Moynihan, who coined the alliterative phrase "Defining Deviancy Down" as the title of a 1993 article he published in *American Scholar.* "There are circumstances," Moynihan writes, "in which society will choose not to notice behavior that would be otherwise controlled, or disapproved, or even punished." He notes that "over the past generation . . . the amount of deviant behavior in American society has increased" beyond the tolerance levels of the community. Accordingly, "we have been redefining deviancy so as to exempt much conduct previously stigmatized, and also quietly raising the 'normal' level in categories where behavior is now abnormal by any earlier standard."

Moynihan then posits "three categories of redefinition." He illustrates the first category, which he describes as the *altruistic,* by "the deinstitutionalization movement within the mental health profession that appeared in the 1950s"—an effort, he feels, simply to redefine mental patients as healthy enough to be released. Caused by "good people [trying] to do good," it resulted in a flood of homeless persons sleeping in doorways who, he writes, were "characteristically defined as persons who lacked 'affordable housing'" rather than as individuals with mental illnesses. His second category, the *opportunistic,* he illustrates by focusing on the problem of single-parent families. He cites Richard T. Gill's finding that "an accumulation of data [shows] that intact biological parent families offer children very large advantages compared to any other family or non-family structure one can imagine." Yet there has been astonishingly little outcry, he notes, over a changing family structure that leaves increasing numbers of children in one-parent families—and, correspondingly, little willingness to recognize the impact of these changes on a child's ability to function well in an educational system. His blunt and notably cynical explanation for this apparent blindness is that "there is good money to be made out of bad schools." His third category, which he calls the *normalizing,* is the tendency to accept as normal what previous generations would have regarded as deviant in the extreme. His illustration: "the growing acceptance of unprecedented levels of violent crime."

If in fact our culture has a tendency to normalize deviant behaviors—and there are, predictably, scholarly objections to Moynihan's thesis—that fact has ramifications for the expression of courage in the moral realm. For if the moral realm has shrunk so that much of what was once seen as immoral is now greeted with tolerance or even approbation, there will be less need for moral courage. That change, while it may appear to be happening in broad, overarching social movements and trends, in fact can influence the way individual decisions are made. Where, several decades ago, a university student who witnessed his classmates cheating might have agonized over whether to speak up, today that behavior may have been normalized to the extent that it provokes little more than indifference, even among students who themselves would not cheat. The challenge to moral courage, then, is that if the "deviancy" that once stimulated a morally courageous response can be redefined as "mainstream," it may appear that no boldness in defense of principle is needed. Those who lack the courage to be moral may, in fact, find themselves quite adept at redefining circumstances in this way.

Altruism

The title Moynihan chose for his first category, the altruistic, describes still another kind of challenge to moral courage—not one that makes it more difficult, but one that causes it to be needed in unforeseen ways. That may sound surprising: how can the desire to do good, and the actual expression of that goodness, require courage to set it right? It does so not by making moral courage harder to express but by creating conditions in which its expression is suddenly needed, sometimes in ways unimagined by the altruists. Two examples illustrate this point.

The first involves Raphael, an eighteen-year-old from a developing country who, through a bizarre set of circumstances, found himself invited to spend the spring of his senior year living with an affluent family in the United States and attending their excellent public high school. The family lived in an upscale suburb, where both parents worked in professional positions. Their one child, a son, was severely disabled, and while they loved him dearly, it was clear that he could never provide them with the normal sense of filial affection and pride for which they longed.

Their home was spacious, however, and their gregarious and community-minded natures welcomed Raphael, who was only too happy to come. While he had not been raised in poverty—his country had millions less fortunate than he—his family was barely in the middle class, though his parents were well educated and his grandparents noteworthy members of his community. By his senior year, Raphael had made his mark. President of his high-school class, he combined an easygoing friendliness with a natural scholastic ability. No one was surprised when the offer to spend a term in America came his way: in the eyes of his peers and the broader community, he was clearly on a track toward success, this invitation being just the latest manifestation.

True to his culture, Raphael also possessed a deep respect for his elders, which showed up as graceful attentiveness and desire to serve those older than he. That quality, he soon discovered, was far rarer in the United States than at home. It helped win him instant approval from his host family, who quickly came to regard him as everything a young man should be. The first few weeks at his new high school confirmed their view: he was a success in every way. What's more, it all seemed so natural. Raphael had never encountered a family of such generosity, nor any two people beyond his own family who seemed so much like parents to him.

Then one evening, a month into his stay, his hosts sat him down after dinner. He was worried at first that he had done something wrong, but they assured him that, in fact, it was just the reverse. They were so impressed by his demeanor, his kindliness, his intelligence, and his love of life that they had a proposition for him: they would like to adopt him, they said, as their own son. As part of the family, of course, he would have everything they could have lavished on their own son: European travel, the finest of educations, a warm and caring family, and all their help in ensuring his success in whatever his life's work might be. There was only one condition: he needed to promise to cut himself loose from his own family and not see them again.

Raphael told me years later that as an eighteen-year-old he was overcome with contradictory emotions. He felt great appreciation for his host family but deep love for his own family. He felt a sense of belonging to his own culture but a recognition that his future lay in moving beyond that culture. He felt a fear of what might happen if he agreed to the adoption and a dread of what might happen if he refused. As he hesitated and demurred, his host parents added a final condition: if Raphael chose not to take them up on their offer, he would have to pack up and return home right away, without finishing the school term.

But in his culture, as Raphael also told me, a young man returning home without finishing his tasks (in this case, completing the school year) would face a massive sense of disappointment, shame, and shattered expectations. Yet in the end, he could not bring himself to leave his own family forever. Using whatever moral courage he could muster against the blandishments of their altruism, he thanked his would-be parents and returned home.

Looking back through the lenses of history, Raphael sees an aspect of this situation that was invisible to him at the time: a kind of manipulative generosity. His hosts were using the devices of philanthropy and affection as they sought to satisfy their own longings for a son they never had at the expense of a friendly but undefended teenager. He remains convinced that their altruism was genuine: they really did think they were offering him a magnificent future. They probably didn't see themselves as manipulative. Yet their kind intentions thrust Raphael into an expression of moral courage far beyond anything he had ever mustered.

Genuine altruism, then, can create real harm if taken past its useful limits, creating situations so damaging that moral courage must come to the rescue. But altruism can also be misapplied. That was the case with

Nate Haasis, a seventeen-year-old high-school senior who had the moral courage—some would call it temerity—to refuse to accept a prestigious football record he had officially won.

On October 25, 2003, during his last game as quarterback for the Southeast High School Spartans in Springfield, Illinois, Haasis was within thirty yards of setting a new conference record for the most yards gained by passes in a career. In the final minutes of play, it was clear that the Spartans could not beat their rivals from Cahokia High, who had a sixteen-point lead. So during the last timeout, with a minute to go, Southeast coach Neal Taylor struck a deal with his counterpart, Antwyne Golliday of rival Cahokia: if Southeast allowed Cahokia to score one more time, the Cahokia players would let Haasis throw one final long bomb. The pass wouldn't change the outcome of the game, but it would shove Haasis into the record books.

The plan worked perfectly. The last pass of his high-school career logged in at thirty-seven feet, and Haasis's name went into the Central State Eight Conference records with 5,006 total yards.

But over the weekend, Haasis began to suspect something was amiss.

"I noticed that something was a little fishy when I saw the Cahokia defenders were not even paying attention to the play, talking to each other," Haasis told ABC News. After learning what had transpired, he sent a letter to the conference requesting that the record be expunged. "It is my belief that the directions given to us in the final seconds of this game were made in 'the heat of battle' and do not represent the values of the athletes of the Southeast football team," he wrote. "In respect to my teammates, and past and present football players of the Central State Eight, it is my hope that this pass is omitted from any conference records."

What led the coaches to this altruistic gesture? Haasis was well liked. He deserved a record. The pass wouldn't affect the score. Nobody, apparently, would be harmed. Besides, there was precedent. In 1998 University of Connecticut women's basketball star Nykesha Sales, despite an injury that kept her from playing that season, limped onto the court at the start of a game and shot an unguarded basket that gave her the school's scoring record. The Illinois coaches simply thought they were doing the right thing. "[Haasis] was leaning toward going to a different school, and he and his parents told me that he went to Southeast because of me," Coach Taylor told the Associated Press. "And when someone does a nice gesture like that, it deserves a nice gesture back."

Not everyone agrees that his zealous altruism deserves praise. The coaches have been criticized for unethical behavior—in effect, for robbing the previous record holder, Griff Jurgens of Glenwood High School in Chatham, Illinois, of his 4,998-yard passing record set in 1998. Haasis, by contrast, had the moral courage to give back a record he had long sought. In a nation hungering for evidence of moral courage, especially among young people, Haasis has been the subject of national news coverage, including a slot on ABC Television's *World News Tonight* as "Person of the Week" for November 7, 2003.

INHIBITORS OF MORAL COURAGE: A SUMMARY

What, then, are the great inhibitors of moral courage?

- An organizational culture that, like NASA's, is "clearly overconfident" and does not invite discussion
- A too-ready sense of political compromise flowing from a need to be liked, to get reelected, or to balance intransigent demands from constituents
- A foolhardy ignorance of danger, a timid unwillingness to endure hardship, or an insistence on physical courage, at times in defense of honor
- Too much reflection, leading away from an impulse to act and toward a rationalization for inaction
- Bystander apathy, where responsibility is diluted by the presence of other bystanders

- The illusory unanimity of groupthink, the apparent normalizing of deviancy, and the excesses of a manipulative altruism

There is, finally, one more inhibitor: different appraisals of the value of an individual. Broadly metaphysical though it is, this last point may in some ways be among the most important. Here's how cultural anthropologist Paul Bohannan puts it:

> When I was in West Africa, one of my assistants came back one evening from bathing in the river. He told me that someone had drowned there. When I asked who it was, he said it was a stranger who couldn't swim. When I asked if anybody had tried to save him, he responded that they had not. When I, in some agitation, asked if *he* hadn't tried to save him, he responded, "He wasn't mine." . . . His cultural tradition had taught him to value the lives of his kinsmen and neighbors—people who were "his." My cultural tradition had taught me to value all human life. The focal length in my tradition was longer than his. But the ideas underlying the incident were the same: you help people. My tradition defined people differently from his.

Defining people differently is surely one of the great inhibitors of courage, moral or physical. If a moral boundary separates us from others—if our values and traditions are wholly apart from theirs—we may conclude that we have no obligation to help. In some cases, that means no duty to express moral courage. Extending the moral boundary, then, opens the possibility of expressing moral courage more broadly: the larger the radius of our moral concern, the more apt we are to act in a morally courageous way. That should come as no surprise. It means only that those who have the most expansive sense of ethics, who see in all humanity a reflection of the core values they themselves espouse, are most apt to be courageous. True morality begets courage, which reminds us of the self-evident fact that, conversely, one of the great inhibitors of moral courage is a lack of morality itself.

Moral Courage Checklist
Step 6: Avoiding the Inhibitors

Like most good things, moral courage is hedged about with imitations, counterfeits, and challenges. What keeps me from being distracted as I seek the morally courageous path? How can I circumvent the detours that would inhibit or quench my moral courage?

Here are a dozen inhibitors to avoid:

1. **Overconfident cultures** that seep into organizations and cut off discussion, tolerate unethical acts, or refuse to hear new ideas from me or anyone else

2. **Compromises** engendered by my desire to be liked, to win promotion or election, or to duck tough but right demands

3. **Foolhardiness** as I forge ahead with chutzpah and quixotic derring-do but without a proper assessment of risk

4. **Timidity** that urges me to flee from situations demanding bold forwardness—a cowardly unwillingness to endure the discomfort that moral courage often requires

5. **Raw courage** that ignores the principled heart of moral courage, substituting instead a misplaced sense of honor or a merely physical bravery

6. **Tepid ethics,** lacking sufficient intensity and breadth to rise above the merely dutiful and tolerant, keeping me from the resounding vision and clarity that often characterize true moral courage

7. **Overreflection,** leading me to rationalize my way out of an expression of moral courage that may have been my first instinct

➤

8. **Bystander apathy** that dilutes my responsibility in the presence of others, letting me excuse my lack of courage because no one else is being courageous, either

9. **Groupthink** that huddles around and staunchly defends a bad collective decision that no one in the group, acting alone, would have countenanced

10. **Normalized deviancy,** leading me to redefine some wrong behaviors as acceptable rather than take a morally courageous (though perhaps unpopular) stand against them

11. **Altruism,** which can challenge my moral courage when expressed in excess (as with manipulative generosity) or when misapplied (as with well-intentioned meddling)

12. **Cultural differences,** persuading me that the boundaries of my moral concern need not extend to include *those people* who are so radically different from me

If I avoid all these, am I home free? Not necessarily. There's a courage of denial needed to escape these pitfalls. But there's also a courage of affirmation that requires proactive, engaged, and positive steps. Avoiding detours doesn't necessarily prove I chose the best road in the first place.

CHAPTER EIGHT

Learning Moral Courage

*Suddenly and surprisingly we can become an example to others—
and those others to us: they hand us along, become a source of moral
encouragement to us, arouse us and stir us, move us to do things
when we might otherwise not be provoked, and they have the will to
act in pursuit of purposes we have come to regard as important.*

—Robert Coles

Can moral courage be learned, or is it innate? Do some people arrive in
the world with their moral-courage software already installed, while others haven't got it and never will? Do the experiences cited so far in this
book pertain only to a predestined few, the chosen ones with a gene the
rest of us never got? Or can moral courage be nurtured, taught, practiced,
and attained on a broad scale?

I think it's the latter. As in all learning, two things are important: the
substance or idea of what's taught and the pedagogy or methodology
through which it's learned. So far, this book has explored the substance of
moral courage—the core values that drive the assessment of risk, the
adherence to principle, and the willingness to endure. These can all be
apprehended intellectually—so much so that, as with ethics of any sort,
individuals who may have no discernible moral compass can be taught to
bandy about the language of moral courage with glib facility. To turn the
conceptual into the practical, to lift moral courage out of theory and into

application, requires something more: a hands-on, street-corner pedagogy.

That training can come in many ways. But it appears to be under-
girded by three modes of learning and teaching:

1. *Discourse and discussion,* where the language of rational inquiry clarifies the idea of moral courage and renders it explicable and relevant
2. *Modeling and mentoring,* where real-life exemplars demonstrate
   moral courage in action and chart pathways of human endeavor
   that others can follow
3. *Practice and persistence,* where learners can discipline themselves
   through direct, incremental skill building that increases their ability to apply moral courage

While most morally courageous actors bear evidence of having
learned in all three modes, some appear to have focused more on one of
these modes than on the other two, as the following examples suggest.

DISCOURSE AND DISCUSSION:
SYMBOLS IN SANTIAGO

The cross and the fish appeared mysteriously one weeknight in 1976
while Mónica Jiménez de Barros was traveling overseas on business.
Hastily painted in black on the redbrick garden wall behind her low, tree-
shaded house in suburban Santiago, Chile, the symbols were positioned
in unavoidable view of her living-room windows. Her husband, Juan,
was a busy engineer who, even during the sunny November evenings of
the Southern Hemisphere's spring, had little reason to glance out back
while she was away. Coming home late, sorting the mail and stacking it
for her on the table, he would get a quick bite of supper, spend a bit of
time with their young children, and head for bed.

So he was never quite sure how many days the ominous markings had been there before he saw them. Had he opened one peculiar letter, he would have discovered. But it was addressed to her. She remembers reading it on her return, after he had pointed out the graffiti. "We are going to kill you and your family," it said, mentioning a time that, because of her delay in reading it, had already passed. "We are following you. Take care of your children."

The letter needed no signature. In those days, three years after the 1973 coup that left former president Salvador Allende dead in the presidential palace in downtown Santiago, the government was firmly in the hands of General Augusto Pinochet, who, she says, "lived on our same street before he became president." The letter and black symbols, she knew, bore the hallmarks of his armed forces.

In recent years, human rights organizations have exposed the grisly toll of Pinochet's sixteen-year rule: several thousand murders and disappearances, forty thousand detained and tortured, and hundreds of thousands fleeing into exile. Pinochet himself has been indicted for international crimes against humanity, escaping punishment only because of his poor health.

At the time, however, the extent of his administration's systematic brutality was unclear. Long a prosperous, independent nation, Chile arrived at the middle of the twentieth century with a well-earned tradition of stability, an array of democratic institutions, a widely respected judicial branch, and an essentially honest commercial and political system that even today remains almost unique on the continent for its low incidence of corruption. But the turbulent 1960s brought Communism into prominence across Latin America. Leading the trend was Fidel Castro, who took power in Cuba in 1959, nationalizing industries, collectivizing agriculture, and developing a Marxist-Leninist state with close ties to the Soviet Union. With the election of Allende in 1970, a committed Marxist arrived in La Moneda, and socialist experimentation took hold in Chile. The next year, after a monthlong visit by Castro, Allende reestablished relations with Cuba, despite a convention by the Organization of American States proscribing such recognition by any Western Hemisphere nation.

For the next two years, as their country careened dangerously into economic instability, Chileans found their government increasingly under the shadow of international Communism. To many of them, the armed forces seemed the last holdout against that danger. So when the coup came and the junta took charge, it was not without a good deal of popular middle-class support.

Still, Jiménez and her husband weren't naive. One night shortly after the coup they learned just how different their country had become when, after hearing noises in the street, they went outdoors to find soldiers chasing a man across the neighboring rooftops. Coming back indoors, they found more soldiers methodically and unapologetically searching their house—a situation that would be repeated many times in the future, with the military, she says, "going in and out of houses whenever they wanted."

Two years after the coup, in an effort to evaluate the human rights situation, Chile's Catholic bishops asked Jiménez, then a professor of social work at the Catholic University of Chile, to preside over a twenty-four-person Justice and Peace Commission formed the year before. "To accept this request," she remembers, "was on one hand an honor and on another a risk." Her very willingness to serve would, she knew, "convert me automatically into an enemy of the state" and expose her to surveillance, threats, and possible loss of her position at the university. She had long discussions with her husband and with her colleagues in the School of Social Work at the university, she recalls, and in both places "the values triumphed." What drove her to accept the offer and join the commission, she said, were the values "of respect for human dignity and of solidarity with those who were being followed and having their human rights abused," as well as "the values of truth, of liberty, and of civic responsibility."

In the year before the cross and the fish appeared, those values sustained her as she went about documenting human rights abuses. But as the commission's investigations began implicating the army and the secret police, or DINA, she heard of other commission members being threatened. So she was not surprised when she read the letter that night.

In the end, the death threat proved empty. Jiménez's work on the Justice and Peace Commission lasted ten years. In the run-up to the election that would ultimately bring Patricio Aylwin into the presidency in 1990, she formed a nationwide organization, Participa, that was credited with registering enough voters to ensure that Pinochet was finally removed.

Jiménez subsequently served as one of the seven members of Chile's National Commission on Truth and Reconciliation. That, too, took moral courage—not because of death threats but because the very idea of granting immunity from prosecution to state-sponsored murderers in return for their complete truth-telling enraged so many Chileans. "We were repudiated by the military government, we were threatened by the intelligence services, we were criticized by right-wing elements and by the media," she told me. "Our results were discussed and deprecated by the judiciary and by the armed forces. But today nobody doubts this clarification of the truth." Yet the final report of the Chilean National Commission, published in 1991, notes that "with the passing of time there can be no doubt that the facts established in the report have come to be widely accepted in Chile as the truth."

But on that day in November of 1976, with the stark symbols on her garden wall and the letter in her hand, what kept Jiménez going forward? That could have been a turning point. With young children and a husband to protect, she would have been forgiven for pulling up stakes right then and there. She already had an international reputation: the trip that kept her from reading the death threat, in fact, had been to Rome for work with the Vatican on issues of peace and justice. A fulfilling career beyond Chile was not impossible. Besides, plenty of their friends were already living in exile in countries like Sweden that provided a sympathetic haven and comparably sophisticated standards of living. What was it that allowed her moral courage to triumph?

When she talked it over with her husband, Jiménez recalls, they agreed that they had to "do what we think we have to do in accordance with our values." They agreed they were "not going to be afraid." They agreed that from that point on they needed to behave as though they were constantly being followed—as though, she says, "they're knowing what you're doing." They made it a policy "always to be well informed," not to take unnecessary risks, and to take good care of themselves. But they also recognized that "if you have to do something, you have to do it." It was a matter, she says, of "living by our internal convictions" and doing "what God has planned for you"—to "live life according to our values" rather than "according to the symbols" on the wall.

"Moral and physical courage were necessary," she writes in an e-mail to me summarizing her response to the situation. "Great commitment to the values, good analysis of the risks, care and protection at certain moments and courage in others where the liberty of the people was at risk. To overcome difficulties, strength and vision were focused on the outcome [and] on the values, not on the obstacles that the military regime and its repressive forces were putting in place."

Woven through her comments, in other words, are the elements of moral courage we've been exploring: a recognition of the role of moral and not merely physical courage; a conviction about the values and principles that most matter; a clear risk assessment; a willingness to endure difficulties and dangers based on a combination of experience, character, faith, and intuition; and an avoidance of the pitfalls of timidity and foolhardiness. These are the core attributes of morally courageous action. But something else was at work here as well: the support of another person, in this case her husband. The fact that they could, as she says, "converse" about the issues was crucial.

In determining whether and how to express moral courage, in fact, discussion is a hugely important tool. In the end, the action itself may be solitary, carried out by the individual alone. But the commitment to action frequently arises from focused discourse with an engaged and compassionate listener. That suggests still another distinction between physical and moral courage: the former can happen alone and in silence, while the latter takes place in the context of a community where words and ideas matter.

That's not surprising: *ethics* and *morality* describe interpersonal qualities, typically expressed in the relations of an individual to the surrounding group. For the individual struggling in isolation, we use other words. The activity of the proverbial hermit in the wilderness, grappling alone with grand ideas and having no companionship beyond the objective elements of the world or an inner thoughtscape of the mind, is more apt to be described with words like *meditation, introspection,* or *prayer.* The term *moral courage,* by contrast, springs more readily to mind to describe situations where the individual rubs up against the collective expressions of humanity.

Perhaps for that reason, moral courage is also learned in part by watching others express it—as Jim Baker discovered in a business setting in Indiana.

MODELING AND MENTORING: COMPETITIVE COURAGE

There's never been a coup in Columbus, Indiana, which is 5,100 miles from Santiago, Chile—even farther, some would say, in mental mileage. But that night in 1988, as James K. Baker halted his car on the winding woods road to his lakeside home a few miles from town, his headlights picked up some words that Mónica Jiménez would have recognized. He had been stopped unexpectedly by a barrier of logs and brush deliberately dragged across his road. The message scrawled in the gravel on the road in front of it said, "Tomorrow you die."

As chairman and chief executive officer of Arvin Industries—now ArvinMeritor, an Indiana-based Fortune 500 manufacturer that at the time had fifteen thousand employees, plants in sixteen countries, and a strong presence in the automotive industry—Baker discounted the literal meaning of the message. It was, he rightly understood, part of the hyperbole that sometimes attends a labor strike. But he didn't discount the sentiment behind it. The strike itself, at two of Arvin's nearby plants, arose from what Baker still regards as "the toughest decision I ever made as CEO."

By 1988, following years of decline in heavy industry that gave the American Midwest its "Rust Belt" label, the region had clawed its way back into profitability. Competition was still stiff. But the automotive industry had regained some of the luster it had lost when Japanese cars, flooding into the U.S. market in prior years, had made Detroit's offerings look dowdy, pricey, and poorly made. With the turnaround, wages for manufacturing workers had begun to rise. There were still plenty of unskilled workers available for $8 an hour. But because "times had been a little fat in America," as Baker recalls, the typical unionized Arvin worker was making about $11 an hour.

Japanese vehicles, however, had already made their mark with American consumers. Some, like Nissan and Honda, were being assembled at plants in the Midwest, and the Japanese were determined to expand their foothold. So in the mid-1980s, Japanese suppliers began setting up factories in the United States. Their plan was to produce exhaust systems, brakes, electrical parts, and other components for Japanese carmakers in America. But they also set their sights on Detroit's "Big Three"—General Motors, Ford, and Chrysler—where Arvin did much of its business.

In those days, Baker recalls, a Japanese firm setting up in Indiana "could have all the workers they'd want at $8 an hour"—$3 less than Arvin was paying. The impact of that $3 differential fell out in two ways: on the company and on the workers. From the company's perspective, Baker explains, an exhaust system that might sell for $100 contained about $55 in materials, $25 in labor, and the rest in overhead and profit. In an Arvin plant, that $25 labor expense would buy just over two hours of time. In a new Japanese-run plant, it would buy more than three hours. It was not hard to see how the Japanese, operating with that price advantage, could undersell whatever Arvin could produce.

Which is exactly what started to happen. In 1988, in a startling development, Japanese competitors succeeded in winning some significant trial contracts with the Big Three for work that Baker thought was coming to Arvin. Yet that was the year that Arvin had also launched an aggressive international initiative. "I believed the risks involved [in that initiative] would increase by an order of magnitude," Baker told me, "if our base business in the United States became unprofitable." It was clear that something had to be done—fast—if Arvin was to retain the U.S. car-makers' business.

As Baker saw it, his company had three options:

1. It could, under U.S. law and without contravening its union contracts, close down its American factories and shed all its $11-an-hour workers. It could then reopen plants one hundred miles or more away from the original plant and hire new workers at $8 an hour.
2. It could persist in its current course and watch its business decline.
3. It could ask the union to recommend to its membership a wage cut in the neighborhood of $3 an hour.

For Baker, none of these options was pleasant. The first he saw as tremendously disruptive, not only for the company, which would have to assimilate new plants and workers all at once, but especially for the workers who would have been let go in a move that, while legal, would strike few people as ethical. The second option, while not fatal, would radically reshape the company into nonautomotive lines of business, abandoning its decades-old and carefully nurtured relationships of trust with the Big Three. Yet Baker was especially concerned about the third option—the impact on the workers of the $3 cut. He knew, of course, that Arvin was a prime source of jobs for unskilled workers who may or may not have finished high school. In those days, he recalls, training consisted of "handing new workers a pair of gloves and telling them to report to a foreman, and by two o'clock that afternoon they'd be up to speed." But just because they were unskilled did not, in Baker's mind, mean they were dispensable. "I've always felt a huge responsibility to keep food on the dining tables of 'my' employees," he says.

As his thinking moved toward that third option, he was acutely aware of the impact of such a wage cut at the personal level. "If a man working in an Arvin factory got $11 an hour—and in those days most of them were men—that meant he was grossing $22,000 a year," he explains. "That meant his wife also had to work, and perhaps she was bringing in $18,000. That's a total income of $40,000, which meant a pickup truck for him to drive to work, and a second car for his wife, and a tract house for their family. And it still left enough for them to take a week's vacation to Grandmother's house in Texas, or a week at the shore."

But when you ask him to take a $3 cut, "you're asking him to take $6,000 off the family income," he says. The family gives up their vacation, and he gives up his truck and instead carpools to work. "That $6,000 pays for those things they really look forward to," he observes. Could he ask workers accustomed to a particular lifestyle to accept a lesser one—even though he knew that if they quit and sought other work, they would not be able to match the wages they'd enjoyed at Arvin?

His own executive team was "pretty mixed" on what they ought to do and not sure whether any of the options would work. But Baker's decision was to ask for the wage reduction. Did he think, I asked him, that another CEO in his position would necessarily have had the courage to make that call? Some, he felt, might have chosen to lower wages by only a dollar—a less courageous move that, in his mind, would have stirred up resentment in the workforce without achieving the cost reductions necessary to save the business. Still others might not have been willing to make the cut that year, choosing instead a wait-and-see approach.

Baker could see it from both sides. In the end, however, he and his team gathered the union leaders from the seven plants that would be affected and laid out the charts and graphs that made their case. Recognizing the enormity of the challenge, the union leaders didn't stand in their way, though they refused to endorse the plan. Instead, they said, "*You'll* have to sell it to the membership."

In the months ahead, five of the seven plants went out on strike, some for short periods but several for five months. During that period, he recalls, his mailbox on the state highway near his driveway was destroyed three times—"not a big deal," he says, "but just another prank" meant to intimidate him and his team. On another occasion, his vice president for automotive engineering was sitting in his office—with the exterior stone wall of the building behind him, topped with several feet of glass—when a bullet ripped through the window above his head. And one evening shortly before he found the message on his gravel road, Baker recalls that he and his wife were guests of the mayor of Columbus, who was hosting a delegation of Japanese officials interested in locating business in the city. The dinner was held at City Hall—a building that also houses the Police Department—and although Baker parked his car in the City Hall lot, they came out after dinner to find all the car windows broken and the tires slashed. But all that, he feels, goes with the territory of courageous leadership. There are times when, as he says, "if you really mean it, you have to be willing to take the strikes."

Was he confident that things would turn out well when he took that stand and asked for a wage cut? "I knew it would be a tough sell," he says, "but I knew it was going to work out." How? Because the only other option he could see was that the workers would walk off the job, and the company would then begin rehiring—causing serious delay and disruption but ultimately making Arvin more competitive. And competitiveness, for Baker, was the principle that undergirded his decision making and gave him confidence.

"When people come up through the business organization, as I did, one of the lessons they learn many times over is that you've got to maintain your competitiveness," he says. Arvin's founder, Q. G. Noblitt, had a saying that has become something of a mantra around the company: in Baker's paraphrase, "you can either sell a better product for the same price, or sell the same product at a little lower price." In a tough competitive atmosphere, Baker notes, "if you try to sidestep your responsibility to be competitive, you've been had." That, as he says, was "the background of my choice"—the underlying conviction that allowed him to endure the hardship of his morally courageous stand, trusting that remaining competitive would benefit everyone in the long run.

Can you learn moral courage? I ask him. Without a moment's hesitation, he says, "Very definitely." You can learn it, he says, just as you learn leadership and ethical behavior. "You're not born with any of these things," he observes, but you take them on by watching the behaviors of "the elders you become associated with" in your career. To this day, he credits his success to the "giants" in the corporate world—"some of the most outstanding people in the state of Indiana"—who had been drawn to the close-knit, competitive, but fundamentally ethical culture of Arvin and became in turn "the models from which I could learn." Because Arvin was "a friendly company" where executives were "not aloof," he had ample opportunity to see them in action on a daily basis. That, he says, contributed far more to his understanding of moral courage than his formal education.

By the time Baker retired as CEO in 1993, the rightness of his choice five years earlier had become apparent. The Japanese auto-parts suppliers had been "contained" without making any significant inroads with U.S. carmakers. Even the union leaders agreed that the wage cut had been necessary. But the most important result, Baker recalls, was that "Arvin management started treating the employees better." Knowing how much their workers had sacrificed, managers went to much greater lengths to provide whatever nonfinancial benefits they could to make life better for them, and the environment "became more harmonious."

Executive decision making reflects such a complex and integrated set of vectors that it is impossible to disaggregate it into its components. But suppose you could. Suppose you were able to separate out a single vector—like moral courage—from the interplay of forces that combined to produce Baker's decision to cut wages. It's not hard to imagine that same level of moral courage being expressed by someone else. That person may have had a different educational background, social upbringing, or political leaning, in a different part of the world and even in a different language. But given that same aptitude for courage, he or she might well have made the same decision as Baker did. By contrast, it's hard to imagine that same stand being taken by someone who had *not* been subjected to a constant enrichment culture of mentoring and modeling by individuals who were expressing moral courage in their quest for competitiveness within an ethical framework. Even though this person was exactly like Baker in all respects but that one, he or she could well have made a very different decision.

Had the examples not been there—from the heroes, the father figures, or, as Baker calls them, "the giants"—could his leadership have developed as it did? Would his confidence have been there—based on long years of experience as well as a developed character and a clear set of intuitions—to reinforce his convictions about the rightness of his choice? Some of the mentoring was formal and prescribed, reflected in regular performance reviews as he took on new managerial responsibilities through the years. But much of it must have come through quiet observation over the years—undiscussed, perhaps even unconscious, but formative nonetheless.

The organization had raised him, and now he was sustaining its future.

Practice and Persistence: Courage in the Hood

Jesse Cottonham was raised by a different kind of organization: San Francisco's Hunters Point, near the old navy shipyard in a crime-ridden area of low-income housing projects and high unemployment. So the day he saw a woman in the neighborhood flattened by a single punch from a man, he didn't think twice before intervening.

As Cottonham recounted the occasion to me, it was just another sunny day on the streets. His partner, Kai, was a journeyman with Pacific Gas and Electric Company (PG&E), one of the nation's largest combined natural gas and electric utilities, serving northern and central California. That summer afternoon, Kai had wheeled his big brown utility truck into position at the corner of Mendell and Jerrold. His task for the next hour, with Cottonham as his younger helper, was to monitor the nitrogen in an underground transmission line to make sure it stayed cool enough. With nothing to do but wait, the two of them were sitting in the cab reading when the drama started to unfold.

In his peripheral vision, Cottonham spotted a young woman with an infant strapped onto the front of her body walking quickly along a nearby street. Suddenly a man about her age came careening down a steep dirt slope into the street ahead of her, cutting her off with threatening gestures and a string of blunt words. Their argument grew more violent. "It looks like he's going to hit her!" Kai exclaimed in alarm.

Whereupon the man reared up and slammed his fist into her face, knocking her and her baby to the ground.

As Cottonham reached for the door handle, Kai said, "Oh, no, Jesse, don't get involved—let's call the police." Cottonham looked at him as if to say, "Are you crazy?" Then he was out of the truck, headed for the altercation.

Putting himself between the two of them, he said to the young man, "Oh, no, man, you're not going to do this in front of me!"

"This is my bitch and my baby!" the young man snarled menacingly.

Cottonham didn't budge. "Hey, it's not worth it, dude," he told him. "My partner's in the truck and he can call the police any time."

But as he helped the woman up—a "tiny lady," he recalls—it was clear that she, like her assailant, was spoiling for a fight. "If you really want to help me," she snapped at Cottonham, "just hold my baby!"

But Cottonham stayed between them. "You just go on where you were going," he told her. "And you," he said to the young man, "you just go back on up the hill." They looked at him angrily, but he stayed put and kept repeating his commands with quiet authority. And within a minute, as quickly as the situation arose, it was over. She went her way, he went his, and Cottonham climbed back into the truck.

In the twelve years since, Cottonham has worked his way up to the position of distribution troubleshooter. He now drives his own PG&E truck—one of the big rigs with a cherry picker on the back, which he parks at his home in the same neighborhood where he was raised and where he now responds to service calls. But he hasn't lost the courage to intervene. Sometimes, he says, he'll see a crowd gathered around a couple of kids who are fighting. He just drives his truck slowly into the middle of the fight, climbs out, and tells them to respect each other and break it up.

"I'm not asking them to stop—I'm *telling* them," he says. "But I'm giving them respect. I can talk to them like I'm their daddy. They respect that because I make them accountable for what they do."

"Around here," he chuckles, "I'm known as 'the PG&E guy.' "

Cottonham's story combines moral and physical courage. More accurately, it exemplifies the use of physical courage in the service of moral courage. But it also indicates something more: a lifelong understanding of the hood, a native speaker's skill with the nuances of its language and gestures, and a practiced, persistent ability to express moral courage. Cottonham didn't suddenly "get" courage that sunny day, after years of timidity. Something had built it up within him over the years through practice and persistence. What was it? I asked him.

He was raised, he tells me, in the housing projects by a mom and a dad. Today, he says, that's rare: a lot of the kids he works with come from single-parent households. But in his day a lot of his friends had both parents at home. Looking back, he feels the key influence on him was his father.

"He always told me to be a gentleman," Cottonham recalls. "No matter what, you never hit a woman. You don't need to, because a man can always overpower a woman. I can remember getting beat up by girls because I was afraid to hit them back!"

His father taught him to defend himself, but never to throw the first punch. He also learned to defend his family, including his two little brothers. It was a rough neighborhood, he recalls, and he did his share of fighting. "But every fight I ever got in," he says, "was because somebody was beating up my little brothers, who were probably mouthing off!"

Another influence on him was the church. The black churches in his community reinforced his respect for women, he says, and for family. His church also taught him that "if you defend yourself, God will protect you." In fact, Cottonham recalls that as he and Kai sat in the truck that day, Kai was reading the newspaper and he was reading the Bible. Now a deacon in his church, Cottonham is deeply involved with church-related activities in his neighborhood, working with a nonprofit boys' mentoring group called the Daniel Discipleship Project that he helped found in 1999. Fittingly, its motto is "A boy has to *see* a man to *be* a man."

But underlying all is Cottonham's lifetime of experience in the culture of the hood. How did he know, I asked him, that the young man who punched the woman wasn't armed? Part of it, he says, was that the attacker was wearing only a T-shirt, pants, and tennis shoes—he had no real place to hide a knife or a gun. But Cottonham also just "knew," the result of years of grooved and confident intuition. He wasn't so sure about the woman. Given her small physical frame but large desire for a fight, he suspected she might have "had something on her." So he never gave her the chance to use it.

Finally, Cottonham was adept at the language of his culture. "You learn how to defuse situations with certain words that you can use without backing down," he says. Adjusting his language to the conditions in front of him, he instinctively found the right tone to use with the young man. Projecting a sense of calm authority—finding words that came across as neither an easily scorned request nor an enraging peremptory command—he let his instincts guide him in what to say and how to act.

What lies behind this minute of courage at Hunters Point, then, are decades of practice, intuition, understanding, and experience. This was not the first time Cottonham had intervened, nor would it be the last. Working from no formula, he trusted that his intuitions—and his God— would tell him how to act once he put himself into the picture. Well aware of the risks, his quick and almost unconscious scan for weapons helped mitigate the danger. So did the presence of Kai in the truck. But risk was there, undeniably. That risk was physical in part. Yet given his role in the community—where even at that time, as a thirty-two-year-old new father himself, he was coaching basketball and working with neighborhood youth—it was also a risk to his position. Had it all gone wrong that day, he would have risked not only bodily harm but a wounding of his principles, his sense of rightness, his reputation as a graceful mediator and effective intervenor.

What were the principles that drove him forward? As he describes the culture of the neighborhood, I hear him articulate three. The first comes from his upbringing: you protect women. The second comes from "the village mentality" that says "you look out for each other's kids." Cottonham says he "tries to live by that philosophy." The third comes from his application of moral courage to his work. As a frontline employee in customer relations, he says he learned early on that there are times when he needs to take the customer's side rather than pass a problem along to someone else after a halfhearted and perfunctory attempt to resolve it. "Integrity is doing it right the first time," he says, "and not having to go back."

Can moral courage be taught? I ask him. The question seems almost silly, steeped as he is in his work with young people who, he says, are regularly learning what courage is all about. He tells the mentors who work in his program—and the judges, police officers, electricians, plumbers, teachers, elected officials, and business leaders who visit his kids to relate how they progressed from the hood to their present positions—that mentoring requires them to set solid personal examples. He tells them, "This makes me more accountable for what I do and this will raise the bar for you, too." The best teaching, he feels, is by example. "We have too many leaders who fall," he says. "If our young people say, 'All the people we look up to fall,' then they're going to say, 'It's okay to fall.'"

But does the teaching work? After a moment's reflection, he recounts a recent incident in which he helped take seventy-five kids on a retreat. Some of them had never been outside the city. Because the group included both boys and girls, he was alert to the fact that, as he says with a chuckle of understatement, "we were going to have that little mix." His prayer ahead of time, he says, was simple and direct: "Lord, just give me the insight to know what's going on."

One night, finding a young couple behind a locked dormitory-room door, he exercised his moral courage—once again as an intervenor—and had a heart-to-heart with them about the kind of example they were set-ting. "I didn't really bash them," he says. "We just had a moral talk."

Later, he recalls, the young man wrote him a letter that moved him so much he had it laminated. "He told me how hurt he was that he had dis-appointed me," Cottonham recalls. "That was the first sign I'd got that it was really working. And I thought to myself, Man, if I can reach one guy, I can reach another guy!"

REACHING ANOTHER GUY: TEACHING MORAL COURAGE*

From these three examples, then, it would seem that moral courage can be taught. Aristotle would agree. His famous dictum that "we become just by doing just acts, temperate by doing temperate acts, brave by doing brave acts" has formed the basis for centuries of instruction in the virtues. A review of the research, which provides an overview of several offerings but is by no means an exhaustive summary of the available programs, confirms that point. From educators to consultants, from writers to researchers, a consensus exists that people of all ages can bene-fit from instruction in this core value. Not surprisingly, there are some demurrals: a Duke University conference on moral courage and civic responsibility in 2003, sponsored by the Kenan Institute for Ethics, fea-tured a session titled "Three Reasons to Have Doubt About Teaching a Character Trait Like Moral Courage." That same conference, however, offered two other sessions—"Middle School Visions: A Schoolwide Effort to Promote Moral Courage and Civic Responsibility" and "The Role of Service-Learning in Nurturing Moral Courage and Civic Respon-sibility in K–12 and University Classrooms"—making the case that cour-age, specifically *moral* courage, could indeed be taught.

But to whom? The elementary school child? The high-school student?

---

* Coauthored by E. Marcus Fairbrother II.

"Brave Acts": Aristotle on Education

"All who have meditated on the art of governing mankind," wrote Aristotle, "have been convinced that the fate of empires depends on the education of youth." Though only a few scraps survive of his work *On Education,* the Greek philosopher makes it clear that education was to be practical and not simply contemplative, that it was closely related to ethics and politics, and that it taught reasoning skills that helped students move from effects back to causes.

But the diamond at the core of his teaching remains the idea that we learn the virtues—courage among them—by imitation and practice. As Aristotle explains it, the "faculties given to us by nature" (by which he means our natural abilities and "our senses") are "bestowed on us first in a potential form; we exhibit their actual exercise afterwards." He uses seeing and hearing as an example of senses that we don't acquire by practice or "by repeatedly seeing or repeatedly listening." On the contrary, he observes, "we had the senses [before] we began to use them[;] we did not get them by using them."

Virtues, however, are acquired by a different means. "We get [the virtues] by first exercising them," he says, noting that we also attain "the arts" in this way. "For the things we have to learn before we can do them, we learn by doing them, e.g., men become builders by building houses, harpers by playing on the harp." That line of reasoning, then, leads him into one of his most-quoted observations, which is that, in a similar way, "we become just by doing just acts, temperate by doing temperate acts, brave by doing brave acts."

Aristotle leaves it to us—indeed, to every age—to determine what those acts are and how we can create the conditions (particularly for youth) that compel us to perform justly, temperately, and bravely. But like his own teacher, Plato, he saw learning as integral to life experience and was keenly devoted to practical, hands-on learning as the route to the wholeness of human experience.

The young professional? The new recruit? The middle manager? The CEO? Who will place the most value on this learning? What are the benefits of such teaching? And if courage in its various forms is a learnable trait or skill, what are the methods that most effectively teach it? Do we acquire moral courage by reading about and discussing courageous people? Do we learn it, as Aristotle pronounced, by doing courageous acts? Can we sing about courage or draw pictures displaying courageous people and their actions and expect to have a better sense of this value held so dearly by so many? Apparently, yes: one can and does learn courage by all these means—and many more.

Predictably, much of the teaching about courage takes place in the classroom. Youngsters from six to nineteen are probably the single largest target audience for training in courage throughout the world. Here are a few examples:

- **The Foundation for Moral Courage,** established in 1992, presents narratives of courageous individuals through the medium of short documentary films. The foundation's first few films feature stories of those involved in the horrors of the Holocaust. *The Other Side of Faith,* for example, tells the story of Stefania Podgorska Burzminski, a sixteen-year-old in Nazi-occupied Poland who risked her life and that of her sister to save a dozen Jewish fugitives.

  More recently the foundation has highlighted the bravery of individuals caught in the atrocities committed after the collapse in the 1990s of the former Yugoslavia. The foundation also produces teachers' guides, conducts a film mentoring program, and sponsors the annual Jan Karski Award for Moral Courage, which "honors individuals whose acts of moral courage embody a shared commitment to universal human values."

- Similarly, the intriguingly named **Giraffe Project** (whose motto is "Moving people to stick their necks out for the common good") uses the stories of courageous individuals to teach courage and citi-

zenship to American students in grades K–12. The organization
has created three editions of its popular curriculum, suitable for
various age groups, with the stories of more than nine hundred
"Giraffes" told through books, audiotapes, and videos. The Giraffe
Project's Heroes Program promotes a three-stage learning process:

1. *Hear the Story,* where students listen to or read the stories of
   numerous Giraffes.
2. *Tell the Story,* where students learn about and create narratives around local heroes in their own communities.
3. *Become the Story,* where students select a local problem and
   undertake a service-learning project to address it, with the
   aim of inspiring others to follow suit.

- The theme of action also pervades of the work of the **Anne Frank
  Trust,** whose video curriculum, *Moral Courage: Who's Got It?* has
  been introduced in the United Kingdom to teach citizenship.
  Named after the author of the world's best-known diary, the trust
  uses the story of its namesake to promote courage—specifically
  moral courage—in young people. The Anne Frank Awards for
  Moral Courage, given to educators, students, or community members, celebrate the fact that "society owes an immense debt to those
  who decide to risk acting with moral courage to confront bigotry,
  racism, and other forms of injustice head on."

  The curriculum centers on the true stories of five individuals,
  told through brief videos highlighting the difficult situations in
  which they found themselves and the ways in which they rose to the
  occasion. The videos begin with the story of Rosa Parks, the African
  American woman in Montgomery, Alabama, who ushered in the
  American civil rights movement when on December 1, 1955, she
  refused to abide by the laws of the segregationist South and give up
  her seat on a bus to a white person. The videos end with the story of
  Sheik, a young Somalian who, forced to cooperate with bandits

raiding his town, warned the townspeople by speaking a local dialect the raiders could not understand. Though he was beaten nearly to death, his selfless actions saved countless others from harm.

Efforts to teach moral courage extend into the home as well. A weekly cartoon called *Courage the Cowardly Dog,* which ran from 1999 to 2002 on the Cartoon Network, featured the clever ploys of a fearful, abandoned dog taken in by an older woman, who loves him dearly, and her failed farmer husband, who can't stand the helpless pooch. Building on this theme but adding interactivity, Disney released a home video game in 2003 called *Finding Nemo: Underwater World of Fun,* which features characters from the hit computer-animated movie and, according to its creators, sets out to "teach courage, perseverance, trust, and helping one another." Even puppets get into the act: the Center for Puppetry Arts in Atlanta presents a one-man show called *Billy Goats Gruff & Other Stuff* that combines several familiar childhood fairy tales, including Little Red Riding Hood and The Three Little Pigs, to "teach courage, fairness and cooperation."

The methods promoted by these organizations to teach youngsters the value and benefits of acting with courage vary widely. But all share a common theme: courage is best understood by hearing about others who exhibit it. Stories of courageous people or fictional characters, most acting locally and a few globally, stand at the center of virtually every organization's curriculum. How teachers are guided to carry forward from hearing to doing is less uniform. And, as in so many areas of education, whether the results actually produce courageous children is still to be demonstrated by assessments and testing.

While it stands to reason that the malleable mind of a child may be the best target for the teaching of values, schools aren't the only places where courage is taught. The armed forces also place a high value on teaching this virtue. With soldiers scattered throughout the globe—young, inexperienced, and frequently far from home—the various militaries of the world share a need for their men and women in uniform to have a solid core of shared values, not least among them courage. The United States Navy puts the term squarely into its motto—*Honor, Courage, Commitment*—and the administration and faculty of the U.S. Naval Academy at Annapolis, Maryland, clearly believe that courage can be learned. Through its Leader of Character Seminars, the academy aims to bring that trait to the forefront in its midshipmen, so that when situations arise in which instinctive action is required, the sailor will take the courageous course without hesitation.

Training in courage is also finding its way into the corporate sector. Based in Israel, the Courage Institute has a network of affiliates throughout the world and preaches the value of courage in the workplace. Courage, proclaims the institute, "isn't what you know. It's reflected in what you do and what you achieve." The institute's founder, Merom Klein, explains that highly effective workforce teams consistently exhibit five key strengths:

1. Candor—"to speak and hear the truth"
2. Purpose—"to pursue lofty and audacious goals"
3. Will—"to inspire hope, spirit, and optimism"
4. Rigor—"to invent new knowledge and make it stick"
5. Risk—"to empower, commit, and invest in relationships"

"These five strengths," the institute states, "equip teams to face new challenges, implement new technology, and solve problems that they've never seen before. Teams with these five factors earn respect. They demonstrate the inner strength to stay on top of their game, even when the pace is fast and the rules keep changing."

Beyond the corporate setting, athletics has also long been seen as a great proving ground for courage. The Australian School of Self-Defence argues on the benefits page of its Web site that martial arts "build character, encourage self-discipline, and teach courage when facing obstacles or adversity." Swimming also teaches courage, according to American

Swimming Coaches Association executive director John Leonard. Every day, he writes, swimmers "get a chance to test their courage (and succeed or fail in that regard) in practice. Courage is a 'developed trait.' Swimming develops it well." And in the summer of 2003, David Frum, a former adviser to President George W. Bush and a journalist with the *National Review Online,* asked readers to share stories of how they tried to teach courage to their children or how their own parents tried to teach it to them. A youth football coach wrote in, explaining that at the beginning of each season he asks his athletes, all under the age of twelve, what they think courage is. Usually, he wrote, they say courage is not being afraid. The coach corrects them, saying that courage is "doing your job despite being afraid. Being afraid is OK. Not doing your job isn't." The speech works, the coach noted, as it "reinforces the team mentality since it makes it clear that it's not just the individual who fails, but the whole group as a result of that individual's lack of courage. It's a way of using peer pressure to encourage some constructive behavior changes."

Nor is courage simply a trait that's actively taught in Western cultures. A whole host of the world's races and religions believe passionately in the value of learning, teaching, and exhibiting courage, including Native Americans. At a Circle of Knowledge seminar held in 2001 at the Buffalo Bill Historical Center in Wyoming, Rose High Bear explained the important role of courage, telling participants that traditional Native American stories "teach courage, respect, honor, and humility" as well as "compassion for relatives and other people." China, too, appreciates courage, especially the courage to admit that you were wrong. Tian Xiuzhen of the *Shanghai Star,* writing about acrobats who after failing to perform a complicated maneuver quickly regrouped and tried again, proclaimed in an editorial that "not everyone is brave enough to admit and get the mistakes right, especially in front of a big audience, although our parents and teachers try to instill this in our character." And a basic Islamic informational Web site in Australia encourages Muslims to teach their children bravery and courage: an article entitled "Courage and the Child" suggests that parents read their children stories of historical Muslims exhibiting courage, teach games that promote courage, and "always encourage [your child] to express his opinion."

This brief *tour d'horizon* makes two things clear: programs that seek to teach courage are ubiquitous, and all face the challenge of proving their utility. Some are more adept than others at distinguishing moral from physical courage. Some seem to engage their learners more actively than others. And some appear to do a better job than others in extending the lessons of courage from the individual to the community at large. This last point is vital. Is moral courage like leaven, providing only a small percentage of the virtues present on any occasion but fundamentally transformative when kneaded into the larger culture of a community? Or does moral courage follow the dictates of Metcalfe's Law of Interconnectivity, which explains that as the number of people connected to the Internet increases, the value of the Internet increases exponentially? Does moral courage, in other words, become a social multiplier whose benefits increase radically as the number of people who learn and exhibit courage grows? Either way, the point is clear: moral courage is a benefit not simply to those who express it but to the entire context in which they are nested.

TEACHING MORAL COURAGE: A SUMMARY

Before setting out to teach anything, good teachers ask three questions: *What? How?* and *Why?* What should be taught? How should it be delivered? And why should it be learned?

The teaching modes explored so far in this chapter address the question of *how*. Discussion, modeling, and practice—along with other methods highlighted in the above review of some available curricula—constitute the ways and means of teaching. They make it plain that narrative is crucial, that active mentoring and real-life exemplification are important, and that practical, hands-on interactivity brings the lessons directly home to students. They also make it clear that the examples can be drawn from history, fiction, news reports, or local community members, and that they can be presented through such media as prose, poetry, films, drama, puppets, audiotapes, lectures, and interviews.

But it's quite possible for powerful curricular methodologies to be deployed in the service of a weak message. Unless the teaching grows out of a clear conceptual framework, the result can be confusing, simplistic, or just plain wrong. Hence the need to know *what* is being taught—the need for a structure of ideas that shapes the topic in ways that bring clarity and focus. Such a structure—a way of thinking about moral courage—has been set out in the earlier chapters. It includes an understanding of core values; of the three circles of principles, danger, and endurance; of the elements of trust that create a willingness to endure; and of the obstacles to taking morally courageous stands. As with any sort of teaching, the addition of the *what* to the *how* lifts the conversation above the level of mere antiphonal chat, where you say one thing and I say another and we imagine that therefore something important has happened. Good, concept-based teaching goes well beyond that. It creates an arena of focused dialogue where the application of a conceptual framework builds toward new understanding.

Developing a new understanding is no mean accomplishment. It doesn't usually happen through the imposition of foreign concepts on a mind unprepared to receive them. Instead it tends to draw out, highlight, and confirm ideas already in place in the student's mind. Among the highest compliments a writer can receive is to have a reader say, "You put into words something I've always felt but could never quite say." That's true for teachers as well. To sharpen the fuzzy and make sense of the vague is one of the greatest achievements of any learning environment, especially when that clarity lets students understand, know, think, and act in ways that help them come to terms with the world in new and transformative ways.

But none of that matters unless a third question is addressed: *why?* What's the point? Years ago, as I sat trembling before my dissertation adviser ready to hear his comments on the draft I had submitted for my first chapter, he responded with what I now see as one of the salient questions of any kind of intellectual discourse. "This is good," he said. "But so what?" Behind every intellectual endeavor that question should be lurking. Why am I doing this? What does it matter? Who cares?

Those questions are really about motive. And while they go to the question of the *teaching* of moral courage, they are also directly relevant to the *expression* of moral courage. Any serious effort to teach moral courage, in other words, must help students address this brooding question, elephantine in size but easily ignored, about *why* I wish to act with moral courage in the first place.

Here three tests are useful. They are based on a perception of risk and benefit, an awareness of a potentially self-righteous response, and the effect on innocent parties. Since these three are related to the dilemma-resolution principles outlined in chapter 4, they can also be called the ends-based, the rule-based, and the care-based tests.

The first of these, the ends-based **risk-benefit test,** asks whether the risk incurred is proportionate to the benefit received. Will this bold stand make a difference? Will my actions be commensurate to the situation? These questions are ends-based because, in accordance with the utilitarian principle of moral reasoning, they focus largely on consequences. If the amount of benefit spread over a number of individuals outweighs the risks to a few that might arise from a particular action, then perhaps the action should be pursued. If, in other words, my acting boldly will produce more good than harm, I can feel some measure of comfort in taking the stand. As in any kind of utilitarian assessment, such calculations are not easily made. The efficacy of the test, nevertheless, lies in its ability to turn my attention toward outcomes, to be sure I'm properly assessing the potential dangers and the rewards.

By contrast, the rule-based **self-righteousness test** asks whether, as I consider doing something that seems morally courageous, I'm really just getting on my high horse about a deeply held personal belief. Could it be that I'm wrong? Am I daring, or am I just stubborn? Like the rule-based reasoning in support of Kant's categorical imperative, this test looks not at consequences but at the principle underlying the action. Is this a principle I would like to see made universal? If everyone in the world were led to take a bold position out of motives just like mine, would the world be a better place? Or would there merely be more stiff-necked inflexibility, more smug self-assurance? This, too, is not an easy test. The line between proper self-regard and intellectual or moral vanity is often blurred. That's especially true in matters of moral courage, where, as we saw in chapter 6, the role of self-confidence and trust in one's own abilities can provide a significant impulse toward morally courageous action.

Finally, the care-based **innocent-parties test** asks who else will be affected by my actions. What impact will my bold stand have on those around me? If I'm truly concerned about my neighbors, my community, and the world at large, will I take this stand? Like the care-based principle of the Golden Rule, this test asks me to put myself in another's shoes and ask what it would be like to bear witness to—or the brunt of—the action I'm considering. This test recognizes that moral courage doesn't usually happen in a vacuum. Such acts often affect the entire community. Would I like to be part of the community in which someone was setting out to do what I'm about to do?

Why are these three tests important? Because the idea of being a morally courageous actor can be appealing—frightening, yes, but at times oddly alluring. For that reason, we need to check our thinking to be sure that our action is proportionate, that we're not being driven by selfish emotion, and that nobody around us is getting hurt unnecessarily.

TEACHING IN ACTION: POLLY'S UNWED VISITORS

Lest the above comments appear focused solely on classroom teaching, it's worth remembering that with moral courage, as with any kind of ethical endeavor, teaching is a constant. The very doing of moral courage is, in some way, the teaching of it. That fact came home to me when I got a note from Polly about the broad ripples created by her family's stand for a controversial aspect of moral courage.

Polly, who grew up in the United States, married Rolf, a college friend from Germany, and settled in California. When their sons were entering their teens, Rolf got a note from his unmarried half-sister in Germany, Helga, asking if she and her boyfriend could come for a visit. Rolf was quick to invite them but added that they needed to know that they would be sleeping in separate rooms.

At first Helga and her boyfriend took his comment as a joke. But as the visit drew nearer, Rolf reiterated his position and made clear his reason for it. Their sons were at a stage where they were not listening to what their parents were saying as much as watching what their parents were doing. Having seen the ravages of licentiousness in the culture around them, he and Polly felt strongly that they needed to transmit a clear message to their sons that sexual activity belonged within the context of marriage rather than outside it.

When Helga realized that Rolf was serious, she began to get other family members involved. "Soon snide remarks, charges of hypocrisy and arrogance, and laughter at our juvenile American values came floating across the ocean," Polly writes. "Great explanations of the differences between our cultures were proposed. 'It's a European thing,' we were told." Finally, when Rolf's father got involved, "it got ugly. We realized that taking a stand for *our* values was being interpreted by them as a judgment on *their* values."

Rolf's response, she reports, was persistently affectionate but firm. He explained that, even though he had not lived up to these values in his younger days, he was trying to present a higher standard to his children. He noted, too, that he was passing no judgment on his family members' lifestyles. As far as he was concerned, they were free to do whatever they wanted when they were by themselves. But when they were under his roof, he simply asked them to abide by his rules.

After months of correspondence, Helga and her family gave in—or seemed to. But when she and her boyfriend arrived, they were still not convinced that Rolf meant what he said. Only after he helped the boyfriend pull out the sofabed in the living room—and then escorted Helga to the back bedroom—did it dawn on them that he really was serious. "They were not pleased," writes Polly with evident understatement.

The two visitors made several side trips while they were there but spent most of the time with Polly and Rolf. "After the initial shock of that first night," she says, "we really had quite a nice visit."

The whole experience, as Polly makes clear, was a challenging one. She and Rolf were forced to clarify their own thinking and decide whether and how to square their values with their actions. Whether or not you agree with their values, one thing is clear: in today's climate, it took significant moral courage to espouse that position and stick to it under the barrage of trans-Atlantic criticism. The risks to family unity were severe. The willingness to endure challenged their own self-confidence. And the principle upon which they stood seemed at times unpopular, perhaps even outmoded.

Or so they thought. "But what happened after this whole episode," Polly says, "is what continues to amaze me. We had no idea how many people were watching us. We knew our children were—and that's what mattered to us. But people would say to us, 'I didn't really know what you would end up doing,' or 'I was in the same situation and didn't think it was a big deal—and now I wish I had taken a stand,' or 'I guess it's more important to stand up for your values, even if it means offending someone.' "

Two of their sons, she writes, are now in college, and many of their friends bring boyfriends and girlfriends home. "Our sons know anyone is welcome," Polly says, "but they also know what the sleeping arrangements will be, even without asking." She notes that "other friends and relatives have referenced us in defense of stands they are now taking. It was a small thing, and yet it has made a tremendous impact."

Which, in the end, is how moral courage typically operates. Though large and daunting to the actor, the issue may seem small in the context of the world's challenges. Yet the impact—the teaching and learning—can be profound. To some, no doubt, the issue that caused Rolf and Polly's agonizing seems (as their German relatives asserted) "juvenile." But the topics it touches upon—sexual freedom, abstinence, promiscuity, marriage, and the attendant issues of birth control, abortion, and AIDS—are at the top of the agenda in many Third-World countries. How moral courage applies to these and other topics in today's news is the subject of the following chapter.

Moral Courage Checklist
Step 7: Learning Moral Courage

Is moral courage a question of nature or nurture? If we're not born with it, how do we get it? Three of the most common methodologies for attaining courage are:

1. **Discourse and discussion**—using rational inquiry to explore narratives about courage, understand what it is, and grasp its relevance.

2. **Modeling and mentoring**—engaging real-life exemplars to demonstrate moral courage in action and to coach, guide, and help chart the path toward it.

3. **Practice and persistence**—finding ways to build our skills by doing courageous things, following Aristotle's famous dictum "we become . . . brave by doing brave acts."

But is this act of moral courage genuine? What are our reasons for engaging in it? Here three tests apply:

- The ends-based **risk-benefit test,** which asks whether the risk incurred is proportionate to the benefit received.

➤

- The rule-based **self-righteousness test,** which asks whether I'm really just getting on my high horse about a deeply held personal belief—whether I'm daring or just stubborn.

- The care-based **innocent-parties test,** which asks who else will be affected by my actions and whether I'd want to live in a community where somebody's doing what I'm about to do.

In a world where moral courage has a certain allure, these are questions worth asking as we test our motives.

CHAPTER NINE

Practicing Moral Courage in the Public Square

I think we would all like to know that there are answers and it will all fit together—and we can make it fit together. I think that's why we go on.

—Lloyd Richards

Moral courage is usually seen as a personal rather than a public attribute. As the examples in this book suggest, it typically unfolds in the private, interior lives of individuals rather than across the consolidated consciousness of a community. "Courage is an intensely personal matter," writes former Procter & Gamble CEO John Pepper in reflecting on his career. "We muster and strengthen it in the depths of our hearts and souls, sometimes during the depth of night." But, I asked him, how do you *get* moral courage? His reply also focused on the individual. "Make sure you know what you really believe in, what you live and die by. And be clear on the mission of your life and the values you want to have guide it."

As we do that, of course, we may still be part of a larger group that collectively manifests moral courage. We may express our courage in relationships with others. Our stories can extend over time or unfold in multiple events. And the meaning of any one incident can sometimes be understood only by examining the fabric of an entire life in a communal context. But to study moral courage is typically to examine the lives and actions of leaders, heroes, and exemplars. Not surprisingly, this book has focused on such narratives.

Yet moral courage can be viewed through another lens, less personal and more topical. Through this lens we see not only the inward concerns of individuals but also the public and civic responsibilities of a community. Through it we spot the strands of moral courage woven into the fabric of entire cultures and nations. Through this lens the great issues of our day, shouting at us from the front pages or buttonholing us around the watercoolers of informal gossip, reveal themselves for what they are: studies in morally courageous action or, sadly, its opposite.

Moral courage, in other words, shows up not only in the cameo portraits of particular people but in the broad landscapes of daily journalism. Scratch hard enough at nearly any topic in the news, and you'll find beneath it a story of the presence or absence of moral courage in the public square.

- **Segregated public schools.** When Don Ingwerson became school superintendent in the greater Louisville, Kentucky, area in 1981, the system was in such racial turmoil that a federal judge had been put in charge of the district and the National Guard had been called in to maintain order. Rebuilding the district and winning the confidence of the community while under severe legal guidelines, Ingwerson realized that, as he told me, "the busing plan, while placing black and white children in the same school, was not addressing the learning needs of the children"—since children were often bused for only a year or two, playing havoc with the consistency of their educational progress. But his staff, speaking from years of experience in the community, warned him that changing the forced-busing plan would be "political suicide." If he advocated for change, he would be seen as insensitive to the needs of black youth, and his "future as an urban superintendent," he said with some understatement, would be "very limited." He was told it was best simply to accept the current situation and blame the legislature and the courts for the impasse. But summoning up the courage to overrule his staff, he set about to create magnet programs and "a voluntary plan" that would get students to *want* to ride buses. He knew it was working when, in 1985, he asked a suburban white parent why her child chose to attend a largely black inner-city magnet school an hour from home. "Because there is more at the end of this bus ride," the mother told him, "than we could find anywhere else." The plan became a national model, and in 1992 Ingwerson was named national superintendent of the year by the American Association of School Administrators.

- **Bureaucratic delays.** Immediately after David Kessler was appointed commissioner of the Food and Drug Administration (FDA) in 1990, he took sharp aim at medical-device manufacturers. Among his first acts, he shut down the angioplasty division of C. R. Bard, a leading developer of medical technologies. Its CEO was paraded from his office in handcuffs and three executives were later convicted on criminal charges. As CEO of Medtronics, Bill George faced a dilemma. His firm was facing delays of up to twenty-nine months in the approval process for new devices. Yet to complain could provoke Dr. Kessler's wrath. In his book *Authentic Leadership,* George recounts a 1992 meeting with Kessler during which one of his fellow manufacturers asked how they could best negotiate the sometimes wide disparities between federal law and the FDA. "Sir," he recalls Kessler retorting, "we deal with lots of criminals in your industry. We have an obligation to seek them out and put them in jail. Next question." Yet by 1993 George had concluded that his industry had to go public with its concerns. "By any measure this was an extremely risky strategy," he writes. But after reform legislation passed Congress in 1996, approval time dropped to less than six months. "In retrospect," George writes, "this story sounds exciting. At the time it was scary. . . . Most companies in this situation would have hidden behind their industry association [rather than] having the courage to speak out publicly against an injustice."

- **International drug trafficking.** When drug traffickers in Colombia need professional killers, or *sicarios,* they recruit teenagers who have creativity and stamina. Now Juan Guillermo Ocampo gets there first—luring kids into classical music programs instead. "Once you put a violin in the hands of a child and teach him to play," insists Ocampo, "he will never pick up a gun." Beginning in 1994 and working in the worst neighborhoods *(comunas)* of Medellín, then one of the world's most violent cities, he faced indifference, suspicion, and malice in starting what has become a string of schools. Now, from the thousands of students trained each year, five hundred come together into a youth symphony. His own modeling of courage has apparently become infectious: these students now serve as respected role models who, he says, can "walk wherever they want" in the turf-conscious *comunas.*

- **Human rights in wartime.** Documenting the tales of thirteen thousand ethnic Albanian women who were raped by Serbian forces in Kosovo, writer Sevdie Ahmeti spent years interviewing women and publishing their stories on the Internet. One night, acting on her husband's warning, she narrowly escaped through a window as soldiers burst through the front door of her home. Although she spent the next three months hiding in barns, cellars, and attics, she refused to leave the country or give up her work. "I am a human rights worker," she told a reporter at Colby College in Maine, adding with mock incredulity, "I leave to save my skin? It is moral to . . . interview people from a distance?" By the time the war ended after NATO intervention in 1999, eight of her family members had been killed. Now, as cofounder and executive director of the Centre for Protection of Women and Children in Pristina, she continues working with women and children suffering the effects of the war.

Ingwerson, George, Ocampo, and Ahmeti were cogs in a vast machinery of events surrounding some of the most challenging public issues of our age. Without these individuals, the issues would no doubt have shuffled ahead. But the courage they brought to bear on their situations set a direction, struck a chord, and kept the momentum moving toward clearer resolutions and a better world. While their contributions were modest by global standards, these people became, through moral courage, an inextricable part of the record of public life in the twentieth century.

But public events also show us, sadly, some appalling lapses in courage—and remind us, by reversal, of some useful lessons.

- **Olympic troubles.** The United States Olympic Committee (USOC) has been beset by reports of bribery, questionable drug testing, and board-level infighting. In May 2002 it faced another blow when its president, Sandra Baldwin, resigned. Ms. Baldwin—no longer "Dr. Baldwin"—precipitously left after learning that a reporter was about to blow the whistle on her résumé. She had never completed her doctorate at Arizona State University—and for thirty-five years had hidden that fact. By all accounts an effective executive as she moved up the Olympic ranks through treasurer and vice president, she had ample time to understand the high-profile nature of her successive posts and to muster the moral courage to correct the deception. But by the time of her election in 2000 as the USOC's first female president and chair, the lie had lain unchallenged for too long—reminding us that the window of opportunity for the courageous rectification of mistakes opens and then closes, and that moral convenience is not moral courage.

- **Unconscious racism.** Routing out old racial prejudices, as William Faulkner knew, takes moral courage—especially when, as in his novels, Southern culture historically set nobility and gentility side by side with racism and intolerance. In December 2002 Senate majority leader Trent Lott, a Mississippi Republican, found himself on the wrong side of moral courage after making apparently pro-segregationist comments at the hundredth birthday party of retiring South Carolina senator Strom Thurmond. His apology only made matters worse. By explaining that he was not using "prepared remarks" but was instead "winging it," he left the impression that his unscripted thoughts and the unguarded utterances he used among friends reflected an unchallenged racism in his thinking. He left his leadership post in disgrace shortly afterward, reminding us that a failure of moral courage can be a career-ending move.

- **Airline safety.** On May 11, 1996, ValuJet Airlines flight 592 crashed into the Everglades, killing 110 people. It turned out that workers for SabreTech, a maintenance company, had improperly loaded aboard 144 uncapped oxygen generators, and one worker, Eugene Florence, had signed off on paperwork saying he had installed the caps. Florence, pressured to move quickly in a corporate culture that cut corners, lacked the moral courage that could have saved 110 lives.

When moral courage instructs us by its absence—as it does in these three examples—it is often because an opportunity was missed. A failure of courage in the public square frequently stems from oversight, stubbornness, or a too-cozy commitment to the convenience of the moment. At bottom, it is a failure to assess risk. If Baldwin, Lott, and Florence have one thing in common, it is that they never correctly assessed the enormity of the dangers they faced. In the end, each could plausibly say, "I had *no idea* it would come to this!"

Some of the issues in the public square, then, involve chicanery, mendacity, perversity, fraud, and a host of other turpitudes. As we watch them emerge—often from a fog of ambiguity into the sunlight of jaw-dropping clarity—we may find ourselves expressing outrage, disgust, sadness, and a range of other emotions. But on one thing we're clear: what we're seeing is flat wrong. That's when we look around to see where the ethical leadership will come from. That's when we long for someone to take a courageous moral stand in right-versus-wrong situations.

But even those who take such stands may not always prevail, as Kathleen Wheaton well knows. She was an operator for Sprint long-distance services who overheard a conference call ten days after the ValuJet crash in which, she says, a top ValuJet executive admitted the company failed to operate the plane safely. She chose to speak up, only to have the judge rule out her testimony as hearsay. Was she right to seek justice through truth-telling? Or would it have been more right to remain loyal to her professional standards of protecting confidentiality and privacy? Her example reminds us that one person's unethical busybody can be another's courageous exemplar.

THE COURAGE OF ENGAGEMENT

Kathleen Wheaton's example illustrates another application of courage— call it the courage to engage—that is called forth by a different kind of public decision making. Those choices involve right-versus-right dilemmas, where the toughest choice is not between one course of action that is wholly right and another that is dead wrong but between two morally powerful rights. In our public lives, where we debate the policies and practices that will determine our collective future, our most common dilemmas arise from right-versus-right issues. That's also true in our private lives. As we try to determine what's best for our family, career, and personal growth, we're not usually torn by decisions between a good and a bad but between two right courses of action. And for good reason. Neither civic policy nor personal endeavor typically presents us with choices where all the angels are on one side. What makes these topics so complex—what turns them into issues requiring moral courage—is the fact that they present us with not *one* but *two* powerful moral arguments.

In such situations, the role of moral courage is not to help us take a stand for right but to help us engage. It is to encourage us to step firmly up to the decision-making process rather than duck responsibility. In the face of right-versus-wrong temptations, it can take courage to say, "This is wrong, and it must be corrected." Had Sandra Baldwin done so, she might still be USOC president. Had Trent Lott done so, he could easily have retained his position as Senate majority leader. And had Eugene Florence done so, 110 people might still be alive. In the face of right-versus-right dilemmas, however, it can take a more subtle kind of courage to say, "This must be addressed. We must think hard, arrive at a resolution, and choose a position—even though there is right on both sides." Failing to engage—standing by, shifting from mental foot to mental foot, taking a wait-and-see approach—is at times the worst kind of failure of moral courage. It's the sort of passive, do-nothing inertia famously derided in a statement attributed to Edmund Burke that "the only thing necessary for the triumph of evil is for good men to do nothing." Or, as the classic 1960s graffito put it, *Not to decide is to decide.*

But how are such right-versus-right issues to be addressed? It can take moral courage to know *what* to think. It can take even more courage, however, to focus instead on *how* to think. In the complex world of public issues, this latter kind of moral courage—the bold willingness to address a multifaceted problem that may have no single right answer—is much needed. What's required, as the following three examples suggest, is the courage of engagement.

SARS AND THE ETHICS OF WARNING: WHEN DO YOU SOUND THE ALARM?

In the fall of 2003, when the epidemic of severe acute respiratory syndrome (SARS) had finally abated, the Ontario Hospital Association at its annual meeting in Toronto heaped well-deserved praise on the nurses and other health-care workers who braved frightening uncertainties to help patients. No doubt about it: they demonstrated individual courage, both moral and physical.

But the way SARS hit Canada is emblematic of the need for an expression of moral courage that goes beyond frontline health-care workers and engages us all. At the beginning of April 2003, Toronto was a benign and welcoming city in one of the world's most peaceable nations. By month's end it was a pariah. Travelers canceled trips. Concerts and conventions evaporated. The hotel and restaurant trade imploded. The reason: a travel advisory slapped on the city by the World Health Organization (WHO).

That advisory, as Canadian officials were quick to argue, struck just as SARS seemed to be leveling off in the city, with no new cases reported outside the hospital system for nearly a week. It happened in the absence of any visits from WHO officials. And it came in contradiction to findings from the Centers for Disease Control and Prevention in the United States, which found no reason for travelers to avoid Toronto.

Was the advisory justified? At issue is a question of moral courage with implications far beyond Canada. When does a word of warning become a promotion of panic? Where's the line between justifiable caution and unconscionable scaremongering? Who has the courage to draw that line? How do you alert people without terrifying them?

Few would disagree that the requirement to alert the unwary is a moral imperative. Knowing the danger and giving no warning is a culpable offense. Yet it can take great moral courage to sound the alarm, knowing the damage that may happen as the public reacts. On the other hand, to provoke exaggerated fear is irresponsible and immoral. Cranking a low-level risk into an international calamity is patently unethical. Yet when the momentum of fright is building and people are running for cover, it can take just as much moral courage to *refuse* to bugle an unnecessary warning.

Such questions face public officials everywhere, from superintendents closing schools for a blizzard to police urging precautions during the Washington, D.C., sniper attacks. It surfaces every time the Department of Homeland Security raises the U.S. terrorism warning another notch. It agonizes health and agriculture officials facing bovine spongiform encephalopathy, or mad cow disease. It clearly touched WHO officials. And on each occasion it calls upon reserves of ethical decision making and moral courage. Those reserves will only become more necessary as this century advances, for three reasons.

- **Media hype.** Panic, like disease, is contagious. It spreads through media sensationalism; publicity is the key to its success. As the omnivorous appetite of the twenty-four-hour global news cycle zeroes in ever more tightly on anything that will bring eyeballs to the screen, such hype may well increase. Had the WHO travel advisory been issued three weeks earlier, it would have come at the height of the U.S. invasion of Iraq. Would the media have cared? Would the advisory have clobbered Toronto as hard? Or would it have been overlooked?

- **Global technology.** The SARS epidemic exemplifies a now-familiar pattern in which technology leverages ethics in unprecedented ways. Fifty years ago, a SARS virus couldn't have circumnavigated the globe so rapidly. Nor could travelers. Nor could a travel advisory by a United Nations organization. These days, globalism connects the world for good and for bad. Will SARS lessen the willingness of corporations to invest in places that, like China, notably erred on the side of nonwarning during that epidemic? If so, would that response then be prudent caution or panicky overreaction? And how will the corporate world express the moral courage to make that call?

- **International terrorism.** There's an odd similarity between terrorism and SARS. Both appear to attack at random, within a civilian population, and without warning. Both engender fear through publicity. Both cause people to hunker down, seek shelter, avoid movement and crowds, disrupt their normal routines, and put plans on hold—all of which slow the economy. Terrorism has prompted us to seek new trade-offs between liberty and lockdown, surrendering a little freedom for a little more security. Will SARS, building on that model, push us even further toward lockdown? If it does, will that shift reflect courageous realism or cowardly capitulation?

Behind these issues lurks another trend: a public indulgence of fear. Horror flicks, ghost stories, roller coasters—think of all we do, willingly and deliberately, to frighten ourselves. Finding a small reason for fear, some will puff it up into a dreaded obsession. All the more reason, then, for public leaders to develop the ethics of warning. Engaging these issues at a deep enough level to find the balance between bland dismissal and terrifying overstatement may be one of the most morally courageous acts of leadership in the twenty-first century.

Sexually Abusive Priests: Is There a Right Way to Handle Wrongdoing?

When the sex-abuse scandal among Catholic priests in the United States flared into global attention early in 2002, one thing was immediately clear: this issue was not new. The fact that men in authority were sexually preying on the young in their trust had been rumored for decades. So had something else: an apparently institutional lack of moral courage in the handling of such cases among the church hierarchy.

By the end of that year, the scandal had claimed the career of Cardinal Bernard Law, who resigned as archbishop of the Boston archdiocese over what the Massachusetts attorney general called an "elaborate scheme" to cover up the issue. But accounts of abuse continued to surface, along with tales of cover-ups among the bishops, payoffs to the abused, and quiet transfers of priests to faraway parishes. Reforms, audits, and Vatican edicts were designed to stop the abuse. Yet the issue continued to generate massive public fascination. Why?

In part because it was not just a "Catholic problem." Predatory sexuality targeting the young was exposed in Protestant organizations and non-religious groups as well. In April of 2002 James Cobble, executive director of Christian Ministry Resources, told *The Christian Science Monitor* that "this problem is even greater with the Protestant churches simply because of their far larger numbers." The issue also surfaced in such nonsectarian organizations as the American Boychoir School in Princeton, New Jersey, and the Boys Choir of Harlem in New York.

True, some Catholic commentators noted that their church provided particularly good cover for such activity. But the fact that it occurred elsewhere, and could involve married as well as unmarried men, suggested that one potential reform—allowing priests to marry—might not fully address the issue. The story, in other words, was big enough that even non-Catholic and nonreligious citizens took interest in it.

In part, too, the fascination arose because this was a story about more than pedophilia. That fact became evident when, just as the crisis was reaching a full and rolling boil in the spring of 2002, readers found church sex-abuse stories running on the same front pages with articles about a United States Supreme Court decision on child pornography. Citing free speech principles, the Court struck down federal laws prohibiting the creation, distribution, or possession of "virtual" child pornography made through computer imaging of young people rather than through filming real children. The Court's decision reminded us that abuse by priests was but one form of a far deeper issue facing society: a growing insistence that sexual freedom should be a proper marker of modern culture, even if it involved the previously sequestered arena of childhood. That insistence required the public to draw ever finer distinctions between sexual practices that were proscribed and those that should be tolerated.

But the fundamental problem facing the Catholic Church was not the presence of sexual abuse. It was the absence of crisis management. The real issue was not that some priests preyed on their charges. It was that bishops and others in authority knew they were doing so and hushed it up in a long, sad litany of denial, deception, and deportation. So it was with former presidents Richard Nixon and Bill Clinton, who met their most crippling challenges not because of the Watergate burglaries or the Monica liaisons, but because each sought to cover them up. In the case of the church, the ire of the faithful was directed less at pedophile priests—who could be forgiven as sick, sinful men needing help—than at a hierarchy protecting itself at the expense of generations of children.

As with SARS, this story had a close relationship with the news media.

It fit well into a nothing-is-sacred form of contemporary journalism, willing to take on powerful institutions where just forty years ago it dared not even mention the sexual escapades of President John F. Kennedy. And it provided an almost textbook case of hypocrisy—St. Paul called it "spiritual wickedness in high places"—which for many people stands as the ultimate collapse of moral conscience. From a secular editor's perspective, in other words, this was a story made in heaven. It had all the elements that sell papers and TV programs: sex, power, and corruption in a famous institution. It had plenty of on-the-street interviews with real people who actually experienced this abuse. It fit the classic dramatic definition of tragedy, dealing with the fall of great men from high places. And, like the worst sorts of computer viruses, it was self-replicating: the more the story was told, the more former victims found the courage to come forth with their own tales.

At bottom, then, the issue of priestly abuse was and remains a many-faceted story of moral courage: the lack of it among church officials who covered up the abuse, the presence of it among the victims who came forth, the anguish over it among churchgoers who saw things and dared not speak up, and the perseverance of church leaders determined to get to the bottom of the issue, whatever the risks to their institution. In many aspects, it's a story of right against wrong. But in the desire of some church officials to address the issue without riding roughshod over the rights of priests—who sometimes stand accused by just one individual recalling decades-old incidents—there are tough right-versus-right dilemmas of truth-telling versus loyalty, of justice versus mercy, of the needs of the individual versus the needs of the community, and of short-term adjustments versus long-term effects. The moral courage needed to address these issues is the courage of engagement, the willingness to cut through all the reasons for inaction and step forward with determination.

THE JAMIE BULGER CASE: FREE SPEECH OR FREEDOM FROM MURDER?

On February 12, 1993, a video camera in a mall in Merseyside captured the opening moments of what would become one of England's most gruesome crimes. It showed the blurred image of a tot being led by the hand away from the camera by a larger boy. The tot, two-year-old Jamie Bulger, had been lured from his mother as she stopped to make a purchase at the butcher shop. His body was later found along a railroad track in nearby Kirkby, victim of a horrendous torture and murder scheme by two ten-year-olds, Jon Venables and Robert Thompson.

The boys were tried in British courts and sentenced to protective custody. Eight years later, when they turned eighteen, they were deemed no longer a threat to society, provided with new identities, and released. At that time, a High Court judge issued an injunction against the news media in England and Wales, making it illegal to publish any details of the boys' new identities or whereabouts. Why? The judge, Dame Elizabeth Butler-Sloss, noted that there remains a "sense of moral outrage" about the case. She cited the determination in some quarters to avenge Jamie Bulger's death—a determination still alive, if ongoing Web site commentaries on this case are any indication. And she called attention to examples of egregious media behavior that, if repeated, could threaten the lives of the boys. For those reasons, she said, she was forced to place the right of life above the right to free expression.

Even for a judge, that's a courageous call. Not surprisingly, the British press frothed into opposition, citing concerns about restrictions on reporting. Several newspaper groups asked the court to lift the injunction, although others recognized the limits of free speech and editorialized in support of the court.

This was no mere teapot tempest. Today's reporters have unprecedented access to long-range lenses, listening devices, and Web-based research tools. More important, international Internet service providers lie outside the scope of Judge Butler-Sloss's injunction. Even if no English or Welsh paper betrayed the boys' identities, they might very well be found out, and the news would be freely available on the Web. And while these Merseyside boys were officially declared to pose no threat to the community, there's a natural desire to know whether you're living next door to a former child-murderer. That desire is not always benign: British vigilantes have been known to firebomb the homes of pedophiles after the tabloids printed their names.

There is, then, a need for courage in the judiciary in protecting these two boys. And there's a need for courage in journalism to ferret out and publish the truth. But the courage of engagement is needed as well. It requires of each of us that we come to moral judgments about the major issues of our time and then be willing to take a stand for our positions—in this case, about the rights of former prisoners.

That may be especially true in the United Kingdom, where the Human Rights Act became law in October 2000 as a way to harmonize Britain's laws with those of the European Union. Under the act, those two ten-year-olds might have been judged too young to be tried. What if that act were to lead the British public to conclude that heinous crimes could never be properly punished on English soil? Would more vigilante squads take the law into their own hands? Following the boys' release, mobs in Wales reportedly threatened to torch the home of a woman wrongfully identified as the mother of one of them. Even Jon Venables's lawyer, Laurence Lee, noted that despite his client's new identity, "his life will never be the same again . . . he'll be hunted down and will always be looking over his shoulder."

The demands of public courage, then, force us to ask whether the culture we're creating is the one we want to live in—and, if not, to act in concert with others to take a stand and change things. Sadly, it sometimes takes a horrific event, like the murder of Jamie Bulger, to cause us to go out of our way to decry vigilantism, demand that the courts be honored even when we disagree, and give public and vocal respect to the concept of the rule of law.

A brief look at these three issues involving SARS, sex abuse, and free speech suggests that the courage of engagement is one of the needs of the hour. As with so many public issues, these three operate in a complex space that, like the world of quantum mechanics, has many more than three dimensions. Disentangling the interwoven strands of courage—noting its degrees of presence and absence among different players—can be a daunting task. But one point remains clear: looking at life through the lens of moral courage, you see things you would not otherwise see and understand interrelations that before were obscure. You engage in a different way.

FORGIVENESS AND PLAGIARISM: TWO GLOBAL THEMES

Ultimately, however, there are issues involving moral courage in the public square that are so large that they set trends, define themes, and shape the thinking of the age. These final two illustrations, from America's heartland and South Africa's poorest neighborhoods, suggest the role of moral courage (or its absence) in its most pervasive and overarching impact. They center on two global themes: plagiarism, or the courage to avoid appropriating others' creative work, and forgiveness, or the courage to forgo blame. These two ideas—about our relations to truth and our relations to others—lie at the heart of what it means to be human. They are related to two of our deepest moral values, honesty and compassion. How they are expressed, as we'll see, is largely a function of the moral courage we bring to them.

PLAGIARISM IN KANSAS

As a second-year teacher of high-school biology, Christine Pelton had no reason to think of herself as a hero. She was just doing her job in the best way she knew: laying out clear expectations for her 118 students, explaining the rudiments of biology, providing challenging topics, and demanding good work. Yet as the fall 2001 semester drew to a close, her moral courage would ignite a firestorm in the pleasant residential suburb of Piper, Kansas, twelve miles west of Kansas City.

That fall the curriculum she was teaching included an assignment that had been a staple of Piper's tenth-grade biology course for a decade. Starting in September, each student was asked to collect twenty different kinds of leaves, study them carefully, write a report on each, and deliver an oral presentation to the class on the results. The project would be worth 50 percent of their overall grade.

At the beginning of the semester, Pelton had asked students and their parents to sign a statement on plagiarism. "Cheating and plagiarism will result in failure of the assignment," the statement read, adding that "all work turned in by the student [must be] completely their own." She had no reason to think her statement was out of line: her own school board's policy, reflected in the student handbook, indicated that first offenders would receive no credit for a plagiarized assignment.

But as the written reports began coming in, Pelton became suspicious. So she ran them through a computer program at the turnitin.com Web site designed to detect similarities between student writing and prose found on the Web. The program scored twenty-eight direct hits. Needing no further proof, she gave each of those twenty-eight students a zero grade for the assignment—in effect failing them in biology that semester.

The response across that leafy and competitive suburb was immediate. Irate parents contacted the principal, Mike Adams, who did some checking of his own and confirmed that the students had indeed plagiarized. Undeterred, the parents swarmed to a December 11 meeting of the school board. They complained that Pelton was a new teacher. They doubted that the students really understood plagiarism. They demanded better grades.

So the seven-member school board, after a closed meeting that the state attorney general later said was illegal under Kansas's open-meeting law, instructed Superintendent Michael Rooney to require Pelton to reduce the penalty. When he reported the board's demand that she reduce the weighting of the project from 50 percent to 30 percent of the grade and deduct only 600 points from the plagiarists rather than the full 1,800 points the project was worth, she resigned.

As a beginning teacher still in a kind of probationary period, she might well have been removing herself permanently from the teaching profession. And in fact she didn't immediately seek another teaching position, announcing plans instead to run a day-care center from her home in nearby Olathe. Yet despite the risks, she hewed to her values. "In explaining her principled stance," writes Michael D. Simpson in the National Education Association *Rights Watch*, "Pelton said that one of the roles of teachers is to teach students 'to be honest people, to have integrity, to listen, to be good citizens. . . . I'm not expecting more than what would be expected of them either at home or down the road.' " On a more practical note, as she explained to *Education Week*'s Andrew Trotter, "I'd lost the kids' respect. I heard kids talking about that if they didn't like what I did in the future, they could go to the board of education and they could change that."

And there the matter might have stood but for the publicity. Over the coming months, the tale of Piper, Kansas, would be spread across national network news. Piper students would be jeered at interschool athletic events. At Kansas State University all twelve deans would sign a joint statement to the Piper school board, saying they expected Piper students who came to their campus to "buy into" their school's honor code "as a part of our culture." Robert E. Hemenway, chancellor of the University of Kansas, would write in his weekly message to the campus community on May 7, 2002, a brief note of praise for Pelton, a KU graduate, "for her display of personal courage, at a time when teaching positions are being cut all over Kansas for budgetary reasons." And by the end of March the school board's vice president, Leigh Vader, would be admitting that "all of us have gotten tons of hate mail, from all over the country. People are telling us we're idiots and stupid."

The good news from the Piper episode lies in the stern and outraged response from the public. Good, too, is the relative simplicity of the issues involved, the fact that they were contained within a few students, and the swift, uncompromising moral courage of Pelton's decision to resign.

But while she could not have known it, her action presaged a much larger debate on plagiarism. Within a month of her resignation, the media was awash with stories that two of the nation's most eminent historians—bestselling author Stephen Ambrose and Pulitzer Prize winner Doris Kearns Goodwin—had plagiarized extensively. And within eighteen months the *New York Times,* which had front-paged the Piper story, found itself embroiled in a plagiarism scandal created by a twenty-seven-year-old reporter, Jayson Blair, who resigned from the *Times* on May 1, 2003. Ambrose was pilloried for appropriating prose not only in his then-current bestseller, *Wild Blue,* but in three earlier books as well. Goodwin was accused of reproducing passages from historian Lynne McTaggert in her book *The Fitzgeralds and the Kennedys: An American Saga* as though they were her own. Blair's editors found him guilty of "frequent acts of journalistic fraud" in which he "fabricated comments," "concocted scenes," and "lifted material from other newspapers and wire services."

Suddenly the issue was not a group of teenagers trying to cut corners for an assignment that even if done right would be quickly forgotten. The issue was the way in which a nation tells itself the collective narratives about its past—and, by extension, its identity. It was, too, the brazen manner in which these passages were kidnapped (the root meaning of *plagiarize*) and passed off as original to these authors—almost guaranteeing that some reader, somewhere, having read earlier books on the same topics, would recognize the similarities and sound the alarm.

That history relies on truth-telling is obvious—and explains why historian Barbara Tuchman, in commenting on the writing of history, observed, "I do not invent anything, even the weather." For those who labor along the slopes where fact can easily slide into fiction—historians, journalists, private investigators—Tuchman articulates the gold standard of professional objectivity.

That doesn't mean such objectivity is easily attained. The boundary between reporting and interpreting is often elusive, sometimes philosophically unknowable. What matters is not only the intent to be original but also the rigorous commitment to truthfulness even when embellishment might intensify the drama. What matters, in other words, is the courage to stick to the task and do it right. Without that sense of integrity on the part of the historian, the public has no basis for trusting the resulting work.

Ambrose apologized graciously and immediately, calling the plagiarism inadvertent. But he never explained how it happened—though he promised to correct future editions of his works—and he died nine months later. Goodwin also apologized, admitting that fifteen years earlier her publisher had settled with McTaggert for an undisclosed sum. But she kept that settlement silent until forced to admit it. Under its terms, Goodwin added numerous notes to the paperback version of her bestseller, *The Fitzgeralds and the Kennedys.* Blair, in a statement following his resignation, referred to unspecified "personal problems." The *Times* investigation noted that in his final months "the audacity of the deceptions grew by the week, suggesting the work of a troubled young man veering toward professional self-destruction."

What should the public make of the ethics of all this? Start by dismissing three arguments that sometimes arise, especially among bright teenagers of the sort Pelton had been teaching.

- "Ownership of property is old-fashioned." This view holds that in the electronic age plagiarism is obsolete, since every created thing should belong to everyone. Such a notion conjures up bizarre analogies. Is every car, for instance, to be driven away by anyone who needs it, regardless of whether somebody else's grandmother is in the backseat? More important, this argument eviscerates creativity. If all art and literature can be freely appropriated, it's commercially worthless. And if nobody can make a living from creative work, only the comfortably rich or the deliberately impoverished will be creative.

- "Plagiarism doesn't count as long as the *intent* is not to steal." As with shoplifting, that argument carries some weight in sentencing offenders but little in determining their guilt. Whatever the motive, the deed has been done. Punishment having been promised, it ought to be exacted. Otherwise, arguments about intent only grease the slippery slope into the land of careless, lazy, and unpunished literary theft. Generations of young students, pushing the envelope in the face of so many distractions, have pleaded, "I *meant* to do it well!"

- "Readers and editors want bright writing in every day's paper and popular books unencumbered by footnotes." In this view, footnotes are a noisome distraction to the flow of the narrative. Tracking down every sentence borrowed from somebody else is mere pedantry. The only thing that matters is speed and sizzle. But if journalism is plagued by uninspired reportage and scholarship is drowning in a swamp of citations, the more obvious remedy entails the writing of prose so lively and original that it need not be lifted from nor credited to anyone else.

Is there, in fact, *any* argument that can excuse rather than simply explain plagiarism? It's not difficult to explain how, in an age of surface impressions and quick fixes, seeming originality passes for the real thing. Where the superficial can be made to look profound, what you seem to be counts for more than what you really are. It's as though success—notably among CEOs, stock analysts, and accounting firms, but also among journalists, historians, and school-board members—goes to those who make things *look* right rather than to those who actually *get* things right. Did students really fail to do their own work? We'll make it look as though they completed their assignments. Was this gripping bit of historical writing penned by someone else? I'll make it seem like my own. Is my reputation as a reporter at risk because I don't know enough to write the story I've been assigned? I'll appropriate a story from another newspaper. In the spin cycle of the information age, what wins in the short term are frequently not enduring facts but evanescent fictions.

Goodwin, reaching for an excuse, claims that her technique got in her way—in writing this book sixteen years earlier, before personal computers were ubiquitous, she took notes longhand and interspersed quotes from others with her own writing. While that tells us how plagiarism can happen, the explanation is in some ways more alarming than the problem. Historians, like bankers, are professionals. Would you trust a banker who, having "inadvertently" mingled your money with that of another client, pleaded poor technique and an inability to keep the funds straight? For a banker, skill with a ledger is a core competency. Similarly, for a historian to know who said what to whom—and whether you or someone else said it—is no mere optional talent. It's a central, bread-and-butter task.

Or at least it is for the professional historian who aspires to popularity. Is there a double standard? When the well-known plagiarize, they quietly settle. When ordinary folks plagiarize, they get dismissed from class or sent packing by their employers—and if that doesn't happen immediately, as in a Kansas high school or a national newspaper, the public roars its disapproval, school-board members are excoriated, and the top editor (as happened at the *Times*) eventually gets the sack. If plagiarism matters, plagiarists in high places owe us more than partial explanations, emended reprintings, and apologies extracted under duress. If plagiarism doesn't matter, then those in low places—high-school biology students and novice reporters, for instance—should be allowed to copy away merrily.

Sorting this out calls on moral courage in a variety of ways. When Christine Pelton resigns, we applaud the presence of moral courage. When her school board bows to parental pressure, we're jarred by its absence. When Jayson Blair self-destructs, we're struck by the lack of editorial courage that should have followed up on earlier suspicions—and there were many—about his work. When Stephen Ambrose and Doris

Kearns Goodwin waffle and equivocate, we're tempted to look for a new term—not exactly *moral idiocy,* but something suggesting our disappointment in finding a void right where the moral courage ought to be. Blair, Ambrose, and Goodwin could have stood up and said, "That's enough." In an ideal world, where the heft and drag of prominence was not so all-encumbering, they could even have resigned. Only one of them, Jayson Blair, did so.

But back in Piper, Mike Adams, the high-school principal, also resigned. His prose does not have the sonorous ring of a historical classic or the driving bite of a bestselling yarn. Instead, it speaks with a direct and simple sincerity. "The problem is, we have become a society that is unwilling to accept responsibility for our actions," Adams told an audience at Kansas State University's "Integrity Week" in 2003. "Right and wrong is no longer clear. We used to believe when we made choices, good or bad, there were going to be consequences for those choices. Now we have parents and adults telling students by their actions [that] they do not have to bear responsibility.

"I am not a hero," he added. "The real hero is a young lady, a young teacher, who had the courage to take a stand, and that is what students, parents, teachers and those in leadership need. They need the willingness to take a stand for what is right."

If the next generation is to learn by doing—rather than merely succeed by copying—taking that "stand for what is right" is essential to educators, editors, journalists, and historians. Sadly, the dominant scholarly mode among today's high-school students may be fabrication and deception: the Gallup Youth Survey for April 2003, for instance, found that among thirteen- to seventeen-year-olds, 67 percent report that "a great deal" or "a fair amount" of cheating goes on in their schools, and nearly half say they themselves have cheated. Was Jayson Blair one of those students? Did he so fully absorb the trends of his school that he slipped easily into plagiarism and duplicity? Did no teacher, perhaps fearing school-board retribution, ever explain to him exactly what's wrong with plagiarism or hold him accountable for doing his own work? In his higher education courses, was he taught by historians who had only a fuzzy grasp on the dangers of literary kidnapping?

In an age when information is so vital and the pressure on it so acute, who is tending the boundaries between fact and fiction, honesty and duplicity, being and seeming? If readers can't have confidence in the honesty of the reporters and historians they read, democracy itself is at risk. And if the moral courage to stand up to plagiarism in public life begins to atrophy—through bad examples at the top and confused responses down through the ranks—how can the reader trust the writing? "Accuracy is all we have," noted the *Times*'s metropolitan editor, Jonathan Landman, commenting on the Blair situation. "It's what we are and what we sell." That's not a bad motto for high schools and historians, too.

FORGIVENESS IN THE VAAL

She sat on a straight chair with her back to us, sobbing. Her audience, facing her on rough wooden benches in the parish hall of a local church, waited patiently. She was partway through telling her harrowing story— a tale of life as a black woman courageously going about her daily life under the apartheid regime in rural South Africa—when the tears caught up with her.

As they caught up with most people. From where we sat up front, behind a head table decorated with a white lace tablecloth and red napkins opened diamondwise, we could see their faces over her gently heaving shoulders. Many were elderly, creased with the enervating dailiness of this dusty, impoverished township of Evaton, thirty miles from Johannesburg, in a farming region known as the Vaal. Others, younger, were poised with promise but already seared with resignation in this job-scarce economy. There were infants and great-grandparents, young men in leather jackets, and middle-aged women in bonnets and Sunday finery. From the front row, four women in blue-and-white vestments led the hymn-singing after each story. Except for us three Americans, all were black.

They had gathered again that October Monday morning in 1999, as they regularly did, for the latest episode of a long, somber national catharsis. Elsewhere, in the nation's major population centers, the Truth and Reconciliation Commission (TRC) had finished its work. Earlier that fall it had released its final report. Its purpose, as Archbishop Desmond Tutu said in his book *No Future Without Forgiveness,* was not to "let bygones be bygones" but to ensure, through eighteen months of sometimes excruciating testimony, that "no one in South Africa would ever again be able to say, 'I did not know' and hope to be believed."

As in Chile and other countries drained by decades of tyranny, in South Africa the TRC's method was courageous. There was to be no general amnesty either for whites from the apartheid government or for blacks from the resistance movements. But anyone who came forward and told all the truth—down to the details of where bodies could be found and returned to their families—would be granted individual amnesty. By seeking facts rather than meting out retribution, the TRC had made sure that the truth would finally come out.

And out it came, in agonizing accounts of murders, rapes, kidnappings, torture, mindless brutality, and shockingly intelligent hatred. "This was the kind of testimony that made me realize that there is an awful depth of depravity to which we can all sink," wrote Archbishop Tutu. "We have supplied God with enough evidence for Him to want to dispatch us all, to wipe the slate clear as He did before with the Flood, and try to make a fresh start."

The phrasing is vintage Tutu. As a man of the cloth and a man of color, his language moves so fluidly between the human and the divine—between the grisly realities of carnage and mayhem and the illuminations of grace and peace—as to suggest that they are somehow one. I remember noticing that use of language in a meeting with him five years earlier at Bishopscourt, the official residence of the Archbishop of Cape Town. I visited him several months before the 1994 election—one of the world's most widely televised, producing the unforgettable images of mile-long lines of black and white voters snaking amicably toward the ballot box to elect Nelson Mandela as their president. When our small delegation was seated in Tutu's salon and the conversation had turned (as it so effortlessly does in South Africa) to politics, I asked him how he could account for what everyone foresaw would be a remarkably peaceful election. Why, after years of intense struggle, was South Africa apparently not going to go the way of Northern Ireland, or the Middle East, or Sri Lanka, or the rest of the world's fiery and vengeance-soaked trouble spots?

He had two answers. First, he replied, every South African household has a Bible—a contention that, if not wholly true, is probably not far from it. Second, the tribes across the nation share a common commitment to *ubuntu,* a Zulu word roughly meaning compassion or respect for others. Traced back to the Zulu maxim, "a person is a person through other persons," it meant, Tutu said, that I am not complete until you are complete, nor happy until you are happy. Revenge, he confidently predicted, would not consume South African blacks once they were in power. They would, instead, forgive.

And forgive they did, although even the TRC—branded by some scoffers as the Kleenex Commission for all the tears it engendered—could interview only a sliver of the afflicted. So every week that fall, in so many of the Evatons across so many Vaals in South Africa, the unheard voices of the overlooked were speaking to one another. We were invited to that church by members of the Khulumani Support Group, a nongovernmental organization with deep ties to this community. That day, they told us, there were four languages being spoken. I sat beside one of the organizers, Traggy Maepa, who whispered translations into my ear as best he could as the tales unfolded.

When the woman in the straight chair reined in her tears and continued, she told how her son was shot dead while his wife was pregnant—and how the police, told of the murder, said, "This thing's not a case!" The next witness, Theodore, told a similar story: his son was murdered, and the police took no action. Another woman told of soldiers telling her that, because she was black, she could no longer run the shop that was her only livelihood. Many speakers told of white-on-black violence. But some had black-on-black tales as well. And those who suffered most, it seemed, were the women. As the testifiers came forward one after another, and the wind rattled the corrugated iron roof and sighed through the ill-fitting steel-framed window, I began to comprehend the immense moral courage of a people who, with every reason to rise in violent hatred against their oppressors, were willing instead to forgive.

Later that day, I talked with Duma Khumalo, one of our hosts. He was well known to the audience—and, indeed, across South Africa—as one of the Sharpeville Six. With five others, he had been accused of murdering a local official during a mob protest in Sharpeville in 1984. Found guilty under a new "common purpose" law that held no one of them accountable for the murder but charged them all collectively, he had come within twenty-four hours of being executed in 1988. He had finally been released in 1991 after the new law was called into question.

Did he feel hatred? "It depends," he told me. He remembered a prison warden who, after one of his hearings, came up and hugged him and shared his address and phone number. And the judge who sentenced him? If he were still alive, "I would forgive him," said Khumalo, because "we were from different areas" and different traditions. The harder thing, he said, is to forgive black-on-black violence—the kind of criminality and political activism that makes blacks not safe in their own townships.

So he understood the swirl of emotions in the parish hall in Evaton. The meetings there had been going on for eight months, he said. For Khumalo, it was all part of the strange but powerful ethic of forgiveness. "It's a complicated situation, forgiveness," he mused. "We want to remember our heroes. We can forgive, but not forget—because if we forget, it may happen again."

Two days later and a world away, I had breakfast in the upscale Johannesburg suburb of Rosebank with one of the TRC commissioners, Fazel Randera. A medical doctor long active in the antiapartheid movement, he, too, understood the delicate complexities of forgiveness in a political situation.

"There's always the argument that the Truth and Reconciliation Commission is there as a compromise," Dr. Randera admitted. By awarding amnesty to those who told all, he added, the TRC had been accused of "trading justice for truth." And while he recognized that feelings still ran deep and that "the forgiveness part is a long ways away," he credited the TRC with moving the country away from retribution and revenge and toward "the new moral society we all want to see."

There's a straight line, it would seem, from morality through courage to forgiveness. It may be, in fact, that one of the highest forms of moral courage is expressed in the ability to forgive those who have brutalized you—to forgive, as Khumalo said, "but not forget." Of the four ways to combine those two terms, I suspect that only the last really makes moral sense:

1. *Forgive and forget.* This common phrase marks a position that, for many, is the easiest way out. But as Archbishop Tutu writes, "the past, far from disappearing or lying down and being quiet, is embarrassingly persistent, and will return and haunt us unless it has been dealt with adequately. Unless we look the beast in the eye we will find that it returns to hold us hostage."

2. *Neither forget nor forgive.* This is the stuff of revenge—and of tragedy. Shakespeare and his fellow Elizabethan playwrights peopled the stage with characters howling for vengeance and bearing their hatreds to untimely graves. The problem with revenge, of course, is that it is never satisfied: there is always someone else ready to avenge the latest murder that was supposed to square the circle and end the violence.

3. *Forget, but don't forgive.* This curious formulation fits those who nurse grudges to such monumental proportions that the animosity outlasts the incident that provoked it. Perhaps the sorriest ethical

void is that inhabited by people who can't remember why they hate someone but still feel the malice.

4. *Forgive, but don't forget.* This, the South African response, is the most difficult. Where amnesty is not allowed to turn into amnesia, the challenge is to honor the memories of those whose blood, as Khumalo put it, "will nourish the freedom of this country." It also demands, as Tutu and the TRC insisted, something from those seeking forgiveness: they must first come forward and ask for it.

Forgiving without forgetting also requires the most moral courage—in part because it is the most controversial option. I got some inkling of the courage required of those who supported the TRC process in a conversation in Johannesburg with a young professional woman of mixed race.

"When you grow up here," she told me, "justice is *such* a key issue. The TRC is kicking against a wall that's thicker than the Chinese wall. You *hate* that commission—it *cannot* be right that [perpetrators] go scot-free!"

Then she paused, as though surprised at her own vehemence. "But at least," she added thoughtfully, "the TRC is making people talk about ethics."

And talking about ethics is what, in the end, determines a culture's moral momentum. Does the rule of law depend, to some degree, on the willingness to set aside eye-for-an-eye formulas about personal retribution, replacing them with forgiveness and compassion? Can that set-aside happen in the absence of moral courage? Without such courage—among sobbing black women and sober TRC commissioners, among fiery young reformers and former death-row inmates—can justice itself survive? The lesson from South Africa may be that there can be no justice without forgiveness, and no forgiveness without moral courage—and that forgiveness may be the only way to secure peace in the coming century. In shorthand, that reads: collective moral courage is essential for world peace.

The Candle and the Closet:
A Closing Parable

Truth-telling and forgiveness, then, are two of the most sweeping themes in contemporary public life. While the above stories illustrate only small parts of these themes, the themes themselves will continue to shape our public discourse on topics as diverse as Iraq, immigration, investing, internment, and a host of other hot-button issues.

But arguably the most crystallizing public event for the coming years will prove to be the terrorist attacks on the United States on September 11, 2001. The collapse of the World Trade Center permanently altered the New York City skyline. Even more powerfully, it changed the moral thoughtscape of America and our willingness to think deeply about topics like moral courage. The intense public cruelty of that day, and the courage expressed in facing it, drove us to the windows of the soul—to new depths of introspection, new ranges of ethical questioning, and new recognitions of the role of moral and physical courage. All across this otherwise pragmatic and down-to-earth nation, the air was filled with oddly metaphysical questions: Who are we? Why are we here? How do we understand our purpose? What can I do?

That last question concerns the individual's role in the face of evil. It's a profoundly moral question. For many people the answer is "I ought to get involved, lend a hand, help out in some way." But there's a nagging doubt. Can my involvement really change the world? Even if I, and all my friends and all their friends, had the courage to band together and help, could we make an impact? Compared to the six billion people in the world today, we're but a rounding error. Can my moral courage really make a difference in the face of so much that violates the ethical canons of humanity?

I'm convinced it can. Let me share a parable.

Some years ago, I interviewed a number of people in the States and overseas for a newspaper series on global education. Among the interviewees were several African American men in their thirties. Each had grown up in a terrible ghetto environment. And each had "made it" and was successful.

Why, I asked them, had they succeeded? Why had they not been gunned down at age eighteen in a neighborhood alley as, statistically, they should have been? Each, using different specifics and a different name, told me essentially the same story: it was old Mrs. Smith in the fourth grade who really turned them around.

"But wait," I asked them. "You've just told me about your schooling, where you had dozens of dreadful teachers. You've just told me about your large and dysfunctional family, where hardly anyone seemed to care. You've just told me about your scores of friends—many now in jail, others now dead—who set all the wrong examples. And now you're telling me that, in the face of that relentless downdrag of depravity, Mrs. Smith alone lifted you up?"

"Yes," each one said, "that's what I'm telling you."

In itself, that fact doesn't surprise us. We all know, intuitively, the enormous power of a single right example. The question is, *Why* should that be so? Why is it not equally true that a child raised in caring, attentive surroundings can meet one bad teacher and be plunged into a life of crime and vice? Somehow that's far less observable.

To understand why, perform the following experiment. Find a closet somewhere in your home that's been closed up for years. It's been shut so tight that no light can get in. If there's any place darkness could grow thick and rich and ugly, this is it.

Now turn off the lights in the room outside the closet and light a candle. Open the closet door, and watch closely. Does that appalling darkness gush forth with such virulence that it extinguishes the candle and plunges you into utter blackness? In the entire history of the world, that has never once happened. Always, unfailingly, the candlelight illumines the closet and dispels the darkness.

That, too, is observable. It doesn't surprise us. But why should it be so?

For one simple reason: light is not the *opposite* of darkness but the *absence* of darkness. If light and dark were opposites, we'd be playing a zero-sum game with the forces of antilight every time we opened a closet. And about half the time the darkness would win. Maybe, if we pulled together a thousand candles, we could just barely defeat such a grisly accumulation of blackness—but only for a while, until the closet forces regrouped and came roaring back to defeat the candle.

Put that way, it sounds silly. Yet notice how our language works to persuade us that darkness and light are equal but opposite powers. We're so used to thinking in terms of opposites—positive and negative charges in electricity, north and south poles in magnetism, up and down, left and right, yin and yang—that we let our metaphors overwhelm us.

"Oh, yes," we assert, without examining our premises, "the world is made up of opposites." And then we take the next logical step. "Light and dark," we say. "They're opposites, too. Even night and day are evenly balanced—in the course of a year, there's about as much of one as of the other. Therefore darkness is the opposite of light."

That mistake might be relatively harmless, were it not for one final logical misstep. We seize on light and dark as our principal metaphor for good and evil, right and wrong. We imagine that they, too, are opposites. We think of ourselves as locked in combat with the powers of wrong that are balanced on a knife-edge against the forces of right. What will it take, we ask, to defeat such a terrible force? Surely all the goodness in the world, if we could scrape it together, would barely be enough to overcome this equal and opposite power.

But what if we've missed the real message of the metaphor? What if wrong is not the *opposite* but the *absence* of good? Doesn't that explain how old Mrs. Smith could single-handedly overcome the inertia and emptiness of our young friends' ghetto upbringings? Wouldn't it seem odd, in fact, if wrong *ever* seemed to prevail in combat with good? Wouldn't it seem bizarre in the extreme if an absence of something could defeat its presence?

Don't get me wrong. I don't mean to minimize the complexity and perversity of the world's evil. I couldn't possibly overlook the stories in this book—especially those from South Africa, Chile, Russia, Kosovo, and Nazi Germany—that would cry out in objection to such a Pollyanna position. I don't for a moment imagine that the forces of depravity will evaporate just because we shift metaphorical gears—that, for instance, terrorism will instantly disappear because we analyze it in a different way. But I'm equally sure that, until we think clearly about evil, we will never master it successfully. Such clarity begins with the understanding that, however massive the assertions of evil, they bear witness only to an absence, not to an opposite.

And that helps explain something else: that just as a single candle can destroy a whole closetful of darkness, so a single life, lived in the light of goodness and moral courage, can make an enormous difference in overcoming the reverberating void that calls itself evil, blackness, doubt, cowardice, fright, or mere bravado. If wrong really is, in some fundamental way, the absence rather than the opposite of right, is it any wonder that each one of us—expressing our highest sense of moral courage, living it to the fullest, and passing it along to others—really can change the world?

Notes

Chapter One: Standing Up for Principle

1 "You gain strength": Eleanor Roosevelt, *You Learn by Living* (New York: Harper & Brothers, 1960), pp. 29–30.

1 St. Paul's School cancels lacrosse season: Andy Carpenter, "MD School Puts Athletics in Perspective: Lacrosse Season Is Canceled over Player's Sex Tape," *Boston Globe*, April 22, 2001, A14.

3 Juan Julio Wicht expresses solidarity: Rushworth M. Kidder, "President's Letter," Institute for Global Ethics, March 1998.

8 "courage is being scared to death": John Wayne, Brainyquote.com, http://www.brainyquote.com/quotes/j/q104746.html (accessed August 26, 2001).

9 Isaiah Berlin notes that courage "has . . . been admired": Ramin Jahanbegloo, *Conversations with Isaiah Berlin* (London: Peter Halban, 1992), p. 37.

13 Officer Mike Bocelli on bike patrol: Andi Atwater, "Ex-officer Pleads No Contest," http://www.news-press.com/news/local_state/p_031125officer .html (accessed November 25, 2003).

14 Andrew Hamerling fails to abide by his conscience: "NASD Fines and Suspends Banc of America Securities Analyst," NASD Press Release, Washington, D.C., December 9, 2003, http://www.nasdr.com/news/ pr2003/release_03_059.html (accessed January 3, 2004).

18 "I do not invent anything": Barbara W. Tuchman, *Practicing History* (New York: Alfred A. Knopf, 1981), p. 18.

Chapter Two: Courage, Moral and Physical

19   "Courage without conscience": Robert Green Ingersoll (1833–1899),
     American lawyer, orator. Speech, May 29, 1882, New York City.

25   "smale foweles": Chaucer, "General Prologue," *The Canterbury Tales*
     (New York: Rinehart, 1954), pp. 9–11.

25   "I'd such a courage to do him good": Shakespeare, *Timon of Athens* 3.3.24,
     The Complete Works of Shakespeare, ed. George Lyman Kittredge (Boston:
     Ginn and Company, 1936), p. 1060.

25   "courage never to submit or yield": Milton, *Paradise Lost* 1.109, *John Mil-
     ton: Complete Poems and Major Prose,* ed. Merritt Y. Hughes (New York:
     The Odessy Press, 1957), p. 214.

26   "the greatest of all virtues": Samuel Johnson, quoted in James Boswell's
     Life of Johnson, April 5, 1775, cited in William Ian Miller, *The Mystery of
     Courage* (Cambridge, Mass.: Harvard University Press, 2000), p. 5.

26   "courage is not simply *one* of the virtues": C. S. Lewis, *The Screwtape Let-
     ters* (San Francisco: Harper, 1942), pp. 161–62.

27   "courage makes for better stories": Miller, *Mystery of Courage,* p. 8.

27   "courage and its corresponding vice": Ibid., p. 7.

28   "the distinction between heroism and courage": Ibid., p. 74.

28   "no man is a hero to his valet": John Bartlett, *Familiar Quotations,* 13th
     ed. (Boston: Little, Brown, 1955), p. 61.

29   "Oliver Cromwell's hypocrisy neutralized": Compton Mackenzie, *On
     Moral Courage* (London: The Quality Book Club, 1962), p. 11.

29   "Moral courage is readiness to expose": Ibid., p. 12.

29   Mackenzie takes Stephen to task: Ibid., p. 12.

29   "facing the pains and dangers of social disapproval": Henry Sidgwick, *The
     Methods of Ethics* (London: Macmillan, 1913), p. 333, n. 3, quoted in
     Miller, *Mystery of Courage,* p. 254.

29   "the courage of shocking conventional opinion": Mackenzie, *On Moral
     Courage,* p. 101.

29   "letting down the side": Ibid., p. 45.

29   "one of the hardest tests of a man's moral courage": Ibid., p. 139.

30   "The cry of distress": *Wagner v. International Railway,* Court of Appeals
     of New York, 232 NY 176; 133 NE 437 (1921). My thanks to Dan Mollway
     of the Hawaii State Ethics Commission for calling my attention to this
     case.

31   "In nine cases out of ten": Mackenzie, *On Moral Courage,* p. 45.

31   "believe me when I tell you": King Edward VIII quoted in ibid., p. 86.

31 "physical courage was a characteristic of the Hanoverians": Ibid., p. 84.

32 "act of tremendous moral courage" and "a piece of royal willfulness": Ibid., p. 91.

32 "not always easy": Ibid., p. 240.

32 "the capacity to overcome the fear of shame": Miller, *Mystery of Courage*, p. 254.

32 "derision, ostracism, loss of status, demotion, loss of job" and "not trivial": Ibid., p. 258.

32 moral courage . . . can be undone by physical cowardice: Ibid.

32 "decays under the intense and relentless demands of combat," "grows by the doing of deeds," and "Standing up for what we think is right": Ibid., p. 65.

32 "moral courage is the courage of the military leader": Ibid., p. 260.

32 "No doubt the majority of the duels": Ulysses S. Grant, *Personal Memoirs of U. S. Grant* (New York: Library of America, 1990), p. 44, quoted in ibid., p. 261.

33 "big-boned, square-jawed" and "undoubtedly brave when it came to physical danger": Norman Dixon, *On the Psychology of Military Incompetence* (New York: Basic Books, 1976), p. 55.

33 "so busy being gentlemen": Ibid., p. 53.

33 "lost no time trying to rid himself of any direct responsibility": Ibid., pp. 56–67.

33 "It requires greater moral courage": Ibid., p. 396.

34 "moral cowardice, indecisiveness, secretiveness and sensitivity to criticism": Ibid., p. 255.

34 "the enforcing virtue": John McCain with Mark Salter, *Why Courage Matters: The Way to a Braver Life* (New York: Random House, 2004), pp. 42, 43.

34 Compton Mackenzie's spiritual perspective: Mackenzie, *On Moral Courage*, pp. 22, 23.

35 "there is little need to carve out," "people could undertake to support unpopular causes," and "loss of social standing": Miller, *Mystery of Courage*, p. 263.

Chapter Three: The Courage to Be Moral

39 "If humanity is to survive": Václav Havel, speech, September 19, 2002, Graduate Center of the City University of New York.

43 "a keeper of the conscience of their community" and "a center of moral gravity": Rushworth M. Kidder, *Shared Values for a Troubled World: Conversations with Men and Women of Conscience* (San Francisco: Jossey-Bass Publishers, 1994), p. 17. The interviewees were Oscar Arias (Costa Rica), James K. Baker (United States), Shojun Bando (Japan), Derek Bok (United States), Kenneth Boulding (United States), Nien Cheng (China), Jill Ker Conway (Australia), Dame Whina Cooper (New Zealand), John W. Gardner (United States), A. H. Halsey (Great Britain), Le Ly Hayslip (Vietnam), Salim el Hoss (Lebanon), James A. Joseph (United States), Jeane Kirkpatrick (United States), Astrid Lindgren (Sweden), Graça Machel (Mozambique), Federico Mayor (Spain), Newton Minow (United States), Sergio Muñoz (Mexico), Bernard Przewozny (Poland), Reuben Snake (United States), Varindra Tarzie Vittachi (Sri Lanka), Katharine Whitehorn (Great Britain), and Muhammad Yunus (Bangladesh).

47 Values Jenny Smucker tracked: Jenny Smucker, former chair, Character Education Committee of the Heartland Education Community, and Maribeth Badertscher, manager, Community Initiatives, J. M. Smucker Co., telephone interviews with author, Orrville, Ohio, January 9, 2002.

51 State of the World Forum survey results: William E. Loges and Rushworth M. Kidder, *Global Values, Moral Boundaries: A Pilot Survey* (Camden, Maine: Institute for Global Ethics, 1997), p. 9.

52 Executive Values (figure 3): William E. Loges and Rushworth M. Kidder, proprietary survey results (Camden, Maine: Institute for Global Ethics, 1999), p. 11.

53 Executive Values in a Merger (figure 4): Ibid., p. 7.

54 Illinois Community College Board survey results: William E. Loges, Rushworth M. Kidder, and Charles R. Novak, *Leadership and Values: The People of Illinois and Their Community Colleges* (Camden, Maine: Institute for Global Ethics, 1999), p. 14.

54 Commonality of survey results: Ibid., p. 15.

55 Nathan Cummings Foundation survey results: William E. Loges and Rushworth M. Kidder, *Reaching Out: Broadening College-Student Constituencies for Environmental Protection* (Camden, Maine: Institute for Global Ethics, 2000), p. 10.

56 BD survey results: Becton Dickinson, "BD Values Survey Summary," September 2001, PowerPoint presentation.

56 Maricopa Community College survey results: William E. Loges, Rushworth M. Kidder, and Paula Mirk, "Maricopa Values and Ethics Survey" (Camden, Maine: Institute for Global Ethics, 2001, photocopy), p. 5.

58 CARE Bangladesh survey results: William E. Loges, "CARE Bangladesh Values and Ethics Survey" (Camden, Maine: Institute for Global Ethics, 2001), p. 3.

60 Levi Strauss "Ethical Principles": Although not on the Levi Strauss Web site, *Inc.* magazine offers the list at http://www2.inc.com/search/14404.html.

60 McDonnell Douglas code: Kidder, *Tough Choices,* p. 83, note for p. 98 on p. 321.

61 "an academic community of integrity": The Center for Academic Integrity, *The Fundamental Values of Academic Integrity* (Des Plaines, Ill.: Oakton Community College Office of College Relations, 1999), p. 5.

61 "Carolinian Creed": Read the entire creed at http://www.sa.sc.edu/creed/.

61 The Honor Code of the United States Air Force Academy: Read about the code and its history at http://www.usafa.af.mil/pa/media/facts/honor.htm.

61 UC Berkeley Haas School of Business undergraduate code of ethics: http://www.haas.berkeley.edu/undergrad/ethicscode.html.

62 OECD report: Organization for Economic Cooperation and Development, *Trust in Government: Ethics Measures in OECD Countries* (Paris: OECD, 2000), p. 11.

63 "common denominator of culture": George P. Murdock, "The Common Denominator of Cultures," *The Science of Man in the World Crisis,* ed. Ralph Linton (New York: Columbia University Press, 1945).

63 "spiritual values": Abraham H. Maslow, *Religions, Values, and Peak-Experiences* (New York: Penguin, 1970), p. 4.

63 "Being-values": Ibid., p. 91.

63 ". . . the path toward a harmonious global society": Wendell Bell, "The Clash of Civilizations and Universal Human Values," *Journal of Futures Studies* 6, no. 3 (February 2002).

64 "human moralities throughout the world:" Paul Bohannan, *How Culture Works* (New York: The Free Press, 1995), p. 180.

65 Core values definitions: Walker Research Incorporated, "Global Values and Ethics Study" (Indianapolis: June 10, 1994).

66 "core virtues" and "character strengths": C. Peterson and Martin E. P. Seligman, *Character Strengths and Virtues: A Handbook and Classification*

(New York: Oxford University Press; Washington, D.C.: American Psychological Association, 2004).

66 "There is astonishing convergence": Martin E. P. Seligman, *Authentic Happiness: Using the New Positive Psychology to Realize Your Potential for Lasting Fulfillment* (New York: Simon & Schuster, 2002), p. 11. See also Christopher Peterson and Martin E. P. Seligman, "Values in Action (VIA) Classification of Strengths," Values in Action Institute, draft January 4, 2003, http://www.positivepsychology.org/viamanualintro.pdf and http://www.positivepsychology.org/viamanualcourage.pdf.

69 "to see what is right": Confucius, *Analects*, bk. 2, chap. 24, quoted in James Legge, trans., *Confucian Analects, the Great Learning, and the Doctrine of the Mean* (1893; reprint, Mineola, N.Y.: Dover Publications, 1971), p. 154.

69 "no moral value in itself": Susan Sontag, "On Courage and Resistance," *The Nation*, May 5, 2003, p. 12.

71 "deeply concerned about the overreaching of federal law enforcement authorities": Rushworth M. Kidder, "Timothy McVeigh: Moral Courage or Moral Vacuity?" *Ethics Newsline* (Camden, Maine: Institute for Global Ethics), June 4, 2001, vol. 4, no. 23, http://www.globalethics.org/newsline/members/issue.tmpl?articleid=06040107410662.

76 Four tests to distinguish significance: I am indebted to Theodore J. Gordon for these categories.

Chapter Four: The First Circle: Applying the Values

77 Weyerhaeuser hotline: Nancy Thomas-Moore, interview with author, Orlando, Florida, October 1, 2003.

80 Definition of whistle-blowing: Roberta Ann Johnson, *Whistleblowing* (Boulder, Colo.: Lynne Rienner Publishers, 2003), p. 3.

81 Boisjoly's testimony: Ibid., p. 35.

81 European Commission resignation: Paul van Buitenen, *Blowing the Whistle: One Man's Fight Against Fraud in the European Commission* (London: Politico's Publishing, 2000), p. 166.

81 Impact of General Maxwell Taylor's book on JFK: Harry J. Maihafer, *Brave Decisions: Moral Courage from the Revolutionary War to Desert Storm* (Washington, D.C.: Brassey's, 1995), p. 209.

81 "So often, whistle-blowers don't think that far ahead": Dana Gold, telephone interview with author, October 14, 2003.

82 "When we scrutinize the personalities": Heinz Kohut, *Self Psychology*

and the Humanities: Reflections on a New Psychoanalytic Approach (New York: W. W. Norton, 1985). Quotations appear on pp. 5, 6, 10–12, 15–16, 20.

85 For an explanation of "bystander apathy," see Bibb Latané and John M. Darley, *The Unresponsive Bystander: Why Doesn't He Help?* (New York: Appleton-Century Crofts, 1970).

89 The four dilemma paradigms: Rushworth M. Kidder, *How Good People Make Tough Choices: Resolving the Dilemmas of Ethical Living* (New York: Simon & Schuster, 1995), pp. 18–23, 109–50.

90 Explanation of the four dilemma paradigms: Ibid., p. 113.

92 Three resolution principles: Ibid., pp. 154–61.

93 "I ought never to act": Immanuel Kant, *The Moral Law: Kant's Groundwork of the Metaphysics of Morals,* trans. H. J. Patton (London: Hutchinson and Co., 1961), p. 70.

96 "ambiguous undulations": Wallace Stevens, "Sunday Morning," *The Collected Poems of Wallace Stevens* (New York: Alfred A. Knopf, 1965), p. 70.

99 "resulted in his political crucifixion": John F. Kennedy, *Profiles in Courage* (New York: Harper & Brothers, 1956; reprint, New York: Perennial Classics, 2000), p. 58.

99 "few politicians have had the distinction": Ibid., p. 69.

100 "I shall stand by the Union": Daniel Webster, quoted in ibid., p. 74.

100 "what is essentially good": Kant, *The Moral Law,* p. 84.

101 "This is the young lady": Matt Apuzzo, staff writer, "Bowman Placed on Probation," *Standard-Times,* November 13, 2002, http://www.southcoasttoday.com/daily/11-02/11-13-02/a01lo005.htm.

101 "I said, 'Are you guys really' ": Ibid.

101 "I should never have let myself": Ibid.

102 "the flaw in the granite": John F. Kennedy, *Profiles in Courage,* p. 61.

102 "great ego" and "thin-skinned mentally": Ibid., p. 76.

107 "I cannot and I will not recant anything": Martin Luther quoted at http://www.luther.de/en/worms.html.

Chapter Five: The Second Circle: Recognizing the Risks

109 "Gloucester, 'tis true": Shakespeare, King Henry in *Henry V* 4.1.1–2.

110 "the lunatic, the lover, and the poet" and ". . . in the night": Shakespeare, *A Midsummer Night's Dream* 5.1. 21–22.

112 Cody's Books keeps *The Satanic Verses* on the shelves: http://www .lib.berkeley.edu/LDO/bene53/codys/html.

119 "I felt the expressive silence": Francine Kiefer, "Good Germans: One Family's Odyssey in Opposition to Hitler" (unpublished manuscript, 2002), p. 27.

120 "the choice between the United States and England": Ibid., p. 42.

120 "the USA . . . sinks like a stone": Ibid., p. 44.

120 "I have already let father know": Ibid.

121 "Exasperated and impatient": Ibid., p. 46.

121 "I am constantly asking myself the meaning of life": Francine Kiefer, "Good Germans: One Family's Odyssey in Opposition to Hitler" (proposal to publisher), p. 6.

122 "Those eight years in Czechoslovakia": Francine Kiefer, "No Turning Back: One Family's Odyssey in Opposition to Hitler" (preliminary proposal to publisher), p. 17.

122 "the full advantage of mankind": Ibid., p. 4.

122 "Ironically, it is the very day": Ibid., pp. 15–16.

123 "I am in the heating and air-conditioning business": Albert Slottje, e-mail message to author, July 14, 2003.

133 J. Alfred Prufrock: Excerpts are from T. S. Eliot, "The Love Song of J. Alfred Prufrock," *The Complete Poems and Plays 1909–1950* (New York: Harcourt, Brace & World, 1952), pp. 3–7.

Chapter Six: The Third Circle: Enduring the Hardship

139 "Never give in": Winston Churchill, speech at Harrow School, 1941.

139 Tom Armstrong's Mount Logan ordeal: Tom Armstrong Jr., interview with author, Freeport, Maine, December 9, 2002.

147 "Trust inevitably requires some sense of mutuality": Charles Handy, "Trust and the Virtual Organization," in Frederick F. Reichheld, ed., *The Quest for Loyalty: Creating Value through Partnership* (Cambridge, Mass.: Harvard Business Review Books, 1996), p. 40.

147 "Dignity extended to employees": John Dalla Costa, *The Ethical Imperative: Why Moral Leadership Is Good Business* (New York: HarperCollins, 1998), p. 232.

147 "an emotional strength": Robert K. Cooper and Ayman Sawaf, *EQ: Emotional Intelligence in Leadership & Organizations* (New York: Grosset/ Putnam, 1996), p. 84.

148 "integrity . . . creates the trust": Stephen Carter, *Integrity* (New York: Basic Books, 1996), p. 31.

148 "the basis of trust": Warren Bennis, *On Becoming a Leader* (Reading, Mass.: Addison-Wesley, 1989), p. 41.

148 Kouzes and Posner's four questions: James M. Kouzes and Barry Z. Posner, *Credibility: Why Leaders Gain and Lose It, Why People Demand It* (San Francisco: Jossey-Bass, 1993), p. 109.

149 John Gardner's qualification of trustworthy behavior: John W. Gardner, *On Leadership* (New York: The Free Press, 1990), p. 33.

149 "Of all the attributes": Kouzes and Posner, p. 24.

149 "ordinary decency": Elaine Sternberg, *Just Business* (London: Little, Brown, 1994), p. 7.

149 *The Fifth Discipline Fieldbook:* Cited in Cooper and Sawaf, *EQ*, p. 85.

150 "requires three steps": Carter, *Integrity*, p. 7.

150 "Contrary to business school doctrine": James C. Collins and Jerry I. Porras, *Built to Last: Successful Habits of Visionary Companies* (New York: HarperBusiness, 1994), p. 8.

150 "A visionary company": Ibid.

154 "ethic of justice": Quotations are from Carol Gilligan, *In a Different Voice: Psychological Theory and Women's Development* (Cambridge, Mass.: Harvard University Press, 1982), pp. 3, 19, 66, 105, 174.

154 "heroics of action": Quotations are from Mary Beth Rose, *Gender and Heroism in Early Modern English Literature* (Chicago: University of Chicago Press, 2002), pp. xi, xii, xiv, xxi, and 113.

157 Šimon Pánek's Prague protest: Šimon Pánek, interview with author, Prague, Czech Republic, May 14, 2002.

158 "Many in Prague": William H. Luers, "Czechoslovakia: Road to Revolution," *Foreign Affairs,* Spring 1990, vol. 69, no. 2.

162 Krogh's loyalty: Egil Krogh, "Wings of Defeat: Integrity Lessons of a Nixon White House Plumber" (unpublished manuscript, 2003), p. 6.

164 Krogh's statement to the Court: "Statement of Defendant on the Offense and His Role," Presentencing report from the defendant to Judge Gerhard A. Gesell, United States District Court, District of Columbia, January 3, 1974.

168 Terms of Nisha Sharma's dowry: James Brooke, "Dowry Too High. Lose Bride and Go to Jail," *New York Times,* May 17, 2003, p. 1.

168 "Getting his daughter married": Monica Chadha, "Three 'Weddings' and No Dowry," BBC News, November 19, 2003, http://news.bbc.co.uk/1/hi/world/south_asia/3283989.stm.

168 "today in Punjab and Haryana": "What Is Dowry?" *India Together,* http://www.indiatogether.org/women/dowry/pledge.htm.

169 "I'm mad as hell": Paddy Chayefsky, quoted in *The Columbia World of Quotations* (1996), http://www.bartleby.com/66/14/11614.html.

170 "People say now it will be very difficult": Brooke, *New York Times,* op. cit., p. 5.

170 "She said she wants to leave the past behind": "Three 'Weddings,' " Chadha, BBC.

Chapter Seven: Fakes, Frauds, and Foibles: What Moral Courage Isn't

175 "Courage is a moral quality": Lord Charles McMoran Wilson, *The Anatomy of Courage* (New York: Houghton Mifflin), p. 67.

176 "People sometimes make errors": "Mars Climate Orbiter Team Finds Likely Cause of Loss," NASA/JPL press release 99-113, September 30, 1999, http://mars.jpl.nasa.gov/msp98/news/mco990930.html.

177 "The problem here": Ibid.

182 "terrible pressures": Kennedy, *Profiles in Courage,* p. 4.

182 "is founded upon the principle": Henry Clay, quoted in ibid, pp. 4–5.

182 "few if any issues": Ibid., p. 5.

182 "It should not automatically be assumed": Ibid., p. 6.

183 "Mark, the great trouble with you": Ashurst, quoted in ibid., p. 8.

183 "the pressure of [the] constituency": Ibid., pp. 9–10.

183 "the fine art of conciliating": Ibid., p. 5.

185 "upon the instruction" and "excluded him": International Skating Union, press release, Lausanne, Switzerland, April 30, 2002, http://www.isu.org/vsite/vfile/page/fileurl/0,11040,4844-130559-131867-26140-0-file,00.pdf.

186 Le Gougne's failure to act: Selena Roberts, "Early Tears: Sign of Scandal to Come," *New York Times,* February 17, 2002, sec. 8, p. 1.

187 "were 97 miles shy of the South Pole": Dennis N. T. Perkins, Paul R. Kessler, and Catherine McCarthy, "The Race to the South Pole" (unpublished paper, Branford, Conn.: The Syncretics Group, 2003), p. 4. Used by permission of the authors.

187 "the extraordinary leadership and teamwork" and "they all survived": Dennis N. T. Perkins, Margaret P. Holtman, Paul R. Kessler, and Catherine McCarthy, *Leading at the Edge: Leadership Lessons from the Extraordinary*

Saga of Shackleton's Antarctic Expedition (New York: AMACOM, 2000), p. 10.

188 "Scott made a last minute decision": Perkins, Kessler, and McCarthy, "The Race to the South Pole."

192 "prearranged armed fight": "Duel," *Columbia Encyclopedia,* 6th ed. (2001), http://www.bartleby.com/65/du/duel.html.

193 "a copy of the Code Duello": Barbara Holland, "Bang! Bang! You're Dead," *Smithsonian* (October 1997), http://www.smithsonianmag.si.edu/smithsonian/issues97/oct97/dueling.html.

198 "By thinking of things": James Joyce, *A Portrait of the Artist as a Young Man* (New York: B. W. Huebsch, 1916), p. 45.

198 "the working-class section": Bruce Golding, "The Viscome Case: Party Turns to Chaos," *The Journal News,* White Plains, N.Y., October 6, 2002, http://www.thejournalnews.com/viscome/06viscomemain.html.

199 "grabbed Viscome by the neck": Ibid.

199 "I yelled to everybody to call the cops": Ibid.

200 John Colapinto's account: "As Rob Lay Dying," *Rolling Stone,* June 12, 2003, p. 84.

200 "the presence of other people": Bibb Latané and John M. Darley, *The Unresponsive Bystander: Why Doesn't He Help?* (New York: Appleton-Century Crofts, 1970), p. 38.

200 Latané and Darley's four reasons: Ibid., p. 125.

201 For a thorough definition and discussion of "groupthink," see Irving Janis, *Victims of Groupthink: A Psychological Study of Foreign-Policy Decisions and Fiascoes* (Boston: Houghton Mifflin, 1972), http://en2.wikipedia.org/wiki/Groupthink.

202 Examples of groupthink causing failures in decision making: *Groupthink,* (Carlsbad, Calif.: CRM Learning, 1992), video.

203 "turn a blind eye": Rupert Cornwell, "Pressure Builds for Reforms after Senate Finds Enron Directors Knew of Crisis," *The Independent* (London), July 8, 2002, cited in N. Craig Smith and Michelle Quirk, "From Grace to Disgrace: The Rise & Fall of Arthur Andersen" (unpublished case study, London Business School, 2003), p. 10. Used by permission of the authors.

203 "high risk," "pushing limits," and "not one director": John Byrne "No Excuses for Enron's Board," in "Special Report: The Angry Market," *Business Week,* July 29, 2002 (issue 3793), p. 50, cited in Smith and Quirk, "From Grace to Disgrace," p. 10.

203 "a red flag the size of Alaska": Ram Charan et al., "Why Companies Fail," *Fortune* (Asia) 145, no. 11, May 22, 2002, p. 36; cited in Smith and Quirk, "From Grace to Disgrace," p. 11.

204 "Defining Deviancy Down": Quotations are from Daniel Patrick Moynihan, "Defining Deviancy Down," *American Scholar* (Winter 1993), http://www2.sunysuffolk.edu/formans/DefiningDeviancy.htm.

208 "I noticed that something was a little fishy": ABC News, "Winning Values," *World News Tonight*, November 7, 2003, http://abcnews.go.com/sections/WNT/PersonofWeek/pow031107_haasis-1.html.

208 "It is my belief" and "In respect to my teammates": Jim Litke, "Sportsmanship Isn't Dead, Just Hiding," Associated Press, November 5, 2003, http://www.mercurynews.com/mld/charlotte/sports/other_sports/7187143.htm?1c.

209 "[Haasis] was leaning" and "And when someone": Ibid.

210 "When I was in West Africa": Paul Bohannan, *How Culture Works* (New York: The Free Press, 1995), p. 181.

Chapter Eight: Learning Moral Courage

213 "Suddenly and surprisingly": Robert Coles, *Lives of Moral Leadership* (New York: Random House, 2000), p. xiv.

214 Mónica Jiménez de Barros receives a threat: This material is based on a telephone interview with the author on December 19, 2003, and an e-mail on the same date, as well as earlier extended conversations with Ms. Jiménez de Barros in Chile and the United States over a ten-year period.

219 James K. Baker's tough decision: This material is drawn from a telephone interview with the author on December 30, 2003, as well as numerous discussions with Mr. Baker in Indiana and elsewhere over thirteen years.

226 Jesse Cottonham's intervention: This material is drawn from a written account by Pally Cottonham (August 3, 2003) and an interview by the author with Jesse Cottonham on January 8, 2004.

230 "we become just": H. Rackham, trans., *Aristotle: The Nicomachean Ethics* (London: William Heinemann, 1962), p. 73.

230 Duke University conference sessions: Kenan Institute for Ethics, Conference Program, Fourth National Conference on Moral Education in a Diverse Society, December 23, 2003, http://kenan.ethics.duke.edu.

231 "All who have meditated": According to the Library of Congress, the "fate

of empires" quote attributed to Aristotle "is widely spread over the Internet but with no attribution as to the citation from Aristotle's work. Such a situation is an alert that perhaps it is not actually a quotation from Aristotle, but someone's version of a thought in line with something Aristotle wrote" (e-mail to E. Marcus Fairbrother II, January 29, 2004).

231   "faculties given to us by nature": Quotations are from Rackham, trans., *Aristotle,* pp. 71, 73.

232   Focus of the Foundation for Moral Courage: Foundation for Moral Courage Web site, http://moralcourage.org (accessed December 24, 2003).

232   "Moving people to stick their necks out": The Giraffe Project Web site, http://www.giraffe.org (accessed December 23, 2003).

233   Three-stage learning process of the Giraffe Project's Heroes Program: Ibid.

233   Anne Frank Trust's videos: *Moral Courage: Who's Got It? Helping You to Introduce Citizenship: A New Teaching Handbook from the Anne Frank Trust* (London: Anne Frank Trust, 2000), pp. 11, 18.

234   *Courage the Cowardly Dog:* TV Tome Web site, http://www.tvtome.com/ tvtome/servlet/ShowMainServlet/showid-6157/ (accessed December 23, 2003).

234   "teach courage, perseverance": City Software Web site, http://www.citysoftware .com.au/products/productdetails.asp?PartNo=FDN001 (accessed December 23, 2003).

234   *Billy Goats Gruff & Other Stuff:* Center for Puppetry Arts Web site, http://www.puppet.org/perform/billygoatsgruff.shtml (accessed December 23, 2003).

235   U.S. Naval Academy's Leader of Character Seminars: United States Naval Academy Development Seminars Web site, http://www.usna.edu/Char-acterDevelopment/seminars/seminars_index.html (accessed December 23, 2003).

235   "isn't what you know": The Courage Institute Web site, http://www .courageinstitute.org (accessed December 23, 2003).

235   "These five strengths": Ibid.

235   "build character": Australian School of Self-Defence Web site, http:// www.johngill.com.au/benefits.htm (accessed December 23, 2003).

236   "get a chance to test": John Leonard, "Sixteen Values that Swimmers Learn from the Sport," *American Swimming Coaches Association Newsletter,* vol. 2002, no. 4, p. 18.

236   "doing your job": David Frum, "David Frum's Diary—Aug. 13, 2003: Courage III," *National Review Online,* http://www.nationalreview.com/ frum/diary081303.asp (accessed December 23, 2003).

236 "reinforces the team mentality": Ibid.

236 "teach courage, respect": "Plains Indian Seminar—2001 Seminar Overview: Circles of Knowledge," Buffalo Bill Historical Center Web site, http://www.bbhc.org/pis/2001overview.cfm.

236 "not everyone is brave": Tian Xiuzhen, "Acrobats Teach a Lesson of Courage," *Shanghai Star,* November 11, 2001, http://appl.chinadaily.com.cn/star/2001/1122/vo2-3.html (accessed December 23, 2003).

237 "always encourage [your child]": "Courage and the Child," Islamic Information and Support Center of Australia Web site, http://www.iisca.org (accessed December 23, 2003).

239 Three tests of moral courage: I am indebted to Patricia Born for developing these three tests.

Chapter Nine: Practicing Moral Courage in the Public Square

245 "I think we would all": Lloyd Richards, *An Agenda for the 21st Century* (Cambridge, Mass.: The MIT Press, 1987), p. 142.

245 "Courage is an intensely personal matter" and "We muster and strengthen it": John E. Pepper (unpublished manuscript, Cincinnati, Ohio, 2003), p. 346.

245 "Make sure you know": John E. Pepper, telephone interview with author, November 18, 2003.

246 "the busing plan": Don Ingwerson, e-mail and conversations with author, July and August 2003.

247 "Sir, we deal with lots of criminals": Bill George, *Authentic Leadership: Rediscovering the Secrets to Creating Lasting Value* (San Francisco: Jossey-Bass, 2003), pp. 178–79.

247 "By any measure": Ibid., p. 178.

247 "In retrospect": Ibid., p. 185.

248 Juan Guillermo Ocampo's intervention: Quotations appear in the "profile" prepared in 2001 by Ashoka, a global nonprofit organization that invests in social entrepreneurs around the world. Juan Guillermo Ocampo is an Ashoka Fellow. See http://www.ashoka.org/home/index.cfm.

248 Sevdie Ahmeti: The profile of Sevdie Ahmeti was prepared by the Oak Institute at Colby College, Waterville, Maine, June 2003, http://www.colby.edu/oak/fellows/ahmeti.html.

249 USOC president Sandra Baldwin resigns: Frank Litsky, "U.S. Olympic

Chief Quits Over Her Lies on College Degrees," *New York Times,* May 25, 2002, p. 1.

252 "the only thing necessary": Attributed to Edmund Burke. According to *Bartlett's Familiar Quotations,* this quotation has never been located in Burke's writing, but it is attributed to him.

255 "elaborate scheme": Stephen Kurkjian, "Reilly Says He Has Evidence of Coverup by Archdiocese," *Boston Globe,* December 13, 2002, http://www.boston.com/globe/spotlight/abuse/stories3/121302_reilly.htm.

255 "this problem is even greater": Mark Clayton, "Sex Abuse Spans Spectrum of Churches," *The Christian Science Monitor,* April 5, 2002, http://www.csmonitor.com/2002/0405/p01s01-ussc.html.

259 "his life will never be the same": "The Hardest Case," *The Big Issue in the North,* http://www.bigissueinthenorth.com/Magazine/bulger.html.

261 "Cheating and plagiarism will result in failure": Michael D. Simpson, "Taking a Stand for Integrity," *Rights Watch,* May 2002, http://www.nea.org/neatoday/0205/rights.html.

262 "In explaining her principled stance": Ibid.

262 "I'd lost the kids' respect": Andrew Trotter, "Plagiarism Controversy Engulfs Kansas School," *Education Week,* April 3, 2002, http://www.edweek.org/ew/newstory.cfm?slug=29piper.h21.

262 "buy into," "as a part of our culture," "for her display of personal courage," and "all of us": Ibid.

263 Ambrose pilloried: Mark Lewis, "More Controversy for Stephen Ambrose," *Forbes.com,* January 9, 2002, http://www.forbes.com/2002/01/09/0109ambrose.html.

263 Goodwin accused: "How the Goodwin Story Developed," History News Network, http://hnn.us/articles/590.html (continuously updated story), accessed January 2004.

263 "frequent acts," "fabricated comments," "concocted scenes," and "lifted material": Dan Barry, David Barstow, Jonathan D. Glater, Adam Liptak, and Jacques Steinberg, "Times Reporter Who Resigned Leaves Long Trail of Deception," *New York Times,* May 11, 2003, http://query.nytimes.com/gst/abstract.html?res=FB0910FA395B0C728DDDAC0894DB404482.

263 "I do not invent anything": Barbara Tuchman, *Practicing History* (New York: Alfred A. Knopf, 1981), p. 18.

264 Blair's "personal problems" and "the audacity of the deceptions": Barry, et al., "Times Reporter Who Resigned Leaves Long Trail of Deception."

267 Quotes from Mike Adams: Jessica Pitts, "Former Piper High Principal Gives Keynote Speech for Integrity Week," *Kansas State Collegian,*

April 15, 2003, http://www.kstatecollegian.com/stories/041503/new_adams .shtml.

267 Gallup Youth Survey data: Heather Mason, "Are Teens Cheating Their Way to Higher GPAs?," *The Gallup Poll,* April 15, 2003, http://www .gallup.com/content/default.aspx?ci=8200&pg=1.

268 "Accuracy is all we have": Ibid.

269 "let bygones be bygones" and "no one in South Africa": Desmond Tutu, *No Future Without Forgiveness* (London: Rider Books, 1999), pp. 31, 91.

269 "This was the kind of testimony": Ibid., p. 110.

271 Interviews with Duma Khumalo and Fazel Randera: See Rushworth M. Kidder, "President's Letter," Institute for Global Ethics, December 1999.

272 "the past, far from disappearing": Tutu, p. 31.

Story Index

This index allows you to search for an anecdote by name or topic. If you are unable to find a specific story detail, please refer to the general index.

General Index

Institute for Global Ethics

FOUNDED BY RUSHWORTH M. KIDDER IN 1990

Many of the real-life examples used in *Moral Courage* are based on interviews conducted by the author under the auspices of the Institute for Global Ethics, a nonprofit membership organization. The institute offers ethics training, educational curriculums, and management consulting for corporations, schools, government agencies, and nonprofits. It also publishes *Ethics Newsline,* a free weekly Web-based newsletter about domestic and international ethical issues from around the world. For more information about membership and programs, please contact the institute:

Institute for Global Ethics
P.O. Box 563
Camden, Maine 04843
(207) 236-6658
www.moral-courage.org
www.globalethics.org